GEORGE TYRRELL'S

LETTERS

SELECTED AND EDITED BY

M. D. PETRE

AUTHOR OF "LIFE OF GEORGE TYRRELL"

NEW YORK
E. P. DUTTON AND COMPANY
681 FIFTH AVENUE
1920

CONTENTS

                                                                    PAGE

BIOGRAPHICAL INTRODUCTION xi

PART I

I

RELIGION

To PÈRE HENRI BREMOND, S.J.: Nov. 13, 1900 ; Jan. 26,
  1902 ; Feb. 17, 1902 ; March 7, 1902 3
To EDWARD THOMAS, ESQ.: May 5, 1904 ; July 21, 1904 ;
  July 22, 1904 12
To THE REV. J. H. R. ABBOTT: Aug. 11, 1904 . . . 21
To V.: Oct. 18, 1901 ; Jan. 1, 1905 23
To N.: Oct. 15, 1908 26
To A. M. L. C. (Notebooks): about 1908 27
To L. D. (Notebooks): 1908 31
To W. R. H. (Notebooks): 1908 35

II

MYSTICISM

To V.: Nov. 25, 1897 38
EXTRACT FROM LETTER OF BARON F. VON HÜGEL TO REV.
  GEORGE TYRRELL, S.J.: Sept. 26, 1898 . . . 40
To BARON F. VON HÜGEL: Sept. 28, 1898 ; Oct. 5, 1898 ;
  Oct. 7, 1898 44

PAGE

To Père Henri Bremond, S.J.: Oct. 29, 1898; Sept. 16,
    1901 50
To T. Bailey Saunders, Esq.: Oct. 25, 1907 . . . 52
To Mrs. U.: Feb. 22, 1908 54

III

DOGMA AND SYMBOLISM

To Baron F. von Hügel: Feb. 10, 1907 56
To the Rev. G. E. Newsom: Nov. 17, 1908 . . . 61
To A. F. (Notebooks): Nov. 22, 1908 62

IV

INFALLIBILITY

To a Fellow-Priest: Dec. 1900; Jan. 22, 1901 . . 66
To Baron F. von Hügel: June 6, 1900 70
To V.: June 20, 1901; Jan. 22, 1906 70
To Wilfrid Ward, Esq.: Aug. 1, 1901; Aug. 1, 1903 . 72

V

MODERNISM

To F. Rooke Ley, Esq.: Nov. 19, 1900 77
To Baron F. von Hügel: June 16, 1900; Jan. 3, 1902 . 78
To Abbé Loisy: Jan. 27, 1903; Jan. 2, 1904; Jan. 27,
    1904; Oct. 20, 1907 83
To Monsieur A. Houtin: June 24, 1903 87
To a French Priest: Feb. 22, 1904; May 15, 1905 . . 89
To Monsieur J. Augustin Leger: March 15, 1904; Nov.
    8, 1908 93
To Dr. Zdziechowski: June 24, 1903 97
To Wilfrid Ward, Esq.: April 8, 1906 99
To Lord Ashbourne: Dec. 7, 1906 102

PAGE

To ROBERT DELL, ESQ. : May 18, 1905 ; Jan. 16, 1907 ; Aug. 2, 1907 104

To V. : April 11, 1902 ; Nov. 5, 1904 107

To WILLIAM CRAIG, ESQ. : Dec. 2, 1906 110

To BISHOP VERNON HERFORD : April 14, 1907 (?) . . 111

To THE REV. CHARLES OSBORNE : March 30, 1907 . . 113

To AN ITALIAN PROFESSOR : April 23, 1908 ; April 27, 1908 ; June 30, 1908 ; Aug. 24, 1908 115

To ARTHUR BOUTWOOD, ESQ. : Jan. 13, 1909 . . . 118

VI

TRUTH

To THE REV. W. G. TARRANT : Feb. 27, 1908 . . . 120

To C. D. (Notebooks) : 1908–1909 122

VII

ANGLICANISM

To VISCOUNT HALIFAX : July 24, 1897 ; Nov. 19, 1903 . 128

To WILLIAM SCOTT-PALMER (MRS. DOWSON) : Aug. 29, 1907 132

VIII

POSITIVISM

To THE REV. MALCOLM QUIN : Jan. 2, 1907 ; Aug. 8, 1907 ; 1909 ; June 8, 1909 137

IX

PRAYER

To MRS. STRACEY : Nov. 27, 1905 144

To P., Date uncertain 147

To V. : May 14, 1901 ; April 2, 1906 148

To MISS DORA WILLIAMS : June 22, 1904 ; May 30, 1905 . 149

To DR. ISRAEL ABRAHAMS : Jan. 22, 1909 152

PART II

I

PERSONAL

PAGE

To Laurence Housman, Esq.: June 23, 1900 ; Aug. 10, 1903 ; Dec. 6, 1906 ; March 15, 1909 157

To the Rev. T. MacClelland : Dec. 6, 1907 . . . 163

To M. Loyson (Père Hyacinthe) : April 25, 1907 or 1908 . 164

To the Rev. A. Dickinson : Nov. 14, 1908 . . . 165

To Miss Florence Bishop : March 7, 1904 . . . 165

To Miss Dora Williams : Dec. 1, 1904 ; Dec. 15, 1904 ; Dec. 22, 1904 ; Feb. 22, 1905 ; Aug. 8, 1905 ; Sept. 20, 1905 ; Oct. 20, 1905 ; Oct. 29, 1905 ; Nov. 12, 1905 ; Dec. 6, 1905 ; Oct. 26, 1906 ; Dec. 2, 1906 168

To his Cousin Sylvia : Christmas 1905 181

To Sister M. : Feb. 26, 1906 ; June 25, 1906 ; Sept. 1906 . 183

To M. D. P. : June 24, 1908 185

To R. M. S. : Dec. 25, 1904 186

To N. S. : Aug. 1900 ; April 1903 ; June 8, 1905 ; Aug. 14, 1907 ; March 24, 1908 187

To an Italian Professor : Dec. 31, 1907 190

To D. : May 30, 1907 191

To K. : Jan. 1909 192

The Rome Express (verses on a picture post-card) . . 193

II

ETHICAL QUESTIONS

To F. H. (Notebooks) : 1908–1909 199

To V. : May 31, 1901 ; June 24, 1901 ; March 2, 1902 ; May 30, 1902 ; Summer 1904 201

To G. : Nov. 2, 1904 ; Dec. 14, 1904 208

To one who had asked advice : Aug. 27, 1900 . . 211

PAGE

To A. S. R. (Notebooks) : 1908–1909 213

To E. D. (Notebooks) : 1908–1909 215

To Laurence Housman, Esq. : Feb. 17, 1901 . . . 223

To F. M. (Notebooks) : 1908–1909 224

To L. H. (Notebooks) : 1908–1909 228

To Sr. B. (Notebooks) : Jan. 5, 1909 232

To K. : Nov. 15, 1907 233

To Lady Low : April 8, 1906 234

To Miss Dora Williams : Oct. 7, 1904, Nov. 3, 1904 ; Dec.
8, 1904 235

To the Rev. A. L. Lilley : June 1909 241

III

LETTERS OF ADVICE

To Miss W. : Feb. 14, 1900 ; Sept. 28, 1902 ; Oct. 28, 1907. 243

To N. : Feb. 6, 1908 246

To L. R. : May 18, 1907 248

To Mrs. U. : Feb. 18, 1908 ; Feb. 20, 1908 . . . 249

To Mrs. Metcalfe : Date uncertain ; June 29, 1901 . . 251

IV

CHANGE OF FAITH

To L. R. : July 9, 1898 ; Feb. 1, 1907 ; March 17, 1907 ; May
26, 1907 ; April 14, 1909 254

To Sister B. : Dec. 15, 1900 ; July 24, 1904 . . . 262

To a Religious : April 4, 1902 267

To Mrs. S. : July 14, 1903 268

V

LITERARY

To Professor Edmund G. Gardner : March 28, 1902 . 270

To the Hon. Emily Lawless : Aug. 25, 1904 ; March 17,
1905 271

PAGE

To Laurence Housman, Esq. : Nov. 28, 1904 ; Sept. 14, 1908 276

To V. : Jan. 2, 1904. 278

To Miss Dora Williams : Nov. 19, 1904 ; Dec. 31, 1904 ; Jan. 12, 1905 ; Jan. 30, 1905 ; March 6, 1905 ; March 15, 1905 280

To " The Weekly Register " : May 27, 1899 . . . 291

VI

STRAY REMARKS AND SENTENCES FROM CONVERSATION AND LETTERS

Patching—To a Friend who Aspired to a Cardinal's Hat —About Popes—Isolation—Money — Planchette — Scandal — Argument — Love of God — Tigers— Weariness—Poetry—Right Proportion—Modernism — Parousia — Polytheism — Apostolic Weakness— Councils—Polygamy — Acts of Submission — Free Will and Providence—Last Words . . . 298

BIOGRAPHICAL INTRODUCTION

To many the name of George Tyrrell is so familiar that
any account of his life may seem superfluous—to many,
but not to all. Furthermore, the years of stress through
which the world has lately passed have dulled the
memory of many events that stood out conspicuously
in times when thought was not at a discount and
action all that signified. The story of the Modernist
movement was hardly ended before the Great War
began ; a crisis during which deeper and more abiding
interests were inevitably suspended in favour of questions materially urgent and imperative.

But even were Modernism generally remembered,
Modernism is far from being all in the life of Tyrrell.
Indeed it may be said that Modernism did a certain
amount of injustice to his memory, in so far as it
overshadowed other sides of his work and his character.
He was a Modernist, and he gave a portion of his life
to the prosecution of that movement ; but he was other
things besides—he was a man of unusual spiritual
insight ; of moral acumen ; of keen human sympathy
and psychological skill ; of literary power and perception ; of abounding humour and fun. He had been
a missioner and a confessor before he was a writer ;
he was the friend of many for whom his orthodoxy
or unorthodoxy had little importance.

In the following selection of letters an attempt has
been made to give this more varied presentment of him,
to show him in his dealings with widely moral and un-
denominationally spiritual issues ; to show him, also,

in his lighter moments, when he spoke true words in
jest, or hid his meaning under a veil of *persiflage*. It
has always been the conviction of the editor of these
letters that George Tyrrell could have attained fame
in many other ways than that in which, with no seeking
of his own, it came to him—a way of pain and sadness,
on the whole ; a way of heroic effort and, in one sense,
heroic failure.

But his way was appointed him, and his fate was
early decided. Religion was the great overmastering
passion of his life ; a passion in which that life was
used up and consumed. Religion predominates, in his
letters as everywhere else ; but it does not predominate
to the extent of concealing other powers and characteristics.

To give, then, a brief account of his career.

He belonged to a family of which not a few have
gained distinction—we need only recall the names of
Professor Robert Yelverton Tyrrell of classical fame ;
of George Tyrrell's own brother, William ; of his
cousin, Sir William Tyrrell, yet living, and prominent
in political affairs.

George Tyrrell was born in Dublin on February 6,
1861 ; his father, a journalist by profession, died
shortly before his birth, and his mother, a Champney
by birth, made a brave struggle for the welfare of her
children. George Tyrrell, in return, loved her as he
never loved anyone else on earth, and nothing in his
autobiography is more pathetic than the passages
consecrated to her memory.

He was educated chiefly at Rathmines School, under
the direction of Dr. C. W. Benson, whom he afterwards
characterised as the " dearest and best of men ; " and
he matriculated at Trinity College in 1878, but did
not go any further in his university career.

It is difficult, in a few words, to give an account of

his religious development, which he has so poignantly described in his own Autobiography. Shortly, however, it was thus. A pious childhood, under the influence of a devout mother, was succeeded by a period of religious indifference and general carelessness. But about the age of fourteen spiritual instincts again became active. He fell first under the influence of High Church Anglican friends, and attended Dr. Maturin's church at Grangegorman. More and more religious interests began to absorb his mind, to the exclusion of all others ; he grew dissatisfied with the Via Media of the Anglican position, and fell under the spell of the Roman Catholic Church. His friend Father Dolling, the great Anglican missioner, was his spiritual guide for some time ; he joined him in London in 1879, and passed over to the Roman Catholic Church that same year.

Tyrrell's movements were ever nothing if not rapid. Those who knew him personally will remember how quickly and silently he would flit from one room to another, and into or out of the house, his arrival or departure being almost imperceptible. In the same manner with his life and career, each movement was almost instantaneous—he was a Catholic almost as soon as he was a believer, a Jesuit almost as soon as he was a Catholic.

His first experience of the Society of Jesus was in Cyprus, and from there he went to Malta ; this was a time of probation, during which he was to examine the life of the Society and determine whether he should adopt it or not. In spite of many doubts and questionings he held to his first purpose, and entered the Novitiate at Manresa in 1880. From the time of his religious conversion his aim had been to work for the cause of religion in the world at large, and he believed that, as a Jesuit, he would have the best opportunities of doing so. In many ways the Society ultimately proved different from what he had expected ; he maintained that it had become stereotyped, and that the original idea of its founder had lost its inspirational force. Indeed, his *dictum* was that no Order should be allowed to outlive its first members. However, he threw himself very completely into the life just as it was laid before him, and was not only a Jesuit, but one of the most popular members of the Society amongst his own brethren. In community life he was eminently adaptable, unselfish and sympathetic ; qualities of no small value in such a life, as all who are acquainted with religious communities will know.

During the scholastic period of his training he became an ardent student and disciple of St. Thomas Aquinas, and had great belief in the adaptability of that great master's teaching to modern religious needs. Though he had to modify this attitude later on, he remained faithful, on many points, to his first allegiance, and the *Summa* of Aquinas was on his shelves to the end.

After a brief career of mission work—the period of his Jesuit life during which he was probably happiest— he went to London and worked on the writing staff of *The Month*, a review edited by the English Jesuits. There also he began to be known to a wider intellectual circle, and to be sought after as spiritual guide and confessor. His influence in the Society itself had been an ever-growing one, and he had a cluster of Jesuit friends for whom he was the coming man. That influence now began to spread outside the body to which he belonged, and he bid fair to become one of the most prominent religious figures in the Catholic Church in England.

But he was destined to a yet wider fame, to a more strenuous and painful sphere of activity. Partly driven by his own unresting mind, partly influenced

by other minds, and one in particular, he began to face
religious questions from outside the shelter under which
he lived. He was not of those who could enjoy a
tranquillity that was secured by protective methods
which rendered it unattainable to the rest of mankind.
He had not sought religion for the sake of his own soul,
but as a great human cause. His faith must be such
as all men could share, or it was no faith to him.

Therefore to open out before him the problems which
beset modern belief was to invite him into the arena
where those problems could be squarely faced; and
to venture into that arena was, for him, to turn back
no more. " A dangerous man, wandering forth, he
knows not whither " ; this was the way in which he
described himself to a friend at that time. With his
usual rapidity he grasped the subjects at issue, above
all those of exegesis and Church history. Perhaps
at another time moral questions would have interested
him the most, but the wind of Modernism was rising,
and on both sides, consciously or unconsciously, the
struggle was preparing.

Tyrrell began to feel a certain insincerity in his
position. He could no longer say what he meant, nor
do what he felt called to do. He had no right to
compromise the body to which he still belonged, yet
neither could he much longer kick against the pricks.
A new conception of religion was needed for a new
world ; Catholicism must become human or must
cease to fulfil its mission.

The first of his writings to excite suspicion and a form
of censure was an article on eternal punishment,
entitled " A Perverted Devotion," which appeared
in the *Weekly Register*. But once the trouble had
begun it continued. For the detailed account of these
difficulties readers must be referred to the *Life ;* suffice
it to say, in this place, that obstacles were multiplied

to the publication of each new work. It was then that he adopted the alternative of private or pseudonymous publication for several of his books. He maintained that, as member of a religious body, he had no right to compromise others by open publication; but that, by this method, he undertook individually all responsibility, and incurred all the censures that might befall the works in question.

He also determined to withdraw into comparative solitude, and for the last years of his life as a Jesuit he lived, studied, and wrote in the little Jesuit mission-house at Richmond in Yorkshire. It was in 1906 that he finally quitted the Society; a step he took in sorrow, but under the conviction that nothing else was left for him to do.

In 1907 the Modernist movement reached its crisis with the publication of the Syllabus *Lamentabili* and the Encyclical *Pascendi*. Tyrrell wrote two letters in *The Times*, in which he openly criticised the latter document—and these letters drew on him a prohibition to frequent the Sacraments. It is not likely that he failed to realise the possible consequences of his action; but he had, by then, made up his mind that it was his task to speak, whatever the consequences to himself might be. Silence was easy to those who had ceased to care; it was not easy, but it was a duty to those for whom God was the only refuge when the rulers of the Church seemed to be at fault; it was neither easy nor morally obligatory for Tyrrell with his blend of mysticism and practicability, his belief that the Church was the great spiritual guide of mankind, and yet that her human elements needed human control. He had entered the Church, as he had entered the Society, to work for mankind at large; he could not abandon his purpose, he could not separate his destiny from that of the rest of the world.

I have endeavoured, elsewhere, to give some idea of what Tyrrell felt and suffered during those last years. He was no optimist, and he knew that success would never fall to his isolated efforts, and that no single man could alter a great religious organisation. But he was equally convinced that life is given us for effort rather than success, and that it is the lot of some to die outside, and not within, the Promised Land. He was a loyal collaborator with those who had adopted the same cause; he asked little of his friends, but all of himself. He committed faults of temper, but not of cowardice or insincerity.

Some will ask what, then, he meant by that Modernism to which he adhered. He meant, by it, a belief in the religious needs of mankind and in the inherent power of the Catholic Church to satisfy those needs; he meant, by it, the belief that, since the Church existed for humanity, at large, she could and must respond to human knowledge and human requirements. He upheld that faith to the end, though he suffered from recurring doubts; he determined to make the mistake of adhering to that faith, if it was a mistake, rather than the mistake of abandoning it if it was not a mistake.

As to Tyrrell's literary activity, it was comprised in a period of twelve years, from 1897, when *Nova et Vetera* was published, to 1909, when his last work, *Christianity at the Cross Roads*, lay on the desk of the room in which he died.

The last two years of his life were spent mainly at Storrington, with intervals in which he stayed with friends at Clapham or went abroad. He had always been frail and delicate, with recurring attacks of violent migraine. His last illness was sudden and short—lasting from July 6, 1909, to July 15, the day of his death. During those ten days he was conscious for

b

the most part, but unable to speak. Few of those who saw him will forget the pathetically Christ-like pose of the dying head, with its stamp of suffering and sacrifice—a sacrifice that was consummated after death by the refusal of the ecclesiastical authorities of the Church in which he died to grant him Christian burial. For though he had received the last Sacraments, he had made no retractation—nor could he have done so. He died an exile from the Church in whose mission to the world he had never ceased to believe, a mission to which he consecrated the fruitful years of his life. He was buried as an exile in the graveyard of another Church, a Church for which he ever cherished something of the old love, but in which he could not again have found his home. It was sad, but it was not an unfitting end to his career. His faith in the Catholic Church was comprehensive and not exclusive ; for him the word Catholic recalled " the out-stretched, all-embracing arms of Him who died for the whole *orbis terrarum.*" He had entered the Church to work for others and not for himself ; he asked for nothing, and he got nothing, but the exile's grave, with the symbol of priesthood over his head.

TO BE CONSULTED

WORKS OF GEORGE TYRRELL

Longmans, Green & Co. :
    Nova et Vetera.
    Hard Sayings.
    External Religion.
    A More Excellent Way (Collected articles).
    Lex Orandi.
    Lex Credendi.
    Oil and Wine
    A Much Abused Letter.
    Medievalism.
    Through Scylla and Charybdis.
    Christianity at the Cross Roads.

Priory Press, Hampstead :
    The Church and the Future :

Edward Arnold :
    Essays on Faith and Immortality (Posthumous).

Also

Edward Arnold :
    Autobiography and Life of George Tyrrell (M. D. Petre). √

and

T. Nelson :
    Modernism, its Failure and its Fruits (M. D. Petre).

PART I

I

RELIGION

To Père Henri Bremond, S.J.

RICHMOND, YORKS,
November 13, 1900.

MY DEAREST PÈRE BREMOND,

It is because I have so much I should like to say to you that I delay so long in hopes of being able to speak less inadequately; even now I have not ripened my thoughts enough to put them on paper.

I have first to thank you for your most admirable article on Barrès' work (which here and there put my narrow French to the strain. Indeed I can rather feel than define the delicacy for which competent judges everywhere praise your beautiful style). I wondered if, as you wrote, you were struck with, or intended, the remarkable parallelism between "*la théorie des énergies latentes de la patrie française*" and the theory of the latent energies and ideas of Catholicism, so ill-expressed by the outward utterances of ecclesiastical theorists or even by all that goes under the title of external religion. All your analysis on pp. 208 *sqq.* is an almost exact illustration of what I am groping at in my article on the "Mind of the Church." I am no optimist, God knows, but I do believe, not as with faith, but as with science, in the irrepressible energy of such latent ideas; in their power of casting aside every worthless or violently imposed accretion, and of working themselves out to

3

their legitimate finality as infallibly as the roots of a tree make for the water through and round every obstacle. "*Omnis plantatio*, etc.," is, like most of the great Gospel principles, an axiom of science. It was as clear to Gamaliel (Acts v.) as it was to Christ. "Da pacem *in diebus nostris*" is the natural expression of ephemeral beings wearied with the slow grinding of God's mill : but there is more wisdom in Patmore's "I believe in the Christianity of ten thousand years hence"—which is another way of saying : I believe in the latent and undeveloped Christianity of the present, as distinct from its halting expression. I can see already that all that has (alas !) come to be meant by the word "Jesuitism" is going to be swept away, at the cost no doubt of infinite scandal, and apostasy and confusion of mind; that the very tightening and straining of the cords under which we are suffering is prompted by a subconscious recognition of a slipping away of power out of the hands that have held it so long. Had Ignatianism not been supplanted by Jesuitism or Aquavivianism there would have been a slow accommodation of ecclesiastical methods to the changing environment ; but thanks to the "*frangi, non flecti*" policy there must come a sudden bursting of impossible barriers, resulting in inundation and much loss of life. Here the clergy are saved (1) by their unintelligence and ignorance, which makes them blind to the very existence of mental difficulties, (2) by their engrossment in money-getting and parochialism ; but when an intelligent priest comes in contact with doubt he is so ill-prepared to resist the virus that he takes the disease in its worst form. Of course bishops and religious superiors are the last persons he could go to either for guidance or consolation. The number of these "Blanco Whites" is already large and will be daily larger. Meanwhile, as Archbishop Magee once

said of his Anglican confrères : " The bishops are
fighting over the papering of the attics while the
basement story is in flames." The " Roman News "
of *The Tablet* tells us of coming beatifications and other
catch-penny spasms of ecclesiastical vitality ; but of
any sensibility to *the* needs of the day—not a word.
Archbishop Mignot [1] is waking up, and Bishop Spalding, but " what are they among so many ? " The
rest " slumber and sleep " with lamps untrimmed, to
be waked by the cry at midnight to find themselves
without light for themselves or for others. They
are as the French *noblesse* on the eve of the Revolution,
saying " ' Peace, peace,' when there is no peace,"
" marrying and giving in marriage, eating and drinking,
till the flood came and destroyed them all." This is
not prophecy or *a priori* prediction, but a simple statement of what I see going on—unless indeed it be prophecy to predict that a stone that is in process of falling
will come to the earth. What will be left in the recon-
structed Catholicism is more uncertain matter of
prediction. I should say : Everything that is vital
to man's eternal life—social and individual ; all that
remains after the dross has been purged away by the
fire, either in its present form or a better ; not an
emptier Catholicism, but a fuller. And I suppose we
should agree that the incarnation and all its legitimate
developments, the eucharist, the communion of saints,
the sacramental system, a teaching *vox populi*, are
really vital. Even a modified sort of Papal infallibility
may possibly survive the scorching light of criticism.
·I agree therefore *verbo tenus* with the common brag
that Catholicism has nothing to lose, everything to
gain, from science, history, and philosophy; though,
Heaven knows, in a different sense.

I am afraid you allow yourself to be much tormented,

[1] Archbishop of Albi, died in 1918.

and that you do not study the stars enough or try to calm yourself with the thought of how infinitely little all looks from there—this battle of microbes. I have come to regard my internal quiet of soul as more important even than personal religion, of which it is the first condition. God " takes up the islands as a very little thing and measures out the ocean in the hollow of His hand," and I do think we ought to try hard to look at these matters with His eyes—to take up the whole wriggling mass of squabbling humanity in our hand as a very little thing—a matter for quiet and not unkindly curiosity more than for volcanic, self-hurting, useless indignation. Surely it is our sole redeeming greatness that we can thus get outside ourselves and our little pebble of a planet and laugh at ourselves : " *Transeunt omnia et nos pariter cum illis* " *et brevi.*

I also was very charmed with your treatment of Adderley[1] and Co., and sent the article on to Kegan Paul, who admires all your work so much. These " Christian Endeavourers," like so many others, see the evils more clearly than the remedies. One of their great leaders is one of my best and oldest friends, and he has gradually been beaten back and back to see that no radical remedy can be found but in a reconstitution of society and resuscitation of that dried mummy called Christianity. He and his confrères would have been Catholics long ago if the Pope's socialism had been of a less dilettante character and governed by a proper understanding of modern economic conditions ; but now they regard the Roman Church as the bulwark of all they would wish to see destroyed.

I think you are attracted by Newman, Keble, etc.,

---

[1] The Hon. and Rev. James Adderley. See *Ames Religieuses*, Henri Bremond.

because they strove to combine elements so unhappily sundered, namely, the earnestness and spirituality of evangelical piety with an acceptance of those Catholic doctrines which set that piety on a firm basis, and whose real, but with us almost abandoned, use is to feed, elevate, and establish that flame of true devotion. Against the undogmatic evangelicals a charge of sentimentalism and poesy might often be justly alleged; but not against the *Christian Year*, which is altogether " real."

I think, in spite of a thousand difficulties, you and I ought to stick fast, like S. Laurence, to our gridiron for the sake of others, unless it comes to our whole life being an *acted untruth*. That may conceivably be the case some day, and it is better to face it. It might be true only of one's life as a Jesuit, or of one's priestly life, or of one's position as a Catholic. I suppose to call oneself a Catholic is to assert *in actu exercito* that one believes *without doubting* whatever the Church proposes. If I ever came to be unable to say this, save in some non-natural and violent sense, I should of course cease to call myself a Catholic; though I might be a Catholic *spe, non re*. It is peculiar to our religion not to allow doubt, nor to be satisfied with probability. As an Anglican one might truthfully be uncertain about the claims of Anglicanism and look Romewards with hope; or one might even not prefer Anglicanism as being more than a comprehensive institution for Christians of a Catholic tendency. But I don't think I could be an Anglican even of that type were I ever to lose that certainty which the profession of Romanism involves. I think I should keep apart and live as Catholic a life as possible for one out of overt communion, and call myself a Catholic-in-hope and desire. At least, I should be then in the soul of the Church and I should be sincere. I think I should try not to " enjoy " my liberty in any way ; and should go on helping others as much as possible. And if ever the old certainty came back I should seek re-admission at once ; if never, I should die in peace with Him

> " Who made the darkness and the light,
> And dwells, not in the light alone,
> But in the darkness and the cloud."

But at present I see a few steps ahead, and " sufficient to the day is the evil thereof." I say this simply to show us that the worst that could happen to either of us is not so very terrible as it looms to our imagination, especially when mirrored in the minds of those im-mediately around us. Father Rickaby once wrote well :

" Later generations see valid excuses where the earlier saw none. It is not difficult to determine the laws of right conduct and to point out that the action of a given individual has been much at variance with those laws ; yet it is a far cry from law to conscience ; from the objective order to the subjective : from facts as they are in themselves to the same as they appear mirrored in this mind and in that."

To the Same

RICHMOND, YORKS,
January 26, 1902.

Oddly enough, as the present system tumbles daily into greater ruin, I seem to see clearer vistas of a possible reconstruction, through the rents in its walls. Perhaps, like her Master, the Church must die and rise again. To human view, the gates of Hell prevailed against Him on Calvary, and the disciples said : *Actum est,* as they will say when some critical Longinus shall thrust his spear into the heart of the Gospel. Lo !

I send you an unpreached sermon on that text. If you are honest you will return it. Jack [1] is besprinkling the floor with fleas—what vigour!

I was rather charmed with Maillefer [2] as a type of good serviceable piety. Personally I care more for a multitude of such men than for the occasional Saint that Catholicism seems content with. The " hero " or " genius " is never an argument for the *system*— being often produced in spite of, rather than by it. It is the *average* turn-out we should look to when we argue *ex fructibus*. I have been much struck by Dolly Winthrop in *Silas Marner*—as a quite satisfactory fruit of the outgoing Protestantism of fifty years ago.

" If a bit of trouble comes I feel I can put up wi' it ; for I've looked for help i' the right quarter, and gev myself up to Them as we must all give ourselves up to at the last ; and if we've done our part, it isn't to be believed as Them as are above us 'ull be worse nor we are, and come short o' Theirn."

What could be better than a populace imbued with this simple, solid faith, so narrow in compass, but so wide in import! And yet this rude and shrewd piety was not at all uncommon in those days when religion was supposed to be dried up like a raisin. I fancy, wherever men hear Bible-reading, however dully and apathetically, some kind of inspiration is always possible ; and it is just " inspiration " that our mechanical piety lacks. Be sure and revisit us this summer. My book is nearly in print ; and then comes the tug-of-war with His Eminence. [3]

[1] His Airedale dog.
[2] See *Ames Religieuses*, Henri Bremond.
[3] Cardinal Vaughan, Archbishop of Westminster.

To the Same

At present I am in labour with a suddenly conceived synthesis of many thoughts that have been gathering in my mind without apparent connection ; but, as usually happens, all the offspring of one seed. It is utterly unfit for publication this century. We must put religion high above all scientific, historic, and even ethical uncertainties, and free it from that " body of death " to which theologians and apologetics have tied it. As long as it rests on a foundation of sand it cannot be believed, or " lived "—that is my thesis. I do not say religion can be altogether indifferent to positive knowledge ; any more than a snail can be indifferent about its shell ; but the shell is not the snail, which can make itself another as often as one is broken. This, as written, sounds a latitudinarian commonplace ; but I think I can give it a Catholic sense. If L. takes up the history of Wesleyanism for his Doctorate, I hope he will try to explain the reasons of its success and contrast them with the methods of Cardinal Vaughan and Co. Whenever I see a little ugly red-brick Wesleyan gospel-shop, in the villages round here, I say : " Why can't we do this ? Isn't half a loaf better than no bread ? If we can't have our full sacramental and sacerdotal apparatus, at least we could give people the ' bread of the word,' something to inspire and raise their lives—a religion, after all, better suited to their capacity." But no ; all our energy goes into that monstrous red-brick vaunt at Westminster, which it is hoped will lure in a few empty-headed ritualists by the gauds of ecclesiastical parade and ceremonial. I would gladly see it broken up into a thousand, even Wesleyan, conventicles, which would at least do something to Christianise, were it in ever so imperfect a way, the neglected millions.

To the Same

March 7, 1902.

CARISSIME,

As to your *Remarques sur l'Éducation*, etc., which are so entirely to my mind that they are scored under almost from beginning to end. Only yesterday Father C.—one of our Angers tertians—was telling me with reverent awe and admiration how P. Coubé rehearsed his sermons in detail over and over, practising each gesture, emphasis, etc., etc. ; and how P. Somebody else had formed himself on Bourdaloue or on Segneri—till at last the Methodist devil broke loose in me and got control of my tongue : " Good God ! Fancy Jesus Christ, or Peter or Paul, or any man not sodden through and through with artificiality and untruthfulness, mincing before a mirror, pinking and preening his peacock feathers ; practising sighs and grimaces, in order to what ? To cover the hollowness of his heart, the non-existence of his own faith and love, and to excite faith and love in others by a make-believe display of the same in himself." Pulpit rhetoric, I went on to explain, is the surest symptom of religious decadence and death ; of the subjection of faith to form. " But the Society's custom, etc., etc." " Rotten," said I, " rotten to the core ! " Nothing could have been more indiscreet, and indeed a little excessive and exaggerated. But C. is such a perfect S.J. product—a man by nature bright, artistic, attractive, and human, but, by docile submission to the system, dreary, uninteresting, self-centred, emasculated. Could I but excite a spark of rebellion in his heart he might be saved so as by fire ! How far better, from a spirit and character point of view, if such a man could be thoroughly shaken in his faith and pass through a crisis ending in the so-called loss, but really the salvation, of his soul! His passivity goaded me on and on till Jack looked up at me in perplexity at my unwonted vehemence, as though he thought I must have seen a rabbit. At the end of our walk I found myself explaining that Père la Fontaine had formulated the crying need of modern Catholicism, i.e. a liberal infusion of Protestant ideas. Your article came in the evening like a cool, moist leaf laid on the hot wounds of my temper.

To Edward Thomas, Esq.

RICHMOND, YORKS,
May 5, 1904.

MY DEAR SIR,

Your papers both interested me greatly; but there is so much to be explained and defined beyond what was consistent with their brevity that I can only speak with great hesitation.

As I implied in my letter, I am beginning to think that even if Mr. Lang had proved his point, and if the Aruntas could be convicted of some latent monotheism, or else of decadence, yet this " Big Man in the Clouds," the Maker and Ruler of All, would only prove the innate need of man's mind for unification, for a First Cause, for " philosophy " of some kind. That " Big Man " would be only the precursor of the Absolute or of the *Ipsum Esse* of later metaphysicians. He would answer man's intellectual and scientific, not necessarily his religious, need. If, on the other hand, our theism is a development of " ghost-worship," it is a development of what is essentially non-religious. Primitive man fears and propitiates ghosts, as he does wild beasts or demons, or other controlling powers with which he must reckon. This again is the rude

precursor of that practical science by which we now
seek to control Nature (better understood) to our own
interest. There is no *true* (i.e. disinterested, reverential,
self-devoting) worship in co-operative magic, any more
than in co-operative business. Nor is there, *in kind*,
any difference between such gods and the One God
conceived as the supreme Nature-Force who can be
irritated to strike, or coaxed to favour, by certain lines
of conduct. It is only a more cultivated form of the
same error, an outcome of the ceaseless effort to square
popular religion with science and philosophy.

It is, however, a great step towards the truth when
the One God begins to be credited with man's highest
goodness, i.e. the love of right for right's sake. This
step is inevitable sooner or later ; it is the new wine that
bursts the old bottles, shatters the last idol. Right
is the only thing that man feels to be absolutely imperative ; whose claims are limitless ; which demands
complete sacrifice of himself and his own interests.
There is an absolute will revealed to every man in every
dictate of his conscience ; and therefore an Absolute
Being which he cannot think of, or deal with, otherwise
than as (at least and equivalently) personal. With this
apprehension I think man arrives at what he was groping after in his former religions and in his idol-gods
(crude or cultured) ; he transfers all the paraphernalia,
language, ritual, etc., now interpreted metaphorically
and spiritually, to the only worthy claimant. The
direct-line ancestry of our Christian God is to be sought,
not in the theologies it has supplanted, but in the various
stages of man's moral development, whereby he has
come to recognise the dictates of his conscience as the
expression of an Absolute Will, at once immanent and
transcendent, and therefore has come to render to
that Will the adoration formerly given to idols. In
those former religions I see only abortive efforts to

satisfy man's worship-instinct and to find a worthy
object for it.

As you say, anthropology shows us man *always
the same*—always this dumb instinct of worship groping
for its proper object ; always this blurred sense of an
infinite and absolute difference between right and
wrong.   In Christianity these hitherto parallel developments have at last converged, God and Good have
been proved coincident.   But to seek from anthropology a proof of the universality of monotheism is not
much use unless we can show that it is the worship
of the *same* " One God," and not merely of something
analogous.

As to your dilemma : " God, either Subject or
Object," I am not quite clear ; so much diversity of
meaning attaches to those terms.   Dr. E. Caird and
all that school would say : " Neither subject nor object,
but something presupposed to both."   The Object-
God, i.e. a vast something or somebody alongside of,
or above, creation is eventually, I think, an idol, a
part (however principal) of that whole which it is
supposed to account for.   I would say much the
same of any sort of *anima mundi* or all-pervading soul
coming to self-consciousness in man, and to its highest
moral development in the soul of Christ.   For, after
all, that moral development meant the submission
of Christ's finite human will to an Absolute Will revealed in the dictates of Christ's human conscience.
To define God or to " image " Him is, for the same
reason, more impossible than to define or " image "
the thinking *self ;* for to think of it is to give it the
form of an object, to represent it in terms of what it
is not.   We cannot really *face* ourselves.   In this
sense, then, I would say God is an " object " of *Faith*,
not of knowledge, or definition.   We know Him simply
as that Will which we worship in obeying our con-

science. When we say : " *Fiat justitia, ruat coelum,*"
we mean to express our innate conviction that the
destruction of the universe is a less evil (less *in kind*)
than any violation of Right, of the Divine Will ; and
this implies that there is a Being compared with which
the being or reality of the universe (subject and object)
is as nothing. All this, I think (with Kant), is forced
upon us by the fact of conscience. It is an experimental
truth, reached by action, by right-doing.

I fear all this will only show you that we are on
different lines in our quest of God. I quite share your
distrust of merely speculative psychology (as opposed
to that experimental psychology on which our philosophy must wait, no less than on anthropology, if it
is ever to win or deserve credit) ; but in resting my
theism on conscience, I rest it on a fact accessible to
all ; nor do I trouble much how men *formulate* the
implications of that fact, so long as, being true to
conscience, they are true to God whether they recognise
it or not. Men may know nothing of the law of gravitation, but they live by it none the less ; or else they
take the fatal consequences. Ghost-worshippers and
co-operative magicians, in so far as they followed their
dull sense of right and wrong, light and darkness,
were, concurrently with all their superstitious obser-
vances, worshipping the Father of our Lord Jesus
Christ. In that, and not in any remote analogy
between their theology and ritual and those of the
Church, I recognise their rudimentary religion, nay,
their rudimentary Christianity. As to " Environment," I am cordially with you when you say : " Religion and life are one and the same " ; for I hold
religion to be the culmination of life, i.e. of man's
self-adaptation to his environment. The steps from
non-sentient to sentient life, and those from grade to
grade of sentience, from mere associations of remem-

bered experiences to complex predictive science—all is a progress in the range and complexity of self-adaptation to, and conquest of, our environment ; an advance from almost mechanical response to the " here and now " to a response to the " everywhere and always." Faith carries the process beyond the limits of the finite and relative and enables us to adapt ourselves to the infinite and eternal. But then I do not mean (as Max Müller seems to mean) by the " infinite " the mere extensive endlessness of the world of our outward experience ; but that Being or Reality *of another order* presupposed to the universe, and *compared with which* the universe is non-Reality. In that sense I would say, " God is man's ultimate environment " ; not, of course, in the *strictly* biological sense which would imply that God, like Nature, was something to *serve* man's purpose, to be mastered and assimilated by man (though in a mystical sense this is true); but in the sense that " environment " stands for all that on which man depends and to which he must adjust himself, whether it be above him or below him, whether to be obeyed by him or commanded by him.

There are perhaps a few passages in the accompanying reprints that will show you the direction in which I drift—for who, indeed, can pretend to do more in these troubled waters ? No man's judgment is worth having who has not surveyed all the accumulated evidence of observation offered us by anthropology, biology, history, etc., etc. ; and no one mortal life is equal to the task of assimilating all this evidence and seizing its implications. That is the *impasse* to which we have been brought, and which makes one envy the ghost-worshippers and co-operative magicians, or else seek to show that religion and faith, if they are necessary factors of every man's life, must be independent of questionable data, that they must be *implicit* in the life of every good man, whether he can formulate them or not.

Forgive me if I have missed your point too hopelessly, as may well be the case ; for in such matters our irreducible individuality bars mutual understanding as in no other.

NOTE

Students of the above subject would be interested by a comparison of George Tyrrell's suggestions with the views of M. Loisy on magic and religion. The following passage, from his volume *A propos d'Histoire des Religions* (Émile Nourry, 1911), deals with the same question from a similar, though not identical, standpoint : "*Selon les vues que nous venons d'émettre, la magie comme telle n'est ni logiquement ni historiquement antérieure à la religion ; mais magie et religion se distinguent et se séparent, tendent à devenir ennemies par le seul fait que la religion s'autorise d'un principe d'obligation que la magie ne reconnaît pas.*" (*Op. cit.* p. 186.)—M. D. P.

To the Same

RICHMOND, YORKS,
July 21, 1904.

MY DEAR SIR,

I am greatly obliged to you for your comments on my letter, which have enabled me to formulate my ideas with greater precision and, *I think*, to eliminate the remaining differences between us as to the matters therein touched upon.

I was wrong in reserving the word religion to that perfect type in which the definitive was finally realised ; and certainly have for years defended the claims of non-Christian cults to be considered as creations of the Holy Spirit, however distorted through the ignorance and moral backwardness of its human instruments. They are not "abortive" efforts in the sense of failing to relate man effectually to God ; but as failing to reach the *specific* difference of Christianity, which alone explicitly identifies God and righteousness ; divine and ethical goodness. Hence, I have said elsewhere, they stand to Christianity as the lower animals stand to man, with whom they have sentient life in common but not moral and rational life. An "accretion," a new element is found in Christianity (caused by the confluence into it of the ethical and religious processes) which could not have *grown out of* the simpler religions just because (as you say) there was no ethical germ in them to develop. In this sense Christianity is a "*nova creatura*," though the older religions prepared a body for it. I did not mean (as you seem to imply in your note) that "the blurred sense of right and wrong" was always *an element of man's religion*, but that *outside* and *parallel with* the religious process there was always a moral process going on—the two meeting and blending only in Christianity. Even in the legislation of Hammurabi (the source, I suppose, of our decalogue) one misses every vestige of *ethical* sense ; religion and society cared nothing for motives or for character, or for man as a person apart from the community ; "right and wrong" meant simply "permitted and forbidden," "safe or punishable." Yet who doubts but that in so civilised a people and period the moral life was fully awakened and fairly developed in individuals, though Church and State took no account of it ? The two processes, religious and ethical, grew side by side, but with no contact.

Assuming then that bloody sacrifice and communion are as universal as anthropology seems to indicate, and that their end or purpose is communion with the divine, a sharing of the divine life and nature, I should say that the common-generic element, which unites these cults with Christianity under the title of " religion," is just that same end and purpose ; that their specific differences are found in their conception of what that divine nature and life really are.   I never thought or meant to imply that Chemosh or Moloch were mere projections into space of man's fancy, any more than Javeh or the Christian " Heavenly Father "—though in a very true sense all are equally so, and without any prejudice to their reality and truth.   All alike are attempts to picture and embody that divine on which man feels himself dependent, from which he comes, to which he returns.   More than this ; they are the work of the divine *in man* striving for self-expression through the limitations of man's mind and language and art. *It* is the reality of which they all (even the highest) are but symbols.   If our God is truer, more real, than Chemosh, it only means that our conception of the divine is fuller, less inadequate ; that in conceiving it as righteousness, as the source of the *moral*, and not merely of the physical or social order, we have advanced from religious childhood to adolescence.   I dissent from you wholly, however, when you say (in your *Ante Omnia Deus*) that " doing the Will of God is not so much the end of life as its means."   That is Paley's view ; we are to do right not for right's sake, but for the sake of some reward, some further utility hereafter.   Life is action ; will is the action or life of a spirit ; God's life is God's will, His love, His action. To do God's will is to live God's life, or rather to suffer God to live in us ; it is precisely that " communion " of life and nature which is the end of the Christian sacrifice and sacrament ; " He that eateth my flesh hath eternal life."   This identification of man's moral life with the divine life, the recognition of it as "the divine" working in man, is the truth symbolised and groped after by the blood of bulls and goats.

As to your main position, then (the continuity of the old-world religions with Christianity as established by a consideration of the universality of sacrifice and sacraments), I think we are at one. The issues raised in your other paper are, of course, difficult to criticise. Every thoughtful man must fabricate some such synthesis *de omnibus ;* and these syntheses, like the old-world gods, will differ much in character according to the mentality of the fabricator. Yet it is the same "All" in each of us that tries to find utterance, the same Truth that struggles painfully to birth. Yet I feel, more and more, that philosophy must wait upon science and induction ; and that precipitation has done harm in the past.

To the Same

RICHMOND, YORKS,
July 22, 1904.

MY DEAR SIR,

Just a PS. to my letter of yesterday to thank you for the enclosed, which is full of interest. I, of course, see no reason why the tribal interest should not occasion the ethical instinct to outstrip the strictly religious interest in its development ; and I see no reason whatever for calling such altruism "religious" or "quasi-religious." Perhaps it is less common than the converse order. Again, to me it is no difficulty to admit that the religious instinct may lie wholly dormant in the earlier stages of man's development from non-human animality ; just as his rational, ethical and social faculties must do at certain stages. When once religion awakes, its manifestations will present certain characteristics, such as sacrificial and sacramental rites. There is a materialistic sense in which the doctrine of evolution is fatal to religion, i.e. if it explains the higher as but a complicated case of the lower and gives the highest reality to atoms and physical forces. But if it explains the beginnings by the end and makes the higher more real than the lower—in a word, if it views the whole process of the world as a gradual self-discloser of a divine idea, I cannot for the life of me see why religious men are so timid about accepting it cordially and candidly. I suppose they shrink from the amount of reinterpretation of dogma that it will involve ; but for my part I am convinced that the real gains will be overwhelming and the losses altogether imaginary.

That even scientific men should speak of any people as " primitive " shows how deeply the roots of tradition are planted in all our minds.

To the Rev. J. H. R. Abbott

SEGHILL VICARAGE, NORTHUMBERLAND,
August 11, 1904.

Blessed is the man who is so occupied about living and helping others to live that he cannot and need not occupy himself about the laws and the theory of life. But one would need cotton-wool in one's ears and in one's brain, in these days, to keep out questionings about the future : " Whence shall we buy bread, etc. ? " I think it is my interest in the millions, rather than in those who can think for themselves, that keeps my nose to the painful grindstone of study. At all events I have got so tangled in the business now, through one cause or another, that I have resigned myself. The millions of the near future will not be the docile priest-worshipping crowds of dear old Ireland, but will be up in all these questions, now whispered

in the ear among ourselves ; and so we must get ready.[1]
I do not think we have yet the data to answer the
problem of the religion of the future ; but I feel more
and more that it will be a more thoroughly Christian
and more thoroughly " Catholic " form of religion
than yet realised.   The mistake would be to lay down
conditions like S. Thomas and to say : " Except this
or that or the other is secured to me, I will not believe."
We once thought (and how very naturally !) that to
decentralise the earth and turn it into a pebble by
the sea-shore would spell chaos in religion.   Yet surely
our loss was gain.   And so, too, evolution is proving
all gain.   I cannot now see how Christianity could
stand without the miraculous altogether ; yet I dare
not say that they would fall together, or even that
the loss might not again prove gain.   In Ritschl's
form the " value-theory " is very wobbly as a criterion
of belief ; but I think there is a core of truth in it.
Dr. Engels [2] and the author of Lex Orandi use it in
a modified form, having got at it, not from Ritschl,
but from Professor James's Will to Believe.   You can't
sit down and sort existing beliefs as true and false
by it ; but it represents the life-law by which the
collective experience of the Christian people determines
whether beliefs shall live or die, or at least be modified.
I think beliefs are created by a thousand causes good,
bad, and indifferent ; and not always, or often, by some
religious interest.   These causes supply the raw
material from which the religiously useful (and therefore true and conformable to fact) beliefs are slowly
selected by the Church's experience.

I have not read Stather, and should be doubly pleased
to have it from your hands.

---

[1] See *Life*, etc., vol. ii. p. 407.
[2] A *nom de plume* he assumed for *Religion as a Factor of Life*.

To V.

October 18, 1901.

I am delighted with many things in Münsterberg's *Psychology and Life,* and find him supporting much that I have contended for in my *Ethical Preludes,* which is now finished as far as the Oxford lectures went, but needs two more chapters, and infinite notes and interludes. Also an English paper by Eucken in the *Monist* on Hegel is most illuminative after the first section, which reproduces Hegel in his, to me, bewildering word-jugglery. What pleases me is that E. spots the very lacunæ which seemed to me so obvious that I felt I must have misunderstood H. I have thought much of what you say about the Catholic Club and what I might call "Dollingism," without disrespect to my best of friends. I feel, but cannot yet define, the profound fallacy that gives birth to the effort, and I felt it when I wrote against Percy Dearmer in *Liberal Catholicism.* This "civilising" is a condition of religion, just as education is; but it is not religion, it is not the *direct* concern of priests any more than teaching Latin grammar is. I feel that the clergy secretly have lost faith in the value of real *personal* religion, or at least in the possibility of giving it to the masses ; and that they are taking up a new business under the old name. If workmen can't be got to feel the need of priests in any other way at least they shall look to them as "servers of tables" ; as deacons of comfort and discussion ; as "good fellows" who can kick a football with the best, and not bore them about their immortal souls. Of course it does keep them in touch with the clergy, who consider their toil repaid if a good many are thereby kept up to their duties, and if, in consequence of segregation as a "Catholic" Club, the sectarian sense is fostered. A football

victory over a Protestant club is a gain for faith.
When one subtracts the vulgarity and sham, there
is surely a large residue of *real* religion among the
Nonconformist masses, e.g. the Methodism portrayed
in *Adam Bede* is a religion fed directly on the Gospels
and the Psalms, and shaped, so to say, on the best
classical models. It seems largely to secure for the
poor what the sacraments do not. I believe, with
à Kempis, that the two tables are needed—the Word
and the Altar ; but if they are to be divorced I should
let the Altar go first. If we had real care for souls,
and not merely for proselytes, we should do what the
Methodists do and have a prayer-room in every village
and corner where the priest cannot come, but where
devout guildsmen might read the Gospel to the poor
(with notes, if necessary), and perhaps conduct the
stations or other simple and sensible Catholic devotions.
Our apparatus of priest, altar, presbytery, etc., etc.,
is too complicated. If aggression and controversy
were forbidden, we should silently sweep in hundreds ;
but, what is far more important, we should waken
some kind of rudimentary spiritual life in thousands,
Catholics and others, who are dead in formalism or
indifferentism. But who would be the most virulent
enemies of such an effort ? Those who sit in the chair
of Moses.

This is, in the rough, how the thing strikes me ; but,
as I said, I am in search of some clearer analysis.

To the Same

January 1, 1905.

This is my first letter of the New Year. How little
one can forecast how many more and of what sort
have to be written before the end ! The *Orbits*[1] have
come, also the *Revue* and *Allah*. I see you are having

[1] *The Soul's Orbit*, by M. D. Petre.

a sort of burst-out on the strength of your dividend ; but, for Heaven's sake, be careful; I may want a pair of boots before July.

I have read about two hundred pages of *Allah*[1]: so far I am not convinced by Androvsky ; but I have no idea what he is to turn into—perhaps an ex-priest. I have just read Fichte's *Die Bestimmung des Gelehrten* in German. It seemed so dead and platitudinous in English that I can scarcely believe it is the same. Obviously he is the father of Euckenism ; and the sixty pages contain a complete little philosophy of life—somewhat stern and merciless. Also I have read several chapters of Schopenhauer, and am much drawn to him. I think a modified Schopenhauer is my destiny. Réville's *Hist. du dogme de la Divinité de J. C.* has very much depressed me with the futility of the *Lex Orandi* apologetic.

Religion has had *so* little to do with the shaping of the creed ; the Council of Nice seems to have been just as disreputable a business as that of the Vatican ; as purely political in its origin and issue. One is driven back always to the religion of Jesus and away from that *about* Jesus. The parochialism of Christianity gets very oppressive at times ; its ridiculous little world-scheme and its fussy little god, and above all its deplorable history. I suppose it is better than that of the Bororos (see enclosure); but it is only a question of more or less. I feel that as Nature-worship was the first, so it will be the last form of religion in which men will be united—*Furca expellas, tamen usque recurret.* The seed was sown by the hand of Christ Himself. But meantime, while that Ark is preparing, what are we poor devils to do to whom the forms and phrases of the lower Christianity have become intolerable in their unreality and irreverence ?

[1] *The Garden of Allah*, R. Hichens.

I suppose " to work the work of God " *in silence* is the best sort of prayer under the circumstances, i.e. when words have become impossible.

To N.

STORRINGTON, SUSSEX,
October 15, 1908.

MY DEAR FRIEND,

I know what I don't know ; and I should be an ass to pretend competence in any arguments based on chemistry or the higher physics. My own idea was that atoms, electrons, and ether were mere hypothetical entities convenient for the explanation of certain phenomenal sequences or groupings. I did not know that they had ever been got at and established. For myself I regard the God of *scholasticism* in much the same light, *sc.* as a convenient hypothesis for the unification of phenomena in general : nor would I give a brass button for all ontological and cosmological proofs in the world as establishing more than this. They all go to prove an ultimate or primary " phenomenon " which is part of the world and not God. Such an ultimate may well be ether ; but it is as purely an hypothesis as ether is. If we have any ghostly idea of what ether is it is by whittling away *not all* but nearly all the sensible properties of things familiar ; but unless it is a mere word or sound we do leave it some sensible properties, and so it remains part of the sensible or physical world—one of the things to be explained. *Non tali auxilio,* etc.

I am sure it is a mistake to try to prove the existence of God. What I try to prove is that every man, honest or dishonest, does at least subconsciously believe in God by the mere fact that he believes in truth and right and disbelieves in falsehood and wrong. God, for me, is the creative Power that pushes every-

thing on towards its higher development ; the principle
of life and health and growth and truth and goodness.
I know it, as I know electricity—in its effects, not in
itself. It is convenient to *think* of electricity as a
fluid or current, for its effects suggest that image ;
and it is convenient to think or speak of God as an
etherialised, immensified, infinitely wise, good, and
strong man. It works well. What He is in Himself
we cannot know owing to the fact that our minds are
made for the physical, finite, material order of things.

NOTE

The following three letters to A. M. L. C., to L. D.,
and to W. R. H. are taken from Father Tyrrell's own
note-books, in which he copied, or resumed, some of
his own letters. The Editor has no certain knowledge
as to the names which the initials denote, and in some
cases there may be a slight divergence between the
note-book copies and the letters which were actually
sent. It can, however, be positively affirmed that
the letters, being in George Tyrrell's own handwriting,
are as true an expression of his mind as any others.

This note-book origin will always be indicated.

To A. M. L. C. (about 1908)

. . . Your letter moves me to tell you the sort of
hope that is shaping itself in my mind. One seeks
refuge in Catholicism from rationalism in the sectarian
and exclusive sense of the so-called " Naturalists " ;
one accepts the existing conflict between faith and
science or criticism, not as final, but as eventually
superable ; and yet, as rationalists hold confidently
that the unity of truth will be saved by the elimination
of dogma, so the Catholic believes as confidently that
it will be saved by the vindication of Catholicism against

Science. Yet a synthesis dissolves thesis and antithesis alike, while saving their values. The word
synthesis is always on our lips, but not always in our
hearts. Platform controversialists always meet each
with an " open mind," because each is cock-sure of
victory. It is time we began to be in earnest, and to
realise that the synthesis of what are at present called
faith and science will be the death of both.

The conception of miraculous revelation and miraculous religions was necessary to safeguard those instinctive religious intuitions which explicit reason, during
its minority, could not justify, and to lend them that
divine authority and stability that is their due. The
idea that religious truth ought to be rational, that
what is irrational is not true, was also usefully asserted
by the negations of irreligious philosophy. Each
side was right and wrong. What I look forward to
is the gradual absorption of the intuitional truths
of religion into the rational system—their passage
from implicit to explicit reasonableness. For, after
all, it is only through reason in the wide sense that
God, who is Reason, reveals Himself to us. Religions,
like rationalism, are the creations of immature reason.
It was not reason but rationalism (i.e. explicit reason
as exclusive and contemptuous of implicit) that was
enthroned at Notre Dame and was dethroned by the
Church (i.e. implicit reason contemptuous of explicit).
It is reason, in its fulness, that must at last reign there
—the synthesis of what is true in both. Then only will
religion be Catholic when it is coterminous with the
reason of mature humanity. Meanwhile the various
religious traditions guard, mixed with the ore of superstition, those treasures of truth for which, as yet,
rationalism has no place. The Christo-Catholic religion
stands for the best and fullest embodiment of such
traditions. We do well to give and withhold our

adhesion both to the Church and to rationalism, certain that each stands for a product of collective reason from which we have much to learn, and also that each is itself learning more from reason every day. Some of the most corrupt and unreasonable features of the Catholic tradition are perversions of most important truths ; misapplications of fundamental principles. A conclusion may be falsely drawn from true premisses, or truly drawn from premisses of which one is false. At present to deny the conclusion would, for most, mean a rejection of the true premiss. And so as to rationalistic conclusions, blind repudiation is as foolish as blind acceptance. One cause why the Churches decay is just that their more important truths are becoming absorbed into the general mind, while their connection with so much that is corrupt and superstitious in the Catholic religion imperils their general acceptance. And if one follows the trend, not of this or that philosophy, but of philosophy as a whole, it is plain that beliefs in God, in Providence, in Prayer, in Communion, in Redemption, in Immortality, etc., are taking root in a shape congenial to modern thought ; that the place of faith (not as belief in hearsay, but as the basis of life and thought) is being steadily, widely, and clearly recognised ; that the purge of rationalism has done its work in clearing faith of its elements of superstition and restoring its reasonable character. While the churches were almighty there were none free to study religious problems unencumbered by the supposed duty of respecting time-honoured conclusions. Thus religion was made to stand and fall with those categories and methods from which the thought of the world was moving away. Not till the Churches were discredited could men strive to justify religion, unimpeded in their thought. The result has been the firmer establishment of central

truths in a higher and transfigured sense. Rationalism
and the existing Churches are being dissolved and fused
by the higher reason. The old dualism is breaking
down. Not only is the God of Faith and Reason one,
but Faith and Reason are one.

As long as man is man we shall need churches. The
vast multitudes of the unthinking will always have
to take their beliefs on hearsay and from authority.
But they will take them as they take their historical
and scientific beliefs on hearsay—as something that
has been verified by the best collective experience
and reflection, and which they are not only allowed,
but invited to verify for themselves. Moreover, we
shall need churches for all that moral and spiritual
reinforcement which common life and aims and example
and worship and symbolism can give. But the Churches
will come closer to one another in coming closer to
reason as identical with the divine light and love
immanent in man. This breaks down the old dualism
of natural and supernatural, but rather in favour of
the latter. Such seems to be the end—God only knows
how far distant—of all our weary struggles and controversies. Perhaps it is just that Kingdom of God
for which we are told to work and pray, not only that
it may be realised, but that it may be more rightly
conceived. Once it was Jerusalem ; then the Roman
Church ; now it is afloat, seeking a yet nobler, though
perhaps not final, embodiment. Meanwhile we do
best to stick to our several Churches and further them
towards that point of convergence in which their
differences will be explained, and their defects inte-
grated. There are treasures of truth in the dust-heap
of every tradition, and the Roman dust-heap is perhaps
the biggest and richest of all. Even could we do
nothing to mend matters, yet the internal struggle,
with its doctrinal and institutional difficulties, sets

our spirit to work and elicits, at the cost of wholesome
suffering, its best ideals and aspirations. " Mine
eyes gush out with water because men keep not Thy
law "—such tears " are a nobler gift than laughter."
Watered by them, a Church springs up in the soul which
is the ideal that is slowly struggling to realise itself
outside us. It is by thus realising itself in individual
souls, and becoming an object of prayer and aspiration,
that the ideal at last takes flesh in the outer world.
Because prophets had first borne Him in their hearts
Simeon bore the Christ in his arms. God will not
ask us : What sort of a Church have you lived in ?
but What sort of Church have you longed for ? It
seems to me that the Roman Church (not the Papacy)
presents the " suggestion " ; the " broken arcs " of
a more perfect round than any other ; and that the
degree of disrepair and brokenness is comparatively
irrelevant. A fragment by Phidias does more for
æsthetic education than the finished work of his pigmy
followers. A Church, like a man, may fail deplorably,
just because its aim is so much higher than its grasp.
It falls even lower than less ambitious aspirants.

To L. D. (1908)

. . . I should be inclined to say that pantheism is
true as faith, and is false only when it pretends to be
knowledge. The attempts to define our relation to
the divinity as identity, diversity, to determine it as
one or many, as within or without, all assume that God
is " a thing " ; that He is apprehensible or comprehensible in terms of object or subject, of the world
or ourselves. Goethe said that he was theist, mono-
theist, polytheist, pantheist by turns and moods ;
i.e. that he accepted none of these theories as knowledge, but only as phases or aspects of the inaccessible

truth. I think the old scholastic solution of the controversy between realists and conceptualists very applicable to our religious ideas. The universal, they concluded, is "*formaliter in intellectu, fundamentaliter in re*"—founded in reality, fashioned by the mind; a fiction based upon fact. Our religious ideas are not subjective fancies, nor objective realities, but a little of both. The transcendental and unknowable which, as the principle of our spiritual life and growth, becomes for us, so far, immanental and knowable, seeks to express itself in terms of our understanding and language. Like our expression of the beautiful in poetry and art, this expression of the divine has its relative truth, its objective criterion, its development in the individual and collective mind. There is a lower and a higher, a less true and a more true, never a finished truth. The would-be finished truth is a lie, and an idol. What saves our " theologia " from being an " eidolopœa " is the sense of its infinite inadequacy to compass the transcendental. Religion dies with the sense of mystery, and worship becomes mere servility. That is why out theologians are so irreligious. Their treatise *De Deo* is as definite as their treatise *De Romano Pontifice*, and they worship God merely as an arch-pope. If, as they teach, God is at once simple (or partless) and incomprehensible, He must be wholly incomprehensible. Yet they speak as though the inadequacy of our God-idea were merely quantitative ; as though He were comprehensible up to a certain point. The experimental foundation of our God-idea is our own God-needing, God-seeking, God-making instinct. We give it intellectual form in the explanation or cause by which we account for these spiritual perturbations and attractions. These ideas, as fashioned by the understanding, are fictions founded on fact. If we take them as more,

they are idols ; if we realise that they are but adumbrations—shadows cast by a ray of the Light Eternal
struggling through the thick fog of the human mind—
then they are " mysteries of faith." Not arbitrary
symbols, for they are natural formations and correspond,
not to the Light Eternal, but to the form of that which
intercepts it. Finitude is of the very essence of everything we can ascribe to God. We can *say* " infinite
goodness," " infinite wisdom," " infinite power," but
the adjective destroys the substantive and leaves the
mind vacant of any meaning. Only because our God
or Eternal Spirit is always surreptitiously humanesque
and finite can we give Him an indefinite measure (but
still always a measure) of these essentially finite attributes. These names bear the same value as applied
to the transcendent as " birdie " or " blossom " applied
by a mother to her little child. It is plainly man's
religious instinct and duty to find the worthiest possible
idea and name for God : " *Quantum potes tantum
aude ; Quia major omni laude ; Nec laudare sufficis.*"
The higher will always be nearer the truth ; the highest
still infinitely short of it. Every article of the Christian
creed is subordinate to and illustrative of its central
and governing article—" I believe in God "—and is
similarly a mystery or adumbration of superhuman
truth in human terms. When I speak of our God-
idea I include our whole construction of the world and
life in relation to God. Religious creeds are the expression of the collectively elaborated God-idea of a
whole people. They are to be valued by the elevation
of their conception of humanity and of the meaning
of life [1] ; by their degree of divine inspiration and
moral fertility. They are not mere dreams or poetic

---

[1] Have we not here a suggestion towards a " religion of humanity "
of deeper reality and fuller spiritual substance than the various
forms of Positivism can offer us ?

3

fictions, for they are checked by those experiences of which they are the religious interpretation—experience of the inward life, of Nature, of human history. They may idealise, but they must not contradict such experiences. They must be *fundamentaliter in re.* They are of divine and not of human origin in so far as these experiences are God's language of self-revelation ; inadequate, as all language is, to the reality it symbolises, and needing a sympathetic spirit for its right interpretation. Monotheism, pantheism, polytheism have reference only to the humanesque images of God; referred to the transcendent reality they are senseless. Monotheism and polytheism save the idea of personality ; the former seems to satisfy the craving for unity, the latter admits of a greater fulness and variety of human excellences than are compatible in the structure of a single character. The Jewish and Christian God has no æsthetic or artistic sympathies ; no joy or laughter ; is, on the whole forbidding and unattractive. The garment of love with which He has been clothed fits ill. He is still the angry, jealous, volcanic Javeh. An Apollo would lack the sterner stuff of humanity. A whole pantheon is needed to display the many-coloured varieties of our nature ; not to speak of our collective and social life. Here Christianity, with a wise inconsistency, has discovered a trinity in unity and given us three gods, which it asserts are not three ; while in the saints and angels it has found room for the divinisation of every phase and form of the ideal humanity, individual and social. Pantheism sacrifices humanesque personality, but thereby is more conscious of the divine otherness, and finds room in the Deity for every sort of created excellence besides the human. Universal immanence means a transcendence of the human, though falling short of absolute transcendence. So, like Goethe,

I admit the truth and therefore the untruth of all of them—as applied to the Reality. As part of the same creed or God-idea I admit they are incompatible ; but the Christian revelation represents the best compromise, as being a sort of " limited monotheism," tempered by certain polytheistic and pantheistic tendencies.

My private revelation is naturally a simple affair. It gives me the image of a sort of indwelling Christ-God—my conscience, my judge, my other and better self, with whom I converse silently much as I converse with my own mind, and with whom I am often at variance, never at peace. This being, I know, is a construction of my understanding and imagination inspired by and explanatory of the Power within me that makes for righteousness, and of whose real nature I have no idea. . . .

To W. R. H. (1908)

. . . If the Jewish law, good and beneficent in its origin, became at last a soul-stifling tyranny, the reason lay chiefly in the endeavour to win for it a supernatural reverence and sanction by ascribing all its enactments to Moses, and thus winning for them a certain finality and infallibility. Whatever subsequent developments were called for had to be deduced from what was already given ; of which nothing could be abrogated or set aside. Thus not only were the new generations weighted by legislation whose *raison d'être* had passed away, but their freedom to shape laws to their own needs was hampered by the necessity of making them conformable to a great mass of obsolete enactments. Catholicism has been killed by an exactly similar process. Its enactments have all claimed to be, not Mosaic, but Apostolic, and to be therefore irreversible and final. We are not only burdened with a mass of

obsolete ideas and institutions, but are hindered by
them from a free self-adaptation to our present needs.
In both cases revelation is conceived as a once-for-all
occurrence ; and its first and least perfect form of
expression is confounded with its substance. This
is the mistake equally of those who claim apostolic
antiquity for modern innovations, and of those who,
rejecting these as spurious, would impose the apostolic
form of Christianity on later generations. Both
admit the same principle, and differ only as to its
application.   Both alike make God merely transcendent, and exclude His self-manifestation in the life and
thought and action of the community.

This is doubly inexcusable in Christianity, which
not merely threw off the yoke of the law, but, by its
doctrine of the indwelling Spirit, struck at the root of
legalism.   In the primitive Church prophecy and revelation were an abiding process ; nor could any appeal
to the past have been understood.   The Spirit, i.e.
the Risen Christ, spoke daily and continuously through
the mouth of the prophets.   What need to check His
present utterances by those of His mortal days ?   " Lo!
I am with you always," He had said.   The notion,
however, that prophetic utterances were infallible,
final, exhaustive, a rule for all time, never obtained.
The spirits were tried and compared and criticised ;
and the ultimate criterion was the spirit of the collective
Church.   Ambiguity and enigma were of the essence
of prophecy.   The Spirit was always true ; but man's
interpretation and utterance of his inward experience
always fallible and reformable.   Nor was this a serious
injury, since the Spirit was always there to utter itself
anew, and offer itself for interpretation as a living,
abiding, revelational experience of the whole Church.

With the conception of a " faith once delivered to
the saints," a " *depositum fidei*," all this was changed ;

and the work of the Spirit was merely to " assist "
in the rational deductive interpretation of the inspired
utterances of Christ and His twelve apostles ; as it
had " assisted " the Rabbis in the interpretation of
the Law of Moses. The same principle yielded the
same result ; and Catholicism became literally " the
New Law." Had it from the first claimed to be
apostolic, not as depending on, but as possessing equal
authority with Christ and His apostles, as being the
embodiment and collective incorporation of the Risen
Christ or the Holy Spirit ; had it claimed for its dogmas
and institutions, not the authority of apostolic descent,
but that of human and perfectible expressions of
present supernatural inspirations, the course of its
development would have been very different. Loisy
perhaps forgets this, when he tries to justify its actual
developments as the work of the indwelling Christ.
For the false conception of " apostolicity " has steadily
vitiated those developments, and checked their freedom by deference to the very forms of obsolete dogmatic and institutional self-utterances. As provisional
instruments and expressions of unity the monarchic
episcopate or the papacy might have been the work of
the Spirit ; but put forward as primitive and irreversible institutions they clogged recourse in later times
to other and more suitable expedients—equally divine
because in the same divine interest. The divinity
of a dogma or institution is just its aptitude to secure
those divine ends for which the Church exists. What
is divine to-day need not be divine to-morrow. It is
unity of Spirit that matters, not unity of expression or
utterance. The Church has erred, not by thinking too
much, but by thinking too little of herself ; or rather
by priding herself on far lower titles than she possesses.
She has materialised and limited her faith in the resurrection, and in herself as the glorified body of Christ. . . .

II

MYSTICISM

To V.

31 FARM STREET, LONDON, W.,
November 25, 1897.

I think I can agree with you as to the inexpediency
of applying the word mysticism, which usage has
consecrated to mean an exceptional order of things,
to so ordinary a thing as the love of God. As you say,
were we so to extend its meaning we should soon need
a new word to supply its old place. What I rather
meant was that I like the insistence on a certain
continuity between the lowest and highest degrees
of sanctity, and the recognition of the elements of
mysticism in even the most rudimentary form of
divine love. I don't say that I *see* it is so, for that
would involve a clearer definition of mysticism than
I can give ; but I should like to think it were so ;
as I wish by all means to distinguish the supernatural
which continues, perfects, and elevates nature, from
the miraculous and preternatural which implies interference and deviation from the established order.
I noticed this morning on re-reading Aquinas, *De
prophetia* and *De raptu* (*extasi*) (II. ii. 99, 172, 599),
how he inclines to the view. Not that I acquit the
scholastic theologians of an excess of rationalising,
and a tendency to squeeze everything into an Aristotelian framework at the cost of some racking ; but
that Aquinas had a larger infusion of the synthetic

38

spirit, and moreover was a mystic himself. Taking
mystic as simply one who loves God, I think Joly[1]
is justified in saying, *Tous les mystiques ne sont pas
des saints, mais tous les saints sont des mystiques ;* but
I also think it shows that his use of *mystic* is non-
natural and that it is rightly reserved for one whose
love has betrayed certain phenomena dependent on
conditions not always given even when the love is
very intense. But still I take it the mystic belongs
to the genus *lover* and so far can be reduced to the order
of the known. If you choose to specify it as the love
of fruition which has less of faith and more of union,
you leave all the elements *known*, and only vary their
proportions, which is just what I want ; unless you
mean the " fruition " in a very strict sense. M. Joly
would make *mystic* signify the generic notion ; you,
I think rightly, would reserve it to express the
" difference."

I certainly think it is well that the general public
should not hold the *via unitiva* too cheap ; that they
should understand that it is a pearl of great price, to
be purchased only at the cost of great suffering and
death to self ; that *non omnibus datum est* ; that it
is like a summons to leave the common ship and meet
our Lord on the waters ; that as some are called to
give their bodies to the flames for God, so others their
souls. Again, a false mysticism is destruction to
many ; and true mysticism is easily perverted to false ;
so that, like every higher vocation, it is more dangerous.
Awe founded on such considerations is certainly
desirable. But the awe of any remediable ignorance
is not much use, and I think a clearer notion of what
mysticism really is would rather tend to check than to
foster presumptuous familiarity, and would yet create
a desire for an occasional drop, if not a full continual

[1] M. Henri Joly, *Psychologie des Saints.*

draught, of the living water. Frankly, I am afraid the vulgar spirit of the age is telling on common Catholic piety and making the Catechism definition of prayer less and less accordant to facts. One hears priests and even religious speak with a superior contempt of " mysticism " without any attempt to discriminate between false and true ; and sweeping away as illusions every working of the Holy Ghost that does not commend itself to " common-sense." It is in the face of this Philistinism that I like to maintain the thesis that no one can love God truly and well who (as I now put it) has not the elements of mysticism, if he be not a mystic. I do hope you will be able to get a little more light on the matter.

NOTE

The two following letters to Baron F. von Hügel will be better understood by some quotations from the correspondent to whom they were addressed.

In his first letter, of September 26, Baron von Hügel raised certain questions in regard to the general subject of mysticism. In his second letter, of October 3, to which Tyrrell's letter of October 5 is a reply, he dealt specially with the relation of hysteria to the mystical temperament.

By his leave I quote the following passages from the first of the two letters :

From Baron F. von Hügel to Rev. George Tyrrell, S.J.

September 26, 1898.

It seems to me that the mystics—I am, of course, thinking of the ecclesiastically approved ones, and the whole mystical element in the teaching of all saints,

(I say " teaching " deliberately, for I think their practice generally comes round to what I would like to see modified in our present-day theory of the matter) —are profoundly right on the following points :

(1) God, our own souls, all the supreme realities and truths, supremely deserving and claiming our assent and practice, are both *incomprehensible* and *indefinitely apprehensible,* and the constant vivid realisation of these two qualities, insuperably inherent to all our knowledge and practice of them, is of primary and equal importance for us.

(2) This indefinite apprehensibleness becomes an actual, ever-increasing apprehension, more through the purification of the heart than through the exercise of the reason, and without some experience (following, no doubt, upon some light) the reason has no adequate material for effective conclusions.

(3) The primary function of religion is not the consoling of the natural man as it finds him, but the purification of this man by effecting an ever-growing cleavage and contrast between his bad false self, and the false, blind self-love that clings to that self, and his good, true self ; and the deepest, generally confused and dumb aspirations of every human heart correspond exactly to, and come from precisely the same source, as the internal helps and examples of miracle, Church or saint.   The true exceptional is thus never the queer, but the supremely normal, and but embodies, in an exceptional degree, the deepest, and hence exceptional longings of us all.

(4) This purification must take place by man voluntarily plunging into some purifying bath or medium of a kind necessarily painful to the false, surface, immediate, animal man, and necessarily purifying (where willed and accepted) to the true, inner, remoter, spiritual self.

And now I have reached the points where I would part company with them.

(5) They teach, as far as possible (their practice is generally fuller, and about all I want) that the soul gains this purification by turning away from the particular, by abstraction, and absorption more and more in the general, as leading away from the particularity of the creature to the simplicity of the Creator. There seems, I think there actually *is*, no logical place in this theory for science, at least experimental, observing science : and the motives for (ever-costing) reform in and of this visible world are weakened or destroyed.

I would like the teaching to run thus :

(*a*) As the body can live only by inhalation and exhalation, nutrition and evacuation, etc. ; and as the mind can only flourish by looking out for sensible material and then elaborating and spiritualising it : so the soul can live, to be fully normal in normal circumstances, only by a double process : occupation with the concrete and then abstraction from it, and this alternately on and on. If it has not the former, it will grow empty and hazy; if it has not the latter, it will grow earthly and heavy.

(*b*) Humanity at large is under *the strict obligation* (this not simply because of the necessities of life, but *because of its* spiritual perfection) to practise *both these activities ;* but at different periods excesses among the many of one or other of these activities justify and require counter-balancing, rectifying excesses of the opposite kind. And as the many will necessarily only exceed in the concrete direction, the compensating activity of the few will be in the abstracting direction. Still, the most difficult, and yet most complete and most fruitful condition, and therefore the ideal, would be the plunging into the concrete and coming back enriched to the abstract, and then returning, purified and simplified, from the abstract to transform and elevate the concrete.

(c) The occupation with the concrete (I am primarily thinking of experimental science, critical scholarship, etc.) has profoundly changed or deepened its character, in proportion as the idea of law, of certain conditions, inexorably inherent to each observing mind, and all observed matter, has become the necessary key to all work. Nature, history, all subjects of research first of all, now, present us with laws, with things, and neither the clamours of the petty self in front of them, nor, at first sight, the intimations of the Divine Person behind and above them, find here an echo or a place. Nothing breaks the purifying power of the thing, and its apparent fatefulness ; the apparent determinism of the phenomena and the mentally and emotionally costing character of their investigation. I think the God of all phenomena, as of all reality, has now given us in these a purifying medium, which as many will and ought to use as have, in the past, striven to use the medium of abstraction alone.

(d) The recollecting of the soul, and its turning back to its own central necessities and dependence upon God, would, of course, remain exactly as they were, and as absolutely necessary : only the running away from, or minimising or illogical tacking on of an occupation with the world around would cease : it would, on the contrary, have *its normal necessary place in the very theory of spirituality :* and every man would be taught in retreats, etc., that he must *study or work* at something definite and concrete, not simply to escape the dangers of idleness or to take off the strain of direct spirituality, but because, without them, he will, as we now know and see things, avoid one of the two twin means of growing lowly and pure, and of removing himself from the centre of his (otherwise little) world.

It would be easy, 'I think, to show how, even still in St. Catherine's day, science—represented by such fantastic, anthropocentric conceptions as those of Paracelsus—and scholarship, by such pretentious omniscience as that of Pico della Mirandola—could not as yet be the ready-formed purification I think they both can now be easily turned to ; and inasmuch as there was an inherent repugnance to all that is particular and concrete, one would have, I think, however carefully and respectfully, to admit that this was and is a confusion or theoretical misconception : for Blondel is surely right at least where he says that the true Absolute and Universal springs for us from the true Concrete and Particular : God, I like to think with Lotze, is the supremely concrete, supremely individual and particular, and the mental and practical occupation with the particular must ever remain an integral part of my way to Him. And this squares so grandly with the whole sacramental doctrine and practice of the Church. One gets otherwise into a Neo-platonic depersonatising of the soul.

You will please forgive me : it has profited me even if you cannot answer much or anything.[1]

To Baron F. von Hügel

WIMBLEDON,
September 28, 1898.

I am glad to see your intellect is at work again, and though for some reasons I should gladly have deferred answering your most interesting letter till I could have given it deeper thought, yet I had better

---

[1] Baron F. von Hügel was already engaged in the composition of his great work, *The Mystical Element of Religion*.

not keep you waiting. Oddly enough I have quite lately been engaged on a similar study, suggested by W. Pater's *Plato and Platonism*, wherein he confounds the *Ens abstractissimum* of Neo-platonic contemplation and the *Ens determinatissimum*, or as you would say *concretissimum*, of the Christian mystic ; in other words, he understands by " pure being " the last residue of an analysis and abstraction ; the barrenest of all ideas, because the most general ; almost identical with " pure nothingness ; " " a crystal ball suspended *in vacuo*." In this sense " pure being " is incomprehensible for its very emptiness. But as said of God it is the result of synthesis, not of analysis ; and is incomprehensible for its very fulness. The former ghost of a concept causes a rest of hypnotic slumber in the mind, just as does gazing on a speck or bright point where the object's emptiness of all interest drives the mind in upon itself. The latter concept by its fulness of interest draws the mind wholly out of itself in what is properly *ec-stasis ;* the other being simply *stasis*, stupefaction.

Yet, just because of the resemblance between extreme contraries, these concepts are so analogous in many ways that Plato at times slips into the " fulness of being," as in the Symposium and Phædrus ; while many Christian mystics slip into the " *emptiness* " or *minimum* of being in their attempted exposition of their theology and mysticism. This is not quite your point, but it is close to it. I wish very much that you would do more than hint, that you would clearly bring out the fact that, unlike dogma and morals, but like ascetic theology, mystic theology has escaped ecclesiastical supervision to a large extent, touching as it does the interests of a very few ; that it has never (fortunately, I think) been scientifically systematised and provided with definite terminology ; that in some

sense each exponent of it begins *ab ovo* and expresses
the truths in his own way ; that consequently it is not
wonderful if in so subtle and metaphysical a point
as the conception of pure being, or the nature of abstraction, or in the analysis of ecstasy, in matters
where a hair's-breadth divides the North Pole from
the South, certain inaccuracies of analysis should
be found.   Plainly we are to interpret the ambiguity
of the mystic's theory by his practice, which, as you
admit, is satisfactory enough.   Heaven and earth
are not more asunder than oriental and Christian mysticism ; the one looking to nonentity as the *Summum
Bonum*, the other to the fulness of infinite existence ;
the one pessimistic, the other eventually optimist,
or " bonist " as they say nowadays.   I quite agree
with you that our mystics are often poor analysts of
their process ; like all good artists, they are clumsy
art-critics.

All in which you agree with the Christian mystics
is evidently the outcome of the true and " concrete "
conception of the divine personality ; who is apprehended (*as every personality is apprehended*) rather
by a certain *sense* or *gustus* than by any reasoning
process ; and the sensitiveness of this sense (which,
I take it, is simply our whole moral and spiritual
being regarded as attracting and attracted by its like,
as repelling and repelled by its unlike) depends on the
purification of the heart and affections, whereby they
are brought into sympathy with God ; and this again
is the chief end of life and experience and education
of every kind.   And as the heart is capable of indefinite
purification, so God is indefinitely apprehensible,
always infinitely exceeding the greatest apprehension
of even the purest heart.

Whenever mystics seem to say that the concept
of God is reached by *mere* generalisation and abstrac-

tion, rather than by synthesis, they are undoubtedly out of harmony with themselves. As long as we see God *in via*, in an idea or image formed in our own mind, and not in His very substance, that idea will in a *loose* sense be abstract, but is certainly not a personification of the notion of *being in general*. I take it that when I know a man solely from his works (and indeed how else do I know any man ?) my idea of him, of his self and personality, is not the sum of my ideas of his works, nor yet a personification of the most empty idea under which all those works can be classed ; but a most concrete idea of him as the *simple* source of all that is good and intelligent in his works.

This being so, it seems to me a thing beyond any question that the study of nature and art, of science and history, of all that can open the mind and give it more matter to put into its conception of God, is an essential condition of spiritual development. Also that life and love and work, as being no less conditions for developing the soul and making it more universally sympathetic with every kind of goodness and fragmentary divinity, increase its power of apprehending more and more what God is, of whom all other good is a manifestation ; and of filling in and making richer that simple thought of God, the absolute Perfection. This doctrine of work as a clearer of the eye, as a purification of .the heart, is nobly taught by Carlyle and in some measure by Ruskin ; each regarding it as developing the power of true insight. Nor can I doubt that experimental science and criticism act still more efficiently in the same direction. Certainly I know how much I have been helped by every little scrap of secular light to a clearer vision of eternal light.

To the Same

I am certainly far from any view of the difficulty that seems to me satisfactory; but your question is rather what is expedient to put before the muddle-headed public. Plainly the third hypothesis is the least assailable—with a tentative and apparently reluctant suggestion of the fourth. With regard to hysteria I should be inclined to insist that it is but a *name* for the unknown cause of a group of symptoms, that it seems to be at root some disturbance of the normal relations of mind and body—a disturbance of the " balance of power " between them, resulting in the undue dominance of one over the other; that the " prophetic " trance or ecstasy, being confessedly an abnormal state of spiritual exaltation or mental predominance over sense-bondage, may well be accompanied by an hysterical state and tend to produce an hysterical habit in the lower strata of the soul; in a word that, though there seems no immediate connection between the symptoms called hysteria and the higher mental status of intuition, contemplation, prophecy, yet the cause of those symptoms (namely the undue absorption of energy of some kind by the soul at the body's expense) may well be so connected. I should admit hysteria, with the *proviso* that we know little or nothing about hysteria, beyond the grouping of its phenomena. The Old Testament prophets, with their music and incantations and other " hypnotising " devices (not to speak of fasting and watching and other conditions which favoured what *we* should call a morbid or subnormal, and *they* an exalted and supernormal state of mind) must be

compared with and understood by the prophets of
ethnic religions, who were all of the hysterical, abnormal, hyper-exalted temperament, akin to the poetic,
which again has usually something of the woman in
it, something hysterical. I can well understand that
the aforesaid "balance of power" between soul and
body might be destroyed by an excess of animalism
and sensuality just as well, and more commonly,
than by an excess of spirituality, and yet the symptoms
would be much the same. Either heat or cold will
crack a glass vessel : who can say which was the cause ?

To the Same

HARROW,
October 7, 1898.

I don't know that S. Teresa's case offers a real
difficulty ; though it suggests a modification of expression. The ill-balance doubtless has its seat in
the nervous system—that limbo or borderland of the
animal and spiritual ; and consists in an abnormal
development of the nerves that minister to one of
these interests at the expense of those which minister
to the other. Though this ill-balance may often be
caused or *accentuated* by undue use and strain, yet
it is often congenital and constitutional ; or, at least,
the disposition towards it. This accords with what
you said in your last but one of hysteria, that it was
no sure sign of evil. Of course all this is *a priori*
and needs confirmation from physiology ; but as an
hypothesis it seems to harmonise many apparently
contradictory facts. I return on Sunday night. If
you think of sending me the proofs I will give them
my best attention and thought.

4

To Père H. Bremond, S.J.

WIMBLEDON COLLEGE, WIMBLEDON,
October 29, 1898.

Your estimate of Wiseman[1] struck me as altogether happy. It is *not* easy for Frenchmen to understand the incoherent Englishman and his philistine ways ; but you seem, thanks perhaps to your stay in England, to have penetrated the rough cortex and to have found something admirable in its way, underneath. I feel much what you say about the coldness of modern Catholic piety as contrasted with a certain strain of mysticism in Protestants ; but I fancy it is a comparatively new feature on both sides, a reaction in the latter against the dryness of the rationalistic spirit which is the soul of Protestantism ; while Catholics, in opposition to Protestant " fluency," indefiniteness, sentimentality, etc., have insisted on definiteness and rationality to an extreme that has killed mysticism for the time being. Kegan Paul, who knows the English mind well, says that it is only through a revival of mysticism that Protestants will be recovered to the Church. We S.J.s forget that S. P. N.[2] was a thorough mystic, and with our " systematisings " of meditation and our " methods " of loving God (e.g. Fr. Roothaan's analysis of mediation ; and let us say Le Gaudier's terrible machinery of sanctity) have created a fashion which the contemplative Orders have not been strong enough to counteract. Of course, all this applies far more to the English S.J., whose national defect of feeling is emphasised by such a system. Doubtless the Latin and Celtic peoples were

---

[1] See *L'Inquiétude Religieuse*, by Henri Bremond (Paris, 1901).

[2] *Sanctus Pater Noster* (Jesuit appellation for their founder, St. Ignatius).

the better of being brought to order to a certain extent ; but we could ill afford it. Nothing strikes me as more at variance than the spirit of, e.g., a High Mass, and the spirit of private and popular Catholic devotions in this country. The Protestants have put on our mysticism and we have put on their rationalism. I am going to make a wild and presumptuous effort to treat the " Exercises " more or less mystically. If such a work ever passed the censors it would naturally be read by our own people and might tell in some way or other against the dry rationalising tone so prevalent.

To the Same

RICHMOND, YORKS,
September 16, 1901.

I do not envy you your liberty of giving retreats ; partly because of those same unrealities that one has to deal with *ore tenus ;* partly because of the veil of illusion it spreads over one's true self. For the time one is as an actor who sincerely forgets himself in his part ; and, by repetition, this professional self comes, in our own mind, to take the place of the real. Some " Sentimental Tommies " encourage and revel in the illusion ; but even those who fight it most strongly are damaged to some extent. Our whole life, in the pulpit, the confessional, the chair, the parlour, forces us to play a part ; to speak in the name of the Church or of the Society, or of a system and tradition which is *ours*, as our clothes are, but is not *we*. At most we are defending a thesis proposed to us by another. I begin to think the only real sin is suicide, or not being one's self.

I have always felt indignant, as you seem to do, at those who prove so glibly and cheaply that a life of pain and sacrifice is quite easy to those who love

God ; and yet never tackle the real problem, why it is so hard to love God, and why, if He wants to be loved effectually, humanly, sensibly, God so industriously hides Himself from our human faculties. If we can only see Him as revealed in the pulpit-talk of priests, who for the most part are as ignorant and cold about Him as we ourselves are, we are hardly to be blamed if we are unmoved to an enthusiasm which normally belongs only to human passion. All along I have been covertly suggesting the solution that God wants to be loved *in* His creatures and not *apart* from them. I do not say the contemplative *nisus* is illusory or not desirable, but that it is not obligatory ; whereas the love of creatures *is* obligatory. I verily believe this is the teaching of Jesus Christ ; and I don't believe the Apostles knew of meditation, or contemplation, or the prayers of quiet or any other prayer than the *Pater Noster*, i.e. petition for the welfare of man.

Had God wanted us to love Him as we love our human friends He would have given us eyes to see right into heaven. He does not impose the end without providing the means. We owe the current view to Neo-platonism reinforced by scholastic intellectualism. It will all pass away.

To T. Bailey Saunders, Esq.

STORRINGTON, SUSSEX,
October 25, 1907.

MY DEAR BAILEY SAUNDERS,

I have been so *accablé* with affairs, getting excommunicated and the like, that I clean forgot to tell you that I am not going to London and could not meet you on the 16th. I shall be here now till the 7th, and then from the 12th till about the 20th,

when I go to London for a few days and then to Paris
for a few months. I remembered you with a jerk
last night as I was reading Lindsay's capital history
of the Reformation (vol. i. pp. 432 ff.). " The great
truth that had been universally neglected throughout
the whole period of mediæval theology by everyone
except the mystics, that in order to know God man
must be in living touch with God Himself." That
is exactly what I should have said to your inquiry.
Scholastic theology did not touch the mystical life
of the Church, which went on in the old order and
among the laity and was fed by the patristic and
especially the Augustinian tradition. The pious mind
—as represented by à Kempis (bk. i, c. 3)—was averse
to the scholastic " modernists " and found no food in
" genus and species." The encyclical of Gregory IX
(1223), infelicitously quoted against us in the recent
encyclical, was levelled against those scholastic dis-
turbers of patristic tradition. It was only when
scholasticism had become stale and traditional, and
had received a sort of consecration from the execration
of the reformers, that it began to penetrate the general
mind and wither up the mystical life of the Church,
as it has been doing these 400 years—though, of course,
not quite successfully, since the Church cannot now
disown the mystics or the pre-scholastic tradition out
of which Protestantism so largely grew. That is how
I read history ; but I am very incompetent, and von
Hügel could tell you more in half-an-hour than I
could in a year. It is, almost exactly, his subject
and speciality. . . . St. Bernard's scholasticism and
mysticism were kept in water-tight compartments.
They could no more blend than oil and water. So
too Aquinas, who was too near the origins of scholasticism not to have escaped its aridity, and was well
soaked in Augustine. For the rest, it is plain that

scholastic epistemology (*nihil in intellectu nisi quod prius in sensu*) lent itself to a purely external, non-mystical view of revelation, as opposed to Protestant " illuminism " of any sort, and as such favoured the papal tendency and was favoured by it. Again, the centralised hierarchy of modern Romanism is plainly a scholastic conception. It is contained in Aquinas quite explicitly as a logical necessity ; and from the unspiritual idea of Church-authority as " jurisdiction " of the same *genus* (though of a higher degree) as state-jurisdiction comes the whole idea of the Pope as King of Kings and Lord of Lords. I do not say that scholasticism is responsible for the idea (which is rather the fabrication of jurists than of theologians), but that it favours and fosters it ; and that mysticism tends all the other way.

To Mrs. U.

16 OLD TOWN, CLAPHAM,
February 22, 1908.

I can only say to you : " Wait and be silent." Read William Law and the mystics and put dogmatic problems out of your head. If you believe in Christ and wish to be in communion with Him and His, go to Communion " asking no questions for conscience sake." You will *never* be able to accept the opinions of Father V. or of the encyclical. An immense revolution is inevitable ; the old is dead, the new not yet born. We can believe in it, though we shall not live to see it. Do try to realise that God will not examine us in theology or history or criticism, but solely in Christliness of spirit, in sincerity, in faith, hope, and charity. These are the best expressions of revealed truth— better than any statements and definitions. " The power of His resurrection " does not depend on the empty tomb. His new life is that new life to which you are risen with Him. What value would the physical portent of bodily resurrection have, apart from that ? At best it was a sign, symbol, or sacrament of that spiritual reality. Frankly I do not believe a bit in the trance-hypothesis. It is far-fetched and fanciful, and would mean imposture on Christ's part. I don't know of any infidel who now upholds it. It needs only to be stated clearly in order to refute itself. Critics now doubt the fleshly resurrection, but they do not doubt the appearances and spiritual resurrection. But they prove nothing ; and change every day. Leave all that alone. To be a Christian is to believe in the teaching of Christ—not necessarily in the theological amplification of that teaching. Personally I have no other answer to these problems but what I have given you. I believe that the Church will eventually be led into all truth ; and for that reason I wish to belong to her. Even the encyclical will be instrumental, under Providence, in that world of enlightenment, and I see God's finger in it.

III

DOGMA AND SYMBOLISM

To Baron F. von Hügel

February 10, 1907.

MY DEAR FRIEND,

I had rather write what I feel about Z.'s letter, and then we can talk over it. He is instinctively right in regarding the Virgin Birth as a far other *kind* of crux than the physical resurrection. For centuries of developing mariology and devotion to Mary are stultified by its denial—to all seeming ; nor do I see how the " plain man " (that is, ninety-nine per cent. of the Church) will ever be made to see that she has not blundered in a way to forfeit all credit as a doctrinal guide and as a director of worship and devotion. In other words, its denial as historic fact involves that complete revolution in our conception of what dogma is for which Loisy and Le Roy are preparing the way— a " kill-or-cure " remedy to which, however, we are simply *forced* by the results of the historico-critical method. In explaining how a belief could naturally have arisen without being true, we do not prove it false, but we have no reason to say it is true ; and when the alleged fact is miraculous or violently improbable we have so much reason for saying it is false. I have no reason to assert or deny that you had mutton for dinner yesterday ; but I am sure you had not roast bear. To take away the affirmative reasons for the

Virgin Birth is to prove it false—as historic fact ; as false as any alleged violation of the laws of Nature.

Hence I am driven to a revolutionary view of dogma. As you know, I distinguish sharply between the Christian revelation and the theology that rationalises and explains it. The former was the work of the inspired era of origins. It is prophetic in form and sense ; it involves an idealised reading of history past and to come. It is, so to say, an inspired construction of things in the interests of religion ; a work of inspired imagination, not of reflection and reasoning. It does not develop or change like theology ; but is the subject-matter of theology. Of that symbolic and imaginative construction the Virgin Birth is an integral part. It is an element of a complete expression. But it must not be broken off and interpreted alone. All the elements conspire to express one thing—the Kingdom of God. The Old Testament prophets laboured at this construction, and we know, looking back, that their construction was an idealisation of a certain core of historic fact ; and how time only has shown its meaning part by part and distinguished between the literal and the purely symbolic parts of the expression and the mere " cement " or frame-stuff, i.e. all the part of a parable which is merely for the sake of cohesion and is not symbolic of anything. I take the fuller construction of the Christian revelation in just the same sense. The whole has a spiritual value as a construction of Time in relation to Eternity. It gives us the *world* of our religious life. But I do not feel bound to find an independent meaning in each element ; or to determine prematurely what elements are of literal, and what of purely symbolic value— which is the core of historic fact and which idealisation. My faith is in the truth, shadowed by the whole creed ;

and in the direction it gives to spiritual life—in the
Way, the Life, and the Truth.

The "Holy Child of Prague" stands before me
in crown and sceptre and royal cope. Is this, as a
child would suppose, a literal portrait of the boy of
Nazareth ? or is it mere symbolism ? Neither wholly.
There is a core of fact idealised, or artistically completed,
to bring out the true inward significance of Christ's
Kingship concealed by the mere historic aspect of
the boy of Nazareth. I say the same of all the legend-
ary idealisation of the historical Jesus. It is born
of the same impulse which makes his love *visible*
by putting his heart outside his body and setting
fire to it. It is the inward truth of history, but it
is not historic truth. That He was born of a Virgin
and ascended into heaven may be but a "visibilising"
of the truth of His transcendence as divine : "No man
hath ascended but Him who hath descended and who
is in heaven." The Virgin Birth may but teach the
same truth as "He who does the will of My Father,
is My mother," i.e. the soul which, impregnated by
the Holy Spirit, reproduces Christ in its own bosom.
But I do not feel bound to find *how* each bit of the
creed helps to the one truth symbolised by the whole.
I will not tinker or tamper with that work of primitive
inspiration, with the image which truth made of
itself in the mind of a prophetic era. I should as soon
think of touching up the *Cenacle* of da Vinci, or correcting the *Divina Commedia* in the light of critical knowledge of history and science.

When it comes to what Dilthey calls "dogmas in
the *secondary* sense," i.e. to authoritative uninspired
statements as to the sense of revealed, or primary,
dogmas, I am rather at a loss what to say. Theology,
so far as adopted and imposed by ecumenical decrees,
is the Church's *understanding* and translation into

common language of the truths which she feels and
believes and has had revealed to her in prophetic
imagery. When we say " Consubstantial with the
Father " is a *revealed* truth, we certainly do not mean
that the expression is inspired or revealed, as is " Thou
art the Son of God." We can only mean that it is
the rational or philosophical equivalent of a revealed
prophetic truth. Our *faith* is in the revealed truth,
not in its translation. Else we are driven to suppose
that Aristotelian categories and exploded science
and history are matters of faith. I see no way out
of this dilemma, which I first felt in my first *Semper
Eadem* article. What value, then, do I attach to
ecclesiastical definitions ? I hint at my revolutionary
answer in *Lex Credendi*, where I defend the condemnation of Galileo. More distinctly : I believe the
Church is precisely and only the guardian of the deposit
of revelation and that she cannot add to it in any way ;
and that her definitions are simply safeguards and
protections of revealed truths. *What* she says is often
absolutely wrong, but the truth in whose defence she
says it is revealed, and to that truth alone we owe
adhesion. She condemns heliocentricism because it
implies a denial of the inspiration of Scripture. Therefore, scholastically speaking, the *formal object* of her
condemnation is this latter denial ; heliocentricism
is only condemned as seeming to involve that denial.
So, too, in affirming the philosophical concepts of
transubstantiation or of the hypostatic union, she
but protects the simple truths of revelation on which
her affirmation *formally* falls. Who can doubt that
the Zwinglian rationalism has *as a fact* weakened and
impoverished devotion and spiritual life ? In all
controversies the Church must instinctively take the
side that best protects the spiritual life. Her criterion
is purely opportunist. In all her utterances she only

repeats the truth revealed—their *meaning* is just
the revealed truth which they protect. That a lie
should be sometimes protective of truth is a consequence of the view of truth as *relative* to the mentality
of a person or people. Hence, no definition of the
historicity of the Virgin Birth could *mean* more than
that the Virgin Birth was part of revelation. Because
and so long as the denial of its historicity seems to
destroy its religious value, she will and must affirm
its historicity in order to affirm those values. In the
implicit affirmation she is right of necessity ; in the
explicit protective affirmation she may be quite wrong.
Revolutionary as all this sounds, I think it is the only
position quite consistent with the distinction between
assistance and *inspiration ;* and with the Patristic
Semper Eadem view of the Church as simply guardian
of an unchanging deposit. Theology of course develops
like any other science. But the Church is no more
infallible in it than is any other science. About all
of them alike, as also about history, she makes quite
fallible affirmations protective of those implicitly
affirmed revealed truths which are her sole charge and
interest. Thus when I say " the sun goes round the
earth " I mean " the Scriptures are the Word of God "
—for that is all the Church cares about and has any
business to care about.

And now as to Z. : First of all, it is true that certain
religious values depend not merely on ideas and symbols of truth, but on their realisation in history. The
fiction of heroism can never stir or help me as can the
fact. The value of the Gospel is not that it gives us
an ideal life, but that that life was actually lived.
The historicity of His passion is all-important, the
factualness of His resurrection equally so. But the
mode, not equally so. What imports is the triumph
of the Gospel through His death.

The fact of Mary's virginity seems to add little to its spiritual value. " What honours the Mother honours the Son " is the source of all Mary's glorification—down to the Immaculate Conception. In all cases the implicit assertion is the glory and divinity of Christ. This is equally expressed whether by the language of fact or by that of idea and image. These glories of Mary may be but as the crown, sceptre, and cope of the Infant of Prague—the Church's prophetic symbolism of what Jesus really signified. The irregularity of His physical conception might symbolise, but could it possibly constitute the dignity of His person ? The *fact* of the miracle would be perhaps a divine attestation ; but is not the Church's attestation just as divine ? If, however, it be asked, Can this symbolism square with currently approved ideas of what dogma is? the answer is an emphatic No. The question is whether criticism is not forcing us to criticise our notion of dogma, and making a quiet revolution inevitable.

To the Rev. G. E. Newsom

STORRINGTON, SUSSEX,
November 17, 1908.

MY DEAR NEWSOM,

I had to come up to London for a dozen reasons in any case, so there is no claim for damages, and it was a pleasure and a gain to address a new sort of audience.[1] It was useful to see how firmly the educated lay-mind is fixed against dogma in the received sense. To some extent symbolism is only a sop to Cerberus. It will do for the present, to keep the old and new believers in our Church. But eventually men will ask, Why express symbolically what can be said plainly ? and we shall have to criticise and define

[1] Refers to a lecture he had delivered, at Mr. Newsom's request, to a society of Church of England laymen.

the just limits of symbolism. It seems to me that the greater truths dawn on us first through the morning mists and do not admit of more than symbolic apprehension and statement; but when they climb to the zenith the symbol obscures them—nay, imperils them so far as they are identified with the symbol. Again, a good deal of our symbolic interpretation is apologetic afterthought and not quite honest. Incense was a disinfectant; now it is prayer, etc. We should ask, Are we truly interpreting the meaning that the symbol strove imperfectly to express? I think we might say so of the resurrection and ascension of Christ. But then, if we can express it more clearly, why adhere to the symbol? " When that which is perfect is come," etc.; we do not need the dark glass when we see face to face. Altogether it seems to me a very complex problem.

It cannot be denied that the desire of Modernists to hold to the Church at all costs (in which they are right) acts as a bias on their perfect candour and makes them far too ingenious. There is more of the strong Puritan temper in the pig-headed, self-destructive intransigence of Pius X—which I frankly admire and wish were in a better cause. But it is more easy for an absolute monarch to be daring than for his serfs. Courage is, I learn daily, the rarest of virtues; and have ceased to look for it—even in myself. Like rats, we are sometimes at bay and show fight for a moment, and then scuttle off to our holes never to show our noses again.

To A. F. (Notebooks)

November 22, 1908.

Personally I hardly believe that Modernism, however defensible in the abstract, will be able to save the Roman Church. It was right to try the experiment, were it only to prove its futility ; but *sero medicina paratur cum mala per longas invaluere moras.* God's arm is not shortened, and He can raise up seed to Abraham out of the ruins of Rome. Evidently the distinction of esoteric and exoteric must obtain by psychological necessity in every institutional religion. It is another thing to say it should be accepted and organised, rather than combated. There will always be a deeper and a more superficial reading of religion. But deeper and shallower should not contradict one another any more than greater and less. Is it not evident that there is often a difference of yea and nay between Modernist and popular Catholicism ? Can the Christian religion admit the *deliberate* toleration of error, fable, and superstition out of deference to the ignorance of the crowd ? Is it to such toleration in the past that we owe the present embarrassment, that makes truth a scandal ? Has Modernism, which is so largely a return from the esoteric complexity of theology to the exoteric simplicity of the Gospel, any right to consider itself a *disciplina arcani?* Are not its teachings just those by which Christ delivered the starving crowd from the indigestible subtleties of the erudite ? I simply resent the idea that the very best in religion should not be accessible to all equally. I will have no enclosure of the commons that Christ threw open at such cost. Mysteries and symbols are justifiable just so far as truth does not admit of plain statement. For all of us the ultimate truths are mysteries, and can be thought and uttered only in symbol. There is no room here for a division of doctrines into esoteric and exoteric. Experience shows us in ourselves and everything a power that makes for good and a power that makes for evil. What they are, how they are related, how unified, we cannot know. We symbolise the first as an idealised good man

—the second as an idealised bad man. We dramatise their relations as a conflict between God and Satan. The victory of the former symbolises our incurable hope. The best of us can do no better—for self is our ultimate and inevitable category. But have we a right to cover up in myths and fables those simple truths of Christianity for lack of which the crowds are perishing ? If we tell them that Christ's body rose into the clouds, they will only laugh their whole religion to scorn. If we tell them that His self-sacrifice raised Him above His fellows, to the level of God, they will understand and believe and love and imitate. The spiritual truth of the Eucharistic presence is within a child's comprehension ; the carnal miracle of transubstantiation is now a scandal to the meanest intelligence, and men throw away the kernel along with the shell. Truths that dawn on our horizon through the mist of symbol are only obscured by that mist when they attain the zenith. When what is perfect is come we abandon what is imperfect ; nor do we need the darkened glass when we can see face to face. Our symbolism is useful, as a passing ex-pedient, to hold the old and new believers in one com-munion until the day when, the new having leavened the old, it will be possible to be perfectly honest. For in the first place the story of the Ascension was not the earliest expression of the simple truth of Christ's moral exaltation. It was a gross materialisation and obscuring of that truth, which we are only now learning to dematerialise and restore. Secondly, many of our interpretations are after-thoughts, and not render-ings of a truth obscured by the symbol in question. Incense was a disinfectant. Altar-lights were to see by. A chasuble was an overcoat. The original mean-ing is forgotten. We have simply tacked on a mystical meaning. In most of these cases what does symbolism do but obscure what is perfectly obvious, its true function being to clarify what is obscure? I think, then, we do right to have symbolic ideas of God, Satan, hell, heaven, and, in general, of metaphysical realities, but not of historical facts or moral platitudes.

With the purpose of your forthcoming novel I keenly sympathise. More justice should be done to the reactionary mind and temper, which stands for a truth and principle too much overlooked by Modernists. The mutual contempt of youth and age for each other is a mutual injustice and folly. But the *mala fides* of the present régime must not be ignored or condoned. I allow that, compared with the average of his predecessors, Pius X is a morally respectable Pope ; and that he sincerely believes he is doing God's work. But, against Döllinger, I agree with Lord Acton that we must not call a man good who thinks evil is good, or one who sincerely believes that the end justifies the means, or one who is resentful, unjust, or uncharitable. Pure relativity is pure scepticism ; nor are heart and head so divorced that the former can be quite sound and the latter quite rotten. The Curé d'Ars was as ignorant and stupid as Pius X. But, then, he knew himself. He would have conceived God's will and work very inadequately, as we all do, but he would not have attributed his own injustice and uncharitableness to God. A man's conception of God's will is the criterion of his own morality. Else, we confound everything and lapse into ethical indifferentism. Sincerity is not the whole of morality ; nor is a sincere devil-worshipper aught but a devil. The Javeh of the Pentateuch was an image and criterion of the badness as well as of the goodness of ancient Israel. I would say the same of the God of Calvin or of Pius X ; God is the evening shadow of man's soul—its grotesque prolongation.

5

IV

INFALLIBILITY

To a Fellow-Priest

RICHMOND, YORKS,
December 1900.

I was almost sure, but not quite, of the sense in which you sympathised with Keble ; but in such matters one does not speak on a mere hint, for fear of giving mortal offence. I have always felt that the infallibility question, answered negatively, takes away all rational foundation for the sacrifice of that family life which is normally the best thing for the perfect development of a man's life, whether it bring more or less trouble, less or more joy ; and I keenly resent the deluge of pious calumny which is poured forth upon any priest who, on leaving the Church, does what he is perfectly consistent in doing. The " *Cherchez la femme* " witticism is shallow and contemptible beyond words ; but is a favourite weapon of " apologetics." Fr. Tepe's implication always seemed to be : " If you do not admit my argument, it is because you keep a mistress." God forbid that I should practise or counsel any sort of *securité bourgeoise*. I resent very much the attitude, e.g., of my very dear friend Fr. T., whose mind, in these matters, is like his room—one vast mess in which he " pigs " along, quite comfortable and undistressed ; he thinks there is something in it all, but he does not know what,

or where, or try to find out. I am sure it is our duty
to try to bring our mind to order, even were we certain
of eventual failures ; just as in moral matters a man
is bound always to struggle, however hopelessly, to
get his passions obedient to his will. But this very
effort after order is frustrated by fretfulness and the
impatience begotten of disappointed hope. Perhaps
resignation to the hopelessness of success makes one
more patient, more successful. The theologians are
just the enemy at present ; not the infallible Pope.
For they are the middle-men between the Pope and us,
who adulterate the goods to their hearts' content.
At least for myself it is the implicit dogma of the
infallibility of theologians, of the scholar, of the
" *consensus patrum societatis* " (a new " *locus theolo-
gicus*"), that is so alarming. At present I can only
think that the Pope is infallible just when and in so
far as he does give voice to the consentient Church
whose mouthpiece he is. The notion that his particular brain is the organ of the Holy Ghost is an innovation.
The other conception is but a closer definition of what
was always held from the beginning. At this rate
I suppose that, in '54 and '70, the Pope was feeling
and reporting the pulse of the whole Church, but since
then he has made no pretence at such an investigation.
Above all, I resent the *quasi-infallibility* claimed for
more solemn non-ecumenical utterances. Here the
difference between *Est* and *Non* is infinite. As a
rationalist, I should regret that Christ did not confer
on His vicar the prerogative of impeccability rather
than that of infallibility. It would have been a far
greater stay to the Church, and refutation of her
enemies, than the present unverifiable claim. As to
the practical issues of intellectual emancipation it
seems to me practice should follow theory a long way
off ; that a moral system ought to survive its specula-

tive roots, much as a tree retains life after it is felled. The desire of " practical " liberty is so apt to be a bias that, for sake of self-respect, one ought to feel that it has had no voice in the speculative decision.

Further, I think until a Mahometan is perfectly sure that his religion is all wrong, and has accepted some substitute, he ought to practise it fully, just to secure this sense of sincerity. For it is provisionally God's word to him, and his word to God; it is the best *organon*, or medium of communication, he knows as yet, and the worst is better than none. I think you or I should stay where we are until (if ever) it is perfectly clear that we are in conflict with the *authorised* tenets of Catholicism—not taking the judgment of a clique, or " an insolent and aggressive faction," in the matter, but giving ourselves the benefit of every probability of a wider view being tenable later. If the " aggressive faction " were in peaceable possession one might be more alarmed; but the " new world undermines the old " and the ground is shaking beneath their feet. This is what makes them so assertive just now—the sense of power slipping from their senile grasp. Galileo did not doubt that his truth would win, for all the frowns of Pope and cardinals—*eppur si muove*. If, however, I were forced outside by authority, I think I should call myself a Catholic *in spe*, and hope for better things; but I should not feel that the end of the world had come, and that there was no middle between Romanism and chaos. But all this I said before? I have, alas, to say it to so many now that I forget.

Of course a rupture with the S.J. may come any day, but that is a small affair by comparison; yet I will do all I can in reason, for the sake of others, to avoid it.

Yes, for us two the " lines have *not* fallen in pleasant

places " ; but surely we are in good company, when one turns over the pages of history and sees the circumstances ever repeating themselves.

To the Same

RICHMOND, YORKS,
January 22, 1901.

The bishops' pastoral [1] is really worse than it seems. It implies a conception of Church-authority that can in no sense be explained away as a " development," but imports a wholesale innovation—a living, active *Ecclesia docens* ; and a purely dead and passive *Ecclesia discens*—the Pope is not the *inherent* head of the organism, a part of that whole which is the spouse of Christ ; but he is vicariously the spouse of the Church, an *alter Christus*, a distinct personality outside and above the Church. This is heresy. Also there is no limit assigned to his vicarious powers ; he is plenipotentiary ; not a divinely-assisted teacher, but a divine teacher. The Pope is Peter ; Peter is Christ, and Christ is God, and there is no more to be said but *Venite adoremus !* I will at least do my best to get these fallacies well aired and discussed.

.   .   .   .   .

Have you ever read Walter Pater's *Marius the Epicurean*, which I am reading with renewed admiration for the third time ? In spite of his laboured preciosity (he is our Flaubert) he is strangely fascinating ; and gives one that " far-off " and " from-outside " view of life which is so healthy and needful a tonic for those like myself, who are apt to take their part in the drama a little too seriously, and miss the divine humour of it all.

[1] Joint-pastoral of the Catholic Bishops of England: see *Autobiography and Life of George Tyrrell.*

To Baron F. von Hügel

June 6, 1900.

I have been saddening my soul lately by going over the miserable story of the Vatican Council again— Quirinus and James and Fesseler and Newman and Manning. I have been looking for a " way out " ; but so far have not succeeded. I expect ecclesiastical infallibility really means that the Church is infallibly moving through tortuous paths to the right end, even when her back is turned to the goal ; that we are infallibly right in holding to her, and betting upon her winning, though many a hare may seem to outstrip the old tortoise for the present ; that all heresy rises from forgetting the organic oneness of her doctrine, and tearing bits off and judging them as wholes in themselves, whereas they are essentially parts and lose their meaning and intelligibility when isolated.

I have not said quite what I mean, but I am groping somewhere in that direction. But, of course, an " inspired Pope " is fatal to all that view of the matter which supposes that the " organ " of the Holy Ghost is the whole Christian people, and that to " define " a doctrine is but to formulate and register the result of the slow growth of the general mind. I am struck by the apparently *radical* opposition of principle between Vaticanism and anti-Vaticanism ; between viewing the Pope as the *mind* of the Church, and as merely the *voice* of that mind. But I may ask you some day to read what I am writing on the question.

To V.

June 20, 1901.

Did you see P. Grisar's Fribourg address in the *Weekly Register* of June 7 ? How obtuse people are as to the consequences of such admissions ! No one with sense is surprised at myths and superstitions getting round a world-old and popular religion ; the purity of Anglicanism in this respect is due to its unpopularity and low rate of vitality. But the point to mark is the attitude of the guardians of purity of faith and worship in regard to these myths ; how they foster and further them ; how rarely, if ever, they check them ; how they are incorporated into collects and masses and imposed by the highest authority on the universal Church ; how the critical attitude, which is really a reverence for faith, is treated as akin to heterodoxy. All this forces us to see that, outside a very narrow sphere, God leaves us to our own wits and endeavours, and never meant to spoon-feed His Church—which is just what one would rather think, and is in accord with the more intelligent notion of His workings in the natural order. He loves to make things make themselves.

To the Same

TINTAGEL,
January 22, 1906.

I am sure you are right about the experts, and I have been trying to define in my own mind what this " vital contact " consists in. I think it means that, in a well-knit, systematised mind, any new knowledge affects the whole and demands a general adjustment ; whereas a loose-knit mind can hold incompatibles quite comfortably. An expert in any subject is one whose mind is well-knit in that particular matter, and who has built that matter or subject into the general fabric of his thought. Hence he is sensitive to, and his whole mind is shaken by, any new fact bearing on that subject. We have all large quantities of unassimilated knowledge lying loose in our minds, waiting to be sorted and systematised ; and we can leave a new fact in that lumber-room pending examination of its bearings on our systematised knowledge. But to the expert those bearings start into view at once ; and either the fact or his system must yield if they will not fit. We tell the non-expert to wait, just because he has no systematic knowledge in the matter. N.'s crime is not so much in *seeing* the good that comes out of evil—out of prejudice, coercion, intolerance—as in justifying the prejudiced and intolerant, and crediting them with *intending* good through evil; in insinuating that Rome's reaction is secretly motived by a long-sighted desire of progress.

To Wilfrid Ward, Esq.

RICHMOND, YORKS,
August 1, 1901.

MY DEAR WARD,

I have read your *Edinburgh* article with great interest, but would have to write something twice as long to do justice to it. Like your *Doctores Ecclesiæ* I feel that it implies principles that may carry, not us, but those who follow us hereafter, much further than we can now distinctly see. Obviously it points to a radical change of view as to the sphere of ecclesiastical infallibility. This will come about, not through any analysis of theories or refinement of definitions, such as was attempted in the recent *Weekly Register* controversy anent Halifax's article, but simply through the opening up of the past by historical research. It will be impossible to pretend that the Church or the Pope are infallible in departments where they have erred over and over again. It is not individuals, but all that we mean by authority, that for centuries has ignored, if not overtly denied, evolution in the Church, and has projected the present backwards to apostolic times, taking a bird's-eye view of the tree and seeing its crown of foliage thrown, as it were, flat on the earth.

We justly point out to Anglicans that no error in doctrinal detail can be so deadly as an error touching the rule of faith and the nature of the Church herself ; and yet we forget that the mechanical " creationist " view of the Church, still held by men like Gallwey and Humphrey and Lescher, who believe that Christ said the First " Mass " and that St. Paul paid triennial visits *ad limina,* is only a survival of what was once universally held. When history has done its work it will be hard to imagine men ever trusting the Church as she now demands to be trusted—with that naïve faith in the Pope which is just what attracts so many converts to us, desirous of certainty in matters of quite secondary import, or less. I think we shall be drawn back to the view I put forward in the " Walla-washee " romance, [1] so that the Church will infallibly right herself, and that it is safer in a storm to cling to an inverted lifeboat than to sit comfortably in one that is not capsized ; or, paradoxically, it is better to be wrong with the Pope, now, or in detail, than right with his adversaries ; that, taken in conjunction with the whole organism of truth, what were separately a lie is truer than what were separately the truth. This is a hard saying ; but Newman says much like it. Of such details I can say reasonably : " I believe them in a sense, though I don't know what sense : I believe the whole system of which they are the undeveloped parts—rudimentary, grotesque, inexplicable at present ; what they mean I know not now, but later times shall know."

Your *Doctores* raises the obvious question : " Who

---

[1] Published in collaboration with Mr. A. R. Waller under the title of *The Civilising of the Matafanus.*

are the experts, if a distinct class from officials and
not designated by the officials ? " If it is presumption
in me to call myself an expert it were equally presumptuous for me to decide who are experts. But
in no view can one exclude the need of private judgment
somewhere or other. I look for a clearer solution in
recognising that in every realm of thought the active
minds are the few and exceptional and the passive and
receptive are the many : that the Church is for the
many and not for the few, or rather an instrument for
distributing the wealth of the few in a form suited to
the needs of the many. While, for all, the sense of
the Church of to-day is the living rule of faith, those
. who are interested and active-minded will read that
rule for themselves with individual variations ; but
the masses who only ask to. be taught will take the
official formulation literally and without discussion.
The more forward minds will be in sympathy with
the Church of the future rather than of the present.
Were there none such, I don't see how there could be
any evolution, since this demands a principle of variation for selection to work upon. A heresy is only a
rejected variation, but the principle of heresy is a
principle of progress and life.

To the Same

RICHMOND, YORKS,
August 1, 1903.

MY DEAR WARD,

I have read your " Hibbert " article twice,
and find myself in agreement with most of it. My
chief objection is to the use (Balfour is responsible) of
the term " authority " for two things so generically
diverse as intellectual originality and official jurisdiction
in regard to truth. The natural laws of collective
mental growth divide the Church, like every other

society, into the teachers and the taught, the leaders
and the led. No one, I suppose, denies that the young
and inexperienced should listen to the old ; and laymen to experts and doctors. The real problem of
Romanism lies in the assumption that, by mere official
appointment, independent of all personal gifts and
attainments, certain " laymen " should be considered
fit to sit in judgment upon experts, or at least to
determine whether or not the conclusions of experts
are legitimate developments of the common belief.
To do this they receive some divine *charisma* of infallibility. This, of course, is just what our Church
teaches ; and so is quite logical in summing up juridi-
cally what *naturally* only admits of intellectual decision.
It is no use, I think, shirking this " miraculous "
factor in Church authority, or trying to bring the
whole system within the compass of reason. Deny
miraculous infallibility, and still I see that *ex officio*,
as distinct from expert, teachers would serve a useful
purpose like that of schoolmasters ; but their teaching
would not be the supreme rule of doctrine ; the teachings both of Pope and Council would be always revisable
by the judgment of theologians and saints. All that
we most complain of now in the cramping of originality
by officialism is traceable to the Vatican conception
of Church authority ; to the belief that Rome possesses
a short-cut to truth, independent of experience and
reflection ; that her infallibility is *not* explicable by
the natural law of the human mind. Now this is either
true or not true. If it is not true, we must go behind
the Vatican Council and cry " *Peccavimus.*"

Again, I agree with you very much when you make the
saints the teachers of the Church (unofficial, of course) ;
it certainly *ought* to be that those who live the life
should know the truth experimentally and instinctively.
But is it really so ? Are there not saints in every

religion ; nay, in every sect of the Christian religion ? Have not canonised saints swallowed down, even more than others, every current superstition of their place and day ? Is not their very reverence, humility, and obedience the reason of their mental passivity and incapacity for criticism ? It seems to me the truths which feed sanctity are few and simple, and common to all who possess the light of conscience. And then, who is to decide who are the saints and who are the experts ? Men who are neither one nor the other *ex officio*, and whose only claim to inerrancy rests on the supposition of miraculous intervention. But given such intervention, why not dispense with the experts altogether ? Thus I think the mingling of these two disparate conceptions of authority make it impossible to state our position clearly ; and still more to bring it within the limits of philosophy. The importance of Newman's line is that it prepares a philosophic and rationalistic theory of Church authority which will (or may possibly) stand when the " miraculous " theory shall have gone the way of all fond illusions. Then and only then will it be possible to give to " official " teaching (*versus expert*) the respect and value which is its due, and to recognise its necessity and utility—and, indeed, its divine authority.

V

MODERNISM

To F. Rooke Ley, Esq.[1]

RICHMOND,
November 19, 1900.

I was dreaming to-day that there will be no remedy for our present miseries till some independent man, like Maxse of the *National*, to whom excommunication means nothing, starts an organ for the relief of suppressed Catholics. I don't mean for red, passionate onslaughts, but for quiet, grey truth—searching and *unfettered* criticism. Bishops would ban it; but it would not lack a public if the tone were kept up, and if other interests were also provided for. Without the gadfly of ruthless and persistent public criticism nothing can be done. But the criticism of outsiders fails through exaggeration and misunderstanding; while that of insiders is suppressed. What a terror such an organ would be to these cardinals and bishops! And yet, if our religion cannot stand the light, is it worth bothering about? Personally, I believe it is; and that when daylight breaks through—as it must soon —it will work a violent purgation at the cost of great present scandal but with far greater ultimate gain. To withdraw from the S.J. would mean stepping into excommunication, unless I got dispensed, which would be morally impossible. Of course, if my position became absolutely false and lying, then, although

[1] Editor, at that time, of *The Weekly Register.*

retaining my belief in the Roman Church, I should be bound to stand out and face the censure as better men have had to do before now. The scandal this would give to many, who could not understand the motives and justifications, and the triumph it would be for those who have shaken their heads over me for twenty years, make me strive as long as I can to find a *modus vivendi ;* and I do not as yet see that to be a Jesuit binds me to approve of all that has got to be meant by Jesuitism. I was never less idle than now ; the stimulus of a prohibition is quite astonishing ; and the waters are gathering rapidly behind the dam. That they will leak out some way or other I do not doubt. I could return to London if I made a fuss, but on the whole this serves my purpose better. As you will see, this is written as a friend to a friend.

To Baron F. von Hügel

CATHOLIC CHURCH,
RICHMOND, YORKS,
June 16, 1900.

MY DEAR BARON,

I must thank you very much for this delightful book of Bishop Spalding's, which you shall have as soon as I have finished it. It is hard to believe that it is by a Roman Catholic bishop, so full as it is of palpitating sympathy with all that is best and most catholic in modern thought. How few live up to the prophecy " *Ut det illis haereditatem gentium,*" or realise that God will call them to account for all the light that is mingled with but not overcome by the darkness of the world in which it shines. The modern Church strikes me as starving to death in the midst of a wealth of pabulum such as never before was offered for its nutrition and reinvigoration. There are heritages on all sides inviting occupation, and yet we hang back through a timidity which vaunts itself as faith and prudence, but is in reality unfaith and shortsightedness. I have been reading Harnack—in English, of course—and have been impressed with the madness of supposing that we can go on ignoring so plain a fact as the growth of Catholicism out of a germ as unlike Catholicism as a walnut is unlike a walnut tree. It will take all our wits, and more learning than at present, alas! the Church can command anywhere, to show that the outgrowth is a real and legitimate development ; and yet our theologians go on dreaming and romancing about a full-fledged apostolic Catholicism, and are anxious to anathematise the very notion of development by putting Newman's Essay on the Index. Surely we are nearing the stone wall against which we seem fated to bang our heads before we wake up.

NOTE TO FOLLOWING LETTER

Writing from Rome on December 18, 1901, Baron F. von Hügel had referred to the temperament of certain German Catholic scholars :

It is surely (he wrote) a most painful spectacle (and one which if I afforded it would, I know, to my own eyes, spell simply the loss of faith) to find active and very religious intelligences like Ss. deliberately, and with reasons given and assigned, giving the " go by " to that whole central mass of facts and their analysis and thronisation : he has his philosophy before them, he has his otherwise universal historical criticism after them ; and, in the middle, there they are, hedged in and off by reason, yet contrary to reason, from every approach of reason ; and this with a frank declaration that this is necessary, since the Catholic position could not stand the application of these otherwise universally valid principles.

The episode of St. Edmund's bones was well known at the time. Cardinal Vaughan had been notoriously deceived in regard to the authenticity of these relics, and had candidly avowed the error.   .

To Baron F. von Hügel

January 3, 1902.

MY VERY DEAR FRIEND,

Your letter is simply bewildering in the multiplicity and intensity of its interests, and I hardly know where to begin. Also I should trespass not merely on your time, but, what is worse, on your attention, were I to launch out on certain oceans of thought which it suggests, in which my wanderings are too rudderless and haphazard to be worth chronicling. What I am fullest about is what you say about Prof. S.—the manner in which, Loisy excepted, we Churchmen evade the *inevitable* " quid inde ? " that arises out of those data of Biblical investigation that some of us are not slow in collecting. As with St. Edmund's bones, the conclusion will soon be drawn for us by outsiders, and we shall find ourselves with no *modus vivendi* if we now burn the boats that Loisy has prepared for our escape. I have carefully read and studied his *Études Bibliques*, his *Religion d'Israel*, and his articles in the *Revue d'Histoire* on " Genesis and Babylonian Myths " ; whence I draw the principle : Inspiration means the progressive spiritualising and refining of those gross embodiments in which man expresses his own ideas and sentiments about God. Thus the Eucharist is the last refinement of an idea originally gross and superstitious—the idea of sacrifice, partly refined in the Law ; further, in prophets ; finally in Christ. Christ's whole " revelation " was little else but a further correction of the better sort of religion

which He found in Israel. The " Our Father " was not
new in words, but He put a new meaning to it ; no
longer " our " in an exclusive nationalistic sense, but
in an all-inclusive Catholic sense ; no longer the ceremonial taboo of the Sacred Name, but the spiritual
and practical reverence of the Nature for which it
stands ; no longer a zeal for the Kingdom of the
comparatively poorly-conceived Messias of the prophets, but for the Kingdom of God in men's hearts.
S. Paul is plain enough on this point when he distin-
guishes the true from the carnal seed of Abraham, etc.,
etc., and spiritual from fleshly circumcision. The
principle is plain, but we shrink from its consistent
application, because we secretly think the *material*
sense is *true*, and the spiritual *unreal*—the husks appeal
to our mental appetite, but the Manna of Angels is
a thin food for mortal stomachs. But another more
potent reason of Rome's hostility to Scripture criticism
is the fact that nothing which Fathers, Councils, or
Tradition have said of the Church's infallibility is
half so strong as what they have said of the infallibility
of Scripture ; and that, if the latter conception has
to be gravely modified, the former cannot hope to
escape a corresponding modification. Yet both modi-
fications are " insuppressible," and the more obsti-
nately the truth is resisted the more disastrously
will it avenge itself at last, and the Church will have to
" begin with shame to take the lowest seat." [1]

I see the Commission on Scripture is announced in
this week's *Tablet* with much parade of the liberal
character of the proceeding. . . . It is a foregone
conclusion that the *Providentissimus* [2] will be extolled
as all-sufficient, and the liberty of discussion will be
like that at the Vatican Council, and the issue will be

---

[1] See *Life*, etc., vol. ii. p. 189.
[2] Encyclical of Pope Leo XIII on Scripture Studies.

6

the contemptuous toleration of the N—s purchased
by the sacrifice of Loisy. . . . I saw Mgr. Mignot's
address.[1] . . . It is indeed a notable advance on
aught we have hitherto heard from authorities. What
more could we reasonably desire ? But what is one
bishop among so many ? *Vox clamantis in deserto*—
a herald perhaps of a day when others will reap with
joy and ingratitude what he has sown in tears. Men
do not even build up the sepulchres of bygone prophets
whom their fathers have slain, but trample over their
bones.

.   :   .   .   .

S.'s short visit was like a sudden burst of sunshine
to me. But his hopefulness is too obviously physical
in its basis to be solidly reassuring. For one who
begins life with the fulness of popular Catholicism
the disillusionments of criticism are not so costing as
for one who has climbed up somewhat laboriously
to that position at the cost of a good deal of needless
intellectual torture and is now forced step by step
down to the level of sane Christianity. I feel that
S. does not, perhaps cannot, know experimentally
the horrors of pure negation ; that his sense of the
extremest possible issue of honest criticism is more
" notional " than " real." In all else, I felt abundantly
in sympathy with the humour of the man, and his all-
saving sense of the ridiculous—that salt for lack of
which so much corruption has invaded theology.

.   .   .   .   .

Your letters are the epochs of my quiet life ; but
you must not sacrifice for me any fraction of that
energy and attention which is needed for more universal

---

[1] "The Method of Theology." This was a discourse pronounced
by Monseigneur Mignot, Archbishop of Albi, before the *Institut Catho-
lique* of Toulouse, November 13, 1901.

ends; though to keep my head above water may perhaps be indirectly for the service of many and not merely for my own comfort.

To Abbé Loisy

RICHMOND, YORKS,
January 27, 1903.

MY DEAR ABBÉ LOISY,

Father L., whose hand is disabled by neuritis, asks me to write to you to offer his absolute sympathy with you in your present annoyance.[1] Needless to say that I wish to unite myself with him unreservedly in his sentiment. That the blow was not altogether unexpected does not make it lighter. One advantage, perhaps, may be imagined—if Rome confirms the Cardinal's censure her action, as less spontaneous, will be less significant; if she keeps silence her silence will be tenfold more significant. The *déraison* of these violent tactics is that no one's opinion is changed either *pro* or *con.*; and that an antagonism of thought, which is harmless, is transformed into an antagonism of sentiment, which is full of harm, especially now, in France, where union and mutual toleration are all-important in the face of foes who accuse the Church of being the enemy of light and liberty. *Eppur si muove;* facts are stronger than cardinals; nor will the whole Curia be able to prevent the tide of history coming in and sweeping down all barriers that are of sand instead of rock.

[1] M. Loisy's book, *L'Évangile et l'Église*, had been prohibited by Cardinal Richard, Archbishop of Paris, and other French archbishops and bishops.

To the Same

RICHMOND, YORKS,
January 2, 1904.

I was so incredulous about the reported condemnations [1] that I held back the expression of my sentiments in *The Pilot* till three days ago. To-day the article should appear (" L'Affaire Loisy "); and I need not now trespass on your patience to say again what I have said there. When I look beyond the present scandal of thousands, created by this triumph of the scholastic clique, to the future liberation of Catholic thought that will result from this blindly suicidal act of theirs, I can be sorry for the anxiety and annoyance it entails upon you personally, and for those whose faith may be shaken for the moment : but I cannot be sorry for the cause of truth. One always has faith that God can get good out of evil, and light out of darkness ; but in this case it scarcely needs faith to see that " *iniquitas mentita est sibi* " ; that reaction has run its head fatally against a wall of stone.

To the Same

January 27, 1904.

I have only this moment heard of this most painful development. It seems to me that you must hold fast to your distinction between the religious and the scientific aspects and approaches of the same questions, allowing the Church's jurisdiction over the former, firmly denying it over the latter. I think, as to " *L'Évangile et l'Église*," and your other more directly apologetic matter, you should say : " That is the only reconciliation I can see between the Church and Science. If authority condemns it let it show me some

---

[1] The best history of M. Loisy's ecclesiastical career is to be found in *Choses Passées*, 1912–1913 (Union pour la Vérité, Paris).

other. Meantime I admit its right to refuse this or any other proffered defence of its own claims and positions." As to the purely scientific interest, it is out of the Church's jurisdiction. You are bound by your presuppositions and methods. You teach in the Sorbonne not *qua* priest but *qua* critic and expert. To make you resign your profession is obviously *ultra vires*. If they excommunicate you for that, the whole world will give it against them. So, as to publishing, their jurisdiction extends to, and ceases with, the *religious* interest. You can certainly retract, as I may do some day if similarly pressed, all you have ever said in defence of Catholicism by way of apologetic, so far as it means a defence of that authority which now repudiates this same method of defence : " *Ipsi viderint.*" An *unjust* excommunication will not cost you a particle of the loyal sympathy and adhesion of the vast multitude of your friends and admirers ; rather it will intensify and extend your influence for good, and will bring merited shame and confusion on these benighted fanatics who are, under God, the crooked instrument by which the Church is to be brought straight. You will no doubt be overwhelmed with conflicting counsels, and I only offer this opinion as the best that now occurs to me. Whatever you do, I will always believe to be dictated by the sincerest and most disinterested love of truth and of religion.

With every sentiment of affection and loyalty.

To the Same

STORRINGTON, SUSSEX,
October 20, 1907.

I delayed answering your request ¹ (per Dell) till I should have time to read the Encyclical *Perdendi gregis*

---

¹ M. Loisy asked him to note the passages of the Encyclical *Pascendi* which referred to his own works.

over again, for the fourth time—a very disagreeable task, which has occupied several hours. When I first read the document I, like others perhaps, found myself in every paragraph ; but now I see that, in most cases, it is impossible to say whether I, or Laberthonnière, or Newman, or Le Roy, etc., be the culprit. I am, however, morally certain that the passage on the nature of Church authority (" *Jam auctoritatis hujus natura . . . ac religione deleta*") is from the article " *Da Dio o dagli uomini ?* " which appeared in *Rinnovamento* and is reproduced in *Scylla and Charybdis*. Of course it is a *lectio conflata* ; still, both what is said and the manner of saying it are plainly mine. Also I suspect the passage about the conservative and progressive factors of ecclesiastical evolution ("*evolutionem ex conflictu duarum virium evenire dicemus . . .*") is from various utterances of mine to that effect ; yet the sequence seems to point to *lay* presumption ("*Ex his enim pronum est . . .*") and is probably levelled at the editors of *Il Rinnovamento* as inspired by my *exitiosissima doctrina*. Then, dealing with the *subjective* method of the new apologetic, the passage " *Elaborant nempe ut homini persuadeant . . . desiderium et exigentiam*" seems to be levelled at *Lex Orandi*, more perhaps from the *form* than from the *substance* of the passage. But in all cases they are *lectiones conflatæ* and quite impossible to verify. Finally, the passage " *De magisterio ecclesiæ sic scilicet commentantur . . . modernistæ collocant*" is probably meant for me, though it might well be for Ward. But, as I said, I *may* be alluded to in fifty other places which condemn what I hold in common with others.

I feel it will be very easy to pull it all to pieces except the part dealing with the *apriorism* of the critico-historical method, which evades refutation owing to its profound obscurity and confusion. Surely it is a truism to say that *all* investigation must be *a priori* so far as it assumes the validity of the *method* of investigation. The crudest positivist sets out with a philosophy of science and criteriology. Such *apriorism* is universal and inevitable. What we reprehend as *apriorism* is that which begins by determining *the results* of the investigation and shapes its *methods* accordingly. The true critic begins by determining the right *method* (a philosophical effort) and then accepts the results honestly and impartially—whether it be the Koran, or the Upanishad, or the Iliad, or the Bible. I confess my respect for the document does not increase on closer acquaintance. But I am glad that it is so clear and decisive. I trust it will wake up our dreamy and *doctrinaire* " Modernists " to the fact that Rome can never reform herself ; that by the logic of her life she is pledged to this course as far as her own action is concerned ; that if she is to be reformed it can only be, as in the past, by a strong lay revolt issuing in legislative compulsion. I trust the day is not far when wise governments will forbid any man to form the public mind who is not guaranteed against folly and fanaticism by a competent education.

To Monsieur A. Houtin

RICHMOND,
June 24, 1903.

REVEREND AND DEAR M. L'ABBÉ,

I must thank you most cordially for honouring me with a copy of your protest.[1] I have read it with the deepest sympathy, which is shared by all those to whom I have lent it. What strikes us all as particularly hard in your case is that you are censured not, as M. Loisy, for certain *theologoumena* and specula-

---

[1] See *Mes Difficultés avec mon Évêque*, by A. Houtin.

tions ; not for historical assertions relative to some remote and obscure period ; but for a concatenation of recent and indubitable events on which you pass no theological judgment whatever. If the episcopal censorship is used in this way, what can we expect except what is happening under our eyes every day, *sc.*, the defection from the Church of just those whose services are most essential to her at the present crisis ?

The fact is that our officials do not understand the disease of the times, and failing in their diagnosis they can devise no new remedy, but only the old medieval method of repression and moral violence. It is as if one should hope to keep out the advancing tide by barriers of sand. The longer its advance is delayed the more destructively will it rush in at last. Surely in the present crisis of the French Church we may see the fruits of these ignorant tactics, rather than of Freemasonry or devilry, which have thriven only because Churchmen have played into their hands, and prepared an environment for their fruitful development. Certainly the position of those who, like yourself, strive to bring about a saner and more fruitful sort of Catholicism, is one of extreme difficulty and suffering : but it is some consolation to reflect that the story is as old as the Gospel, and older ; and that the service of truth has always been paid with such bitter wages. As one who has already tasted a little of your chalice, and may yet have to taste a great deal of it, I beg to offer you my sincerest sympathy and respect.

To a French Priest

RICHMOND,
February 22, 1904.

DEAR M. L'ABBÉ,[1]

Your letter was forwarded to me by my friend N. . . .

With your difficulties I am in full sympathy ; all the critics of *The Church and the Future*, especially he to whom it was addressed as a letter and by whom it was printed in its present very crude form, find the same flaw in its conclusion. And now, having myself just finished A. Sabatier's very wonderful and inspiring book, *Les Religions d'Autorité et la Religion de l'Esprit*, I ask myself frankly, Am I implicitly a liberal Protestant ; or is Sabatier implicitly a liberal Catholic ? Or is there still an irreducible difference of principle between us ? I believe there is, in that I regard the official *Ecclesia Docens* not merely as *expressing* the mind of the whole Church ; not merely as co-operating in the formation of that mind (as our politicians co-operate, educatively, in forming the political mind of the nation), but also as (in virtue of an implicit delegation) *imposing* the general mind on the individual with an authority that is *moral*, and not purely intellectual, like that of a consensus of experts. In matters of profane knowledge I am *morally* free to disregard the consensus of experts ; it is folly to do so, but it is not sin. It is sin, where the consensus concerns the way of my own salvation ; and where the consensus is in some way the work of the Holy Spirit. This Sabatier ignores, and treats Church authority as purely intellectual and subject simply to the criteria of collective testimony. How

---

[1] This letter is an answer to one from above correspondent, who had written regarding intellectual difficulties of his own, as also on questions raised by the perusal of some of Tyrrell's pseudonymous publications.

then do I take the whole body of official doctrine as it is to-day ? Just as I take the Bible, which I believe to be inspired ; to be a heavenly treasure in an earthen vessel. I owe it a certain inward obedience ; but it is to be, according to my powers, a discriminating, not a blind, obedience. I know that every " infallible " definition is infallibly necessary for the integrity of the total " Word of God " ; but that total " Word " remains necessarily a riddle and a mystery—like Christ's parables, from which each drew some measure of truth and practical guidance for himself. Taken *as a whole* the present *summa doctrinæ* is relatively the best expression of Christian truth yet realised. But if this " rule of faith " is to develop, it can only be because it is assimilated, surpassed, corrected, and amplified by certain individuals. Hence the truth of a single dogma is relative, not merely in the sense that it is capable of better expression, but also because, like a word in the context of a sentence, it has signification only as part of the organic body of truth, and not *absolutely*, or apart from its context in the total " Word of God." The present *doctrine* of authority and of infallibility is infallibly true *in some sense* (like that of three persons in One God) ; no better expression of that sense was possible in 1870 ; but the crude literal sense is already discredited.

To try once more to say what I would ; I look on the *whole body* of official teaching of to-day as the public and authorised expression of the spiritual life of the faithful in its present stage of development. That expression is necessarily imperfect by way of excess and defect, but is approximately and practically adequate. As imposed by the Church, through the officials, with *moral authority*, by way of law, it demands · my outward acceptance and profession of its organic integrity. It also demands my inner assent, to *its integrity*, as *containing* the Word of God, as the soul is contained in the body; it demands my inward consideration and criticism of the meaning and value of its several parts and of their articulation, and even the adaptation of the whole for the needs of my own mind and spiritual life. This is the direction in which I am groping for a solution that will reconcile inward liberty with Catholic unity. The articles *Semper Eadem* [1] may also help you to form your own judgment. They simply attempt to state, not to solve, a very pressing dilemma. My own solution is given in the last ten lines of *Lex Orandi*.

With deep sympathy and respect.

To the Same

RICHMOND, YORKS,
May 15, 1905.

I had not even heard of M. Le Roy's article in the *Quinzaine*, so I can hardly deal satisfactorily with your criticisms of it. I can only say, in general, that (as I said in the preface) the *Lex Orandi* criticism is at best supplementary—a verification of results otherwise obtained. Also, I quite see the impossibility of coercing the unbeliever's mind by such a method of apologetic. But, I ask, does not faith always begin *from within*, as a spontaneous *wish* to believe? Is a *real* (not verbal, or formal) belief in God, in immortality, in free will, *ever* the result of arguments communicated from outside? Is it not always worked out by each soul for itself, the result of its moral conflict? I think this anxiety for an apologetic which will *force* the unbelieving mind to surrender is somewhat " scholastic " and false to experience. Blondel [2] tells us that the best apologetic is that which

---

[1] Republished in *Through Scylla and Charybdis*.
[2] M. Maurice Blondel, author of *L'Action*.

does not seek to convince directly, but which prepares the mind to work out its own convictions. What men are drawn to is Christ and the Christian community; and the secret of the attraction is moral, not intellectualist. It is the attraction of a personality or character. Once drawn to Christ, we take His teaching on trust; not on the strength of arguments. Apologetic is at most a *causa removens prohibens*. Do we not, some of us, take the doctrinal side of Christianity a great deal too seriously? What was Christ's own attitude towards theology and theologians as revealed in the Synoptic Gospels? (e.g. Matt. xxiii. 13–31). It is by the *life* of the Church, not by her theology, that these "incroyants" of yours are attracted or repelled. It was not of theological light that Christ said *Sic luceat lux vestra*, etc.

As regards your strictures of *The Letter to a Professor* [1] I do *not* believe that the theologians are an essential part of the Church's divine institution; or that collectively they are the organ of her developing faith. At most, they attempt to analyse and register a process of growth that takes place in the communion of her *living* members, of those in whom the "Spirit of Christ" is active and dominant. In that growth there is no breach of continuity, but in the analysis or theory of it there may well be such breaches—as when, in National Service, the accumulation of experience demands new hypotheses and new schools. The old hypotheses may be "doctored" and patched up to a certain point, but at last they have to be set aside. This is not to deny them *all* value. The Apostles hoped, at first, that Judaism might develop into Christianity without a complete breach with the old theology and forms of worship; but soon they found that new experiences required new syntheses,

---

[1] Eventually published under the title of *A Much-abused Letter*.

and that part of Judaism which refused to be taken up into the wider religion was left to decay. After all, Christianity *is* continuous with Judaism ; it is a transformed Judaism and nothing more. We forget this because the *name* (Judaism) survives only as the designation of the apostate or schismatic Judaism. We are suffering now from a recrudescence of the same evil *in the same Church*, against which Christ's whole life and death was a protest. Let us by all possible means defer the day of revolutionary re-statement as long as we can ; let us explain, and distinguish, and sub-distinguish the old forms and phrases, so far as we can do so at all honestly and without a graver scandal than that which we seek to avoid. But men cannot live on distinctions for ever, and what *The Letter* means is simply that, *even if things were far worse than they are* (pp. 14 and 33), there is nothing to be afraid of unless we are foolish enough to take theology and theologians at their own preposterous valuation.

To Monsieur J. Augustin Leger

RICHMOND, YORKS,
March 15, 1904.

I feel much ashamed of my delay in answering your three last letters ; but the fact that I have retained them proves that I steadily purposed doing so. Well, of course you know, in substance, the crisis that has arisen for us all about Loisy. I do not see how he could possibly have done otherwise than he did. Submission " pure and simple " is due to God alone—not to a tribunal which is avowedly fallible and whose sphere is avowedly circumscribed to matters of religion. How could he, in conscience, submit in a form that would give away the whole cause for which he stands,

which is, in effect, the limitation of the territories
of science and religion ?   I send you an article I wrote
in *The Pilot* before the excommunication.   Also a
letter from *Romanus* (not very difficult to identify)
to *The Times*.   I confess I feel with you that the *con-
structive* chapter of the new " Apologetic " has yet to
be written.   I have attempted it in an article that I
may send you later.   It seems to me that our estimate
of Church-teaching must be modified analogously to
that of Bible-teaching.   *As a whole*, the Bible still
possesses a certain *moral* and inwardly binding
authority, as being a revelation of the workings of
God's spirit in man, from which we can derive a knowledge of the laws of the life of religion to be applied
to our own need ;   moreover, as distinct from other
spiritual books (e.g. *à Kempis*) the Bible has been
approved and improved by the collective conscience
of the Judæo-Christian Church.   Hence we are
morally bound to yield it inward deference and consideration, to use it as a treasure (contained in earthen
vessels, no doubt) given us by God for our self-nourish-
ment ;   put into our *hands*, however, and not into our
stomachs.   It is for us to masticate and digest.   As
a Catholic I apply all this to the fulness of ecclesiastical
teaching, in which the sacred Scriptures are included.
That teaching is food, divinely guaranteed as *containing*
truth and spiritual nutriment ;   as the Word *made
flesh* and mingled with corruptible and human elements,
but, none the less, divine and venerable.   What we
receive *purely, merely*, on testimony, is *so far* no part
of our mind, i.e. of the living organism of our thought.
It lies on the surface, like seed by the wayside.   Of
such we do not say " I know," but " I have been
told," or " It is said."   Only so far as it fits in with
our own experience, and is verified by its proved harmony with the rest of our knowledge, does it come to

be assimilated and to make part of our mind. Over
the living, inward *penetration* of the mind we have
no more *direct* control than over the formation and
growth of our own bodies ; we can only control the
conditions. If we cannot command our understanding, neither can the Church oblige us to do so.
Hence all she can *impose* upon us is the undigested
food. Her control stops at the outward surface of
our mind. Of her teaching *as a whole* I can say I
believe it is a divine revelation ; that it is true for the
mind of the Church, though as yet, to a large extent,
it is not true for my mind. I don't think intellectual
liberty suffers unless, instead of waiting patiently
on the natural growth of our own mind for a better
understanding of religious teaching, we violently
twist our minds into correspondence with what we
imagine that teaching to mean. I am afraid there
are, as Blondel says, *presque deux Catholicismes*
struggling for ascendency in the Church just now,
and that a synthesis is impossible owing to the utterly
fundamental nature of the point at issue, *sc.*, the nature
and unity and bases of authority. The balance is
secured by a very long right arm with a little weight,
and a very short left arm with a very heavy weight ;
it is numbers versus brains. If the numbers drive
out the brains they will dwindle away just as fast
as education spreads—as spread it must. There is
nothing in the Catholicism of Canada, or Ireland, or
Spain, to hold out against modern education ; and the
clericals know that well enough, and put all their
trust in ignorance and obscurantism. Already Ireland
is developing a strong anti-clericalism of a French
pattern ; and Spain is dry grass waiting to catch fire.
I was struck yesterday by the truth of a remark by
an Italian liberal, that the conflict was less between
Catholicism and Science than between Catholicism

and Christianity ; that is, I fancy, between the pagan and the Christian elements of Catholicism. Pius X, when he speaks and acts from his own *understanding*, is profoundly evangelical and anti-pagan ; but he is of course the victim of his own ignorance and critical inability ; and so becomes the foe of a cause that is really his own.

To the Same

STORRINGTON, SUSSEX,
November 8, 1908.

That was a very disconsolate letter of September 19. I trust it only represented a passing, and not too frequently recurring mood.

I often thank God I was not born and bred a Roman Catholic, and therefore know experimentally that the substance and most vital truth of religion does not stand or fall with the Roman Church. She has no monopoly of the Heavenly Father, who cares for the very hairs of our head. Nor is Jesus of Nazareth her property or invention. If her teachings and institutions can bring us nearer to God, well and good. If they hinder our access, let them go, and I shall not regret them. To have been born and bred a Catholic, to have had the primary religious and moral beliefs amalgamated with so much that is secondary and disputable, is a calamity for those Catholics who are forced to dispute these secondary matters. The baby and the bath are thrown out together. Religion and Catholicism, focd and form, should be kept in water-tight compartments. It seems to me that if the papacy vanished St. Augustine's confessions would lose none of their worth. In the present crisis we should wean ourselves, as much as possible, from the perishable, and cling to the imperishable elements of Catholicism. The papacy must either be radically transformed or absolutely sterilised. If the latter, then God's will be done. Who am I to dictate on what lines God shall save the world ? Could I believe that religion and the Roman Church were identical I should indeed despair. Science will reassert its claims as long as man has a brain. Religion will reassert itself as long as he has a heart.

Ever yours faithfully.

NOTE

Dr. Zdziechowski, then professor in the Jagell University, Cracow, has been a student of Slav literature, and, in particular, of the Messianic movement in Poland. He has also published a work on *Byron and His Age*. The pamphlet to which the following letter refers excited much attention. In it he set forth those evils which, to his mind, imperilled the spiritual action of the Church on the modern world.

To Dr. Zdziechowski

RICHMOND, YORKS,
June 24, 1903.

I am greatly obliged to you for your brochure, *Pestis perniciosissima*, which I have read with great interest, sympathy, and, I hope, profit. The true " Pestis " is undoubtedly to be sought rather in the hard, abstract intellectualism of the scholastic tradition than in such " liberalising " as results from the evangelical spirit of charity. No one can study the Gospels and not see that our Lord was a " liberaliser " in relation to the rabbinical scholasticism of the Jewish Church, and this just because of the *implications* of His universal humanitarian spirit. He was not *explicitly* a theologian, or a revealer of intellectual orthodoxy, but the diffuser of a spirit, or love, which

7

implied a more liberal theology, a wider and worthier conception of God and of man, and of their mutual relations. This spirit was the new wine that eventually burst the old scholastic bottles. Hence your able analysis of the *Zwiespalt* between Mgr. Bonomelli's mentality and his spirit (i.e. between what he has received through tradition, education, and other influences from outside, and what he is, inwardly, by temperament and character) is most illuminative. One sees how his *implicit* theology rebels against his *explicit* theology. I had felt this myself still more deeply as regards Pius X, whose educational influences make him adverse to that liberal movement which is really an expression of his own evangelical spirit. He cannot see that scholasticism is but a branch of the tree of " formalism " ; that it is bound up with the sort of " ecclesiasticism " with which he, as a reformer, is at war. I wish I could think his expressions of sympathy with your views were dictated not merely by kindliness and a general intention of fairness and candour, but also by an intelligent understanding of your attitude. When good men of that sort speak of using the weapons of outsiders against outsiders, they do not really believe that these weapons are better than those of traditional apologetics, but only that they are useful *ad hominem*, for " answering a fool according to his folly." That we have anything to learn from outsiders ; that they have treasured truths and principles that we have neglected, never really enters into the head of a good, simple man like Pius X. On the other hand, some of the results of historical criticism must necessarily seem to him blasphemous and subversive of all his most sacred traditions. So much of that tradition derives from the workings of scholastic curiosity in past ages ; so much of it must crumble away under the touch of honest investigation, that I cannot find it in my heart to blame those who simply stop their ears and refuse to listen to criticism in any shape or form. Few of our "liberalisers" seem to "sit down and count the cost." I do not for a moment mean that we should bargain with truth, or stipulate that a method shall lead us so far and no further ; I only plead for a greater realisation of the issues at stake than is common with our more light-hearted reformers, and a greater sympathy with the *instinctive* (even if not intelligent) repugnances of those whose temples and altars seem doomed to a somewhat ruthless despoliation.

The best hope, as far as I can see, is to be placed rather in the spirit of charity than in the spirit of criticism. As in our Lord's time, so now, that spirit may be trusted to work out its own implications in due season, and to effect noiselessly and quietly what criticism can effect only imperfectly and with much pain and distress of the simple. Here it is that I feel myself so cordially at one with your little book. Mentally I am heart and soul with Abbé Loisy and his school, but I hope far more in the methods of Mgr. Bonomelli, whose theology is to me as an intellectual nightmare : *spiritus est qui vivificat.*

With sincere respect and affection.

To Wilfrid Ward, Esq.

FREIBURG I. BREISGAU,
April 8, 1906.

Many thanks for the *Dublin* and for the kind mention therein. With your own criticism, as with much of the attitude of George Sutcliffe,[1] I agree in the abstract. What I always feel is that Rome has duties as well as rights ; and that, in the concrete, she takes all you

[1] Refers to Mrs. Wilfrid Ward's novel of the Modernist movement, *Out of Due Time.*

say about loyalty, and the value of authority, as a matter of course, but will not hear a word on the subject of those duties which are correlative to her rights. I believe that men would not ordinarily deny her her rights of loyalty and submission if she showed any decent consciousness of her duties ; and that it is because she has for centuries traded on their faith and loyalty, grabbed everything and given nothing, that she has now lost her authority beyond recovery. Of course, I am smarting under the assassination of L.[1] Correlative virtues should always be preached and apprehended and practised simultaneously, measure for measure. When has the Roman Church ever, by word or action, emphasised what she cannot deny, that there are limits to obedience and authority ? When has she ever censured excessive claims on her behalf, or checked the violence of men like Turinaz, or condemned a book as uncharitable and ignorant if it made for her power ? *One* sign of that kind would do more to restore her lawful authority than a hundred self-interested condemnations, however just—*non enim qui seipsum commendat probatus est sed quem Deus commendat.* The truth is she has *no faith* in her heart, she does not believe in her cause, her sole hope is in advertisement. *Real* faith begets faith. Because they detect the tremor in her voice, men cease to believe in her. And then they cannot but feel the " business-value " of her claims. It may be lawful, but is it expedient to tie such disparate interests together ? Not only evil, but the appearance of evil may be wrong. St. Paul thought so, and declined his temporal rights, while claiming them. Mrs. Ward will say I want to make the Pope a Baptist minister. That is to prejudice the case by importing a vulgarisation

---

[1] A distinguished French writer who had recen'ly incurred condemnation.

that is no consequence of my belief. Christ was not vulgar in His poverty and simplicity ; in the robes of Cæsar He would have been vulgar. It is perfectly fair to ask, If Christ, or even Peter, came on earth to govern the Church to-day, *in propria persona*, do you believe for one moment that they would assume the Byzantine pomp of the Vatican, or claim temporal power ? I am afraid if you said *yes* I should not believe you—so perhaps it is not a fair question. To me the mixture of revelation and theology, of spiritual and temporal power, are two manifestations of the same fallacy. I believe in revelation as a man of faith, I believe in theology as a man of reason ; I believe each helps and depends on the other, but that the bastard progeny of their mixture is not *a priori* only, but historically the enemy of both, the parent of unbelief and ignorance. So, too, the authority of Church government is lawful and necessary, it is ministerial to spiritual authority—but it is not " divine " in the same direct sense any more than theological thought is divine in the same sense as revelation. What is due only to the spiritual is claimed for the natural. The Church's chief officer is called *His Holiness*, and *as such* claims what belongs only to the natural ; and thus we get a parallel mixture with parallel ill-results. If I do not recognise myself in George Sutcliffe, so, of course, neither in Paul ; though undoubtedly I am nearer to him of the two. But in no case is he a religious man ; his interest is primarily intellectual and theoretic, whereas I care about a synthesis only because I care about religion. I feel a far deeper fraternity and sympathy with any religious Nonconformist (even a Baptist minister) than I do with Abbé Loisy or Houtin or Gibson ; and if I swear by the Baron or Miss Petre or Laberthonnière, it is just because with them, too, the life is more than the theory; and because, with them, I still hope that Catholicism offers a fuller and richer life than any form of Protestantism, or perhaps than Anglicanism can offer to those who want it. If in any other point I were like Paul, it might be in retiring to save my soul in peace " where the Churches cease from troubling and the weary are at rest "—not to the Dominicans (God forbid), nor perhaps the Carthusians ; but quite away. The book is certainly interesting and actual. I am told that Paul is the Baron, is Gibson, etc., etc. Plainly he is a mosaic ; and probably even that unconsciously. Sutcliffe is more obvious—at least, I think so. I am very pleased indeed to receive it, and still more the sympathetic and friendly letter that accompanies it, which I must answer as soon as I can. As to my vows, I could easily get " secularised " by a little trouble and perhaps intrigue ; but it seems to me rather undignified to petition for favours from those from whom one has suffered unceremonious handling. They ought to see that it does them harm to leave me suspended. For my own devotion I always preferred hearing to saying Mass, and to occupy the layman's part of the Church, being too democratic even to enjoy the " superiority " of sacerdotal dignity. A Roman collar always chokes me, though I wear it still for propriety's sake.

To the Hon. Wm. Gibson (now Lord Ashbourne)

LADY PLACE, STORRINGTON,
December 7, 1906.

MY DEAR GIBSON,
        Thank you most cordially for introducing me to Grégoire, [1] of whom my previous knowledge was

[1] Refers to a life of Abbé Grégoire, the Constitutional Bishop, by Mr. Gibson.

just zero. One rarely meets a really " edifying " book, such as you have given us precisely because you are not thinking of edification. It is manhood that moves us ; not supernatural inhumanity. If Christianity is more than the perfect development of manhood it is of no use to us. And this was a man altogether, and his death stamped him a Christian of the true brand. Again, you have cleared my mind of the popular notion that Gallicanism is Erastian. Not that I am insensible to M. Arnold's plea for Erastianism. It means a reintroduction of the lay mind and voice into Church affairs, albeit in a crooked and undesirable way ; and one would trust the Privy Council for a temperate and practical view of many Church questions rather than the bench of bishops. Still, lay influence need not be State influence, and ought to be purely religious. My own hope is that the lay mind will quietly impose a democratic interpretation on the existing ecclesiastical hierarchy through its growing inability to understand authority in any other way than as deriving from the whole community. That will mean that the pyramid which is now unstably poised on its infallible apex will, without any internal alteration, be dumped down on its base.

It was a happy thought to set his indictment of Absolutism and of inverted Absolutism side by side in the Appendix, so as to bring out the male independence and fearlessness of the man. Six bishops of that sort might save the Church even now ; but, as the Pope observes with joy in his consistorial allocution, the bishops to-day are, thanks to careful selection, as uniform and impersonal as bullets from the same mould ; and the unity is equally miraculous and significant. *Ex uno disce omnes.* He hopes the laity will imitate their pastors.

To Robert Dell, Esq.

May 18, 1905.

I have carefully read and re-read your *C.Q.* article, and I don't see how it could well be bettered. What beats me is the psychology of clericalism. The mentality of a man like Merry del Val, who is plainly not (as Acton would have it) a wilfully bad and immoral man, is as strange to me as that of a Fiji islander. If I wanted to convert him I shouldn't know where to begin. Nor is it altogether stupidity, for, e.g., Gerard and B. are not stupid men. I can only conclude that their clerical education grafts them on to a branch-tradition that has been for centuries diverging from the point of bifurcation and now constitutes a complete and separate culture-system, so knit together that the whole is affirmed or denied with every part. That is what the clericalist feels instinctively ; that is why all detailed discussion with him is idle.

As to the identity of Catholicism and Vaticanism, I say with you, " Heaven forbid ! " But Sabatier's book on the *Religions of Authority*, and still more Sohm's *Kirchenrecht*, make me wonder whether 1870 was not the perfectly logical and historically inevitable issue of the " Catholicising " process which began perhaps with St. Paul, and is traceable in St. Matthew's Gospel—a process arrested in the Greek Churches; repudiated theoretically (not really) by the Protestant sects, and accepted alongside of its contrary by the Anglican compromise. Bourdon thinks that the evil derives not from the necessary Catholicising process but from one element of it ; namely, from the confounding of spiritual with juridical authority ; the authority of the preacher with that of the law-giver. He would retain for the Church and Bishop of Rome a spiritual primacy or leadership such as Paul allows

(Rom. i. 8) and such as Christ exercised by His life and example. But what does history say to such an idea of Rome and her bishops, whose example has been the scandal of the world ?

But I do think that this " juridical " conception of pastoral authority is the root of clericalism ; and that Vaticanism is its ripest fruit. When the fruit is quite ripe it falls to earth ; and I can only trust that some Pope, blind-drunk with a sense of authority, may some day define himself to be born of a virgin in virtue of his prerogatives as Christ's *alter Ego*.

To the Same

MOORHURST, HOLMWOOD,
January 16, 1907.

Many thanks for your most interesting letter. I could rather wish myself over in Paris during this *réunion* week, marked by the third assembly of the bishops, [1] and by that of so many Catholic liberals round Fogazzaro. But my purse was not equal to the strain. G., F., W. and myself have consoled ourselves by a little private ecumenical council of a very revolutionary character. My own personal view, in the light of a careful re-perusal of Döllinger's *La Papauté*, is that our work must be to work within the Church for the unravelling of this gigantic papal imposition ; for the restoration of the hierarchy ; for the inversion of the hierarchic pyramid now unstably poised on its apex and which needs to be planted firmly on its basis ; for the recognition of the *regale sacerdotium* of the Christian people as the fount of all order and jurisdiction. The modern mind, especially as saturated with the ideas of divine Immanence,

---

[1] The attitude to be adopted by the French Church in regard to the Law of Separation was then under discussion.

will soon be incapable of any other way of seeing things. The leadership of Rome must be, as primitively, one of example, not one of coercive right. I could not stay in the Roman Communion if I had to accept the new Vaticanism as part of the system. I can endure it as a heresy or disease. One joined the Church to be delivered from the tyranny of individualism, and to live under the rule of a wide and quasi-Catholic consensus, in which the vagaries of individualism are eliminated and the true developments of mind-in-general made manifest. But one finds oneself subjected to the tyranny of a privileged private judgment ; the election of the cardinals makes the personal ideas of Giuseppe Sarto a rule of truth, and his will is substituted for the canons and customs shaped by the growth of the Christian people. If this is not a revolution and a heresy I don't know what is. The *letter* of the Vatican Council may be Wardesquely interpreted in a Catholic sense ; but surely we must look rather to the concrete movement which gave birth to it and of which it is still the charter. Does Pius X even pretend to represent the mind of the French Church ? It seems to me we must all go straight for this point and regard all other points as secondary and subordinate.

To the Same

STORRINGTON, SUSSEX,
August 2, 1907.

I am rather tied here just at present by visitors. There is at most an off-chance that I shall have to go to London in two or three days to interview the Surveyor of Taxes, who is convinced that I have got £1,000 a year. In that case I'll let you know. It would then be best to take Carshalton on my way to and fro. And so the seven hills have brought forth their little mouse at last. [1] I cannot see (alas !) that they have created a new situation. It is only sixty-five blunders at a go, instead of dribbled out over sixty-five years. The interesting question is, How can the Pope ask us to assent absolutely and eternally under pain of sin (and undoubtedly this is what he and Moyes and the Jesuits intend) to condemnations on which he is unwilling to stake his infallibility ; which are avowed reversible and infallible ? Is it moral to say : I assent eternally and absolutely to what I know to be possibly untrue ? Can it be a sin to say that an avowedly fallible decision is not infallible, and therefore may or may not be true ? If not, then who need hesitate to sign these condemnations as propositions that may or may not be true ? Well, I should hesitate ; for I feel that at least twenty of them could not possibly be true. However, apart from the technical value of the document, its effect on the public mind will be that of a final declaration of war against science, history, criticism, and all that has been gained by years of struggle against the rulers of the darkness of this world. And then there is therein a clearly exercised claim to *direct* jurisdiction over the whole realm of man's natural reason. And that must be flatly denied.

The Church Times last week was excellent, both on the Syllabus and on Acton. If Rome was bidding for the Anglo-Catholic vote she has failed.

To V.

April 11, 1902.

Turinaz interested me very much as showing how he and his school are really responsible for the extravagances of the opposing school. One sees no limit now to the process of disintegration, all confidence in the

[1] The syllabus *Lamentabili.*

competence and sincerity of the episcopate being destroyed by their blind intolerance of even moderate liberalism. The moderate men, being exasperated, cease to exercise restraint on their immoderate disciples, and what might have been an orderly and dignified retreat from untenable positions has become a pell-mell flight. And yet I doubt more and more if there be an honest *via media* with clearly defined limits, such as W. Ward is trying to tinker up out of J. H. N. I find now three millstones with which Catholicism is weighted to destruction, and yet, cut them away, and what remains? They are first the political conception of the Church as embodied in the " court of Rome " and the claim to temporal power ; secondly, the " protection " system, which adapts the environment to the organism and not conversely, and is embodied in Jesuitism ; thirdly, the tyranny of theological schools as embodied in scholasticism. But Catholicism, minus Politics, Jesuitism, and Scholasticism, equals Protestantism ; and with that equation I am not quite satisfied. Have you ever read John Morley's book on *Compromise ;* it is a stronger plea for honesty than I yet feel equal to. But I think his hard sayings apply to those only whose convictions are fixed and subjectively certain, and so I may go on shuffling a little longer. There is also a physical side which he neglects.

To the Same

November 5, 1904.

Yes, in truth ; the only thing now is to steer straight by one's conscience, be it true or false. *That* God stands firm and undeniable when every other Dagon of the intellect or of the imagination lies flat, handless and footless. And how little anything would matter were one quite right with conscience ! *Nam etsi ambulavero in medio umbræ mortis non timebit cor meum quoniam tu mecum es. Pone me juxta te et cujusvis manus pugnet contra me. Si Deus pro nobis quis contra nos?* That seems the beginning, the middle, the end, the core, the essence, the key to all our dogmas, mysteries, sacraments ; to the crucifix and the saints and martyrs ; to faith and hope and charity : " *ex uno verbo omnia, et unum loquuntur omnia.*" If they say more or less, or other, they are naught.[1] And yet I have the horrors on me, and feel tangled in the arms of some marine polypus or giant octopus. The Church sits on my soul like a nightmare, and the oppression is maddening ; much more since these revelations of bad faith and cruel mendacity. I do not wonder that to Savonarola and the medieval mystics Rome seemed anti-Christ. The misery is that she is both Christ and anti-Christ ; wheat and tares ; a double-faced Janus looking heavenwards and hellwards. Hence I do long for *simpler* conditions, when I should not have to do good by stealth, and whisper the truth in holes and corners as though it were obscenity. The grotesque insincerity of my position as a Jesuit appals me at times. During Mass this morning I was planning advertisements : " A Roman Catholic Priest, retiring from the exercise of his ministry for reasons of conscience, desires temporary occupation, literary, secretarial, or even tutorial, which will leave him leisure for writing. Country much preferred. Address XYZ, office of *The Guardian.*" And then something says : No, wait till you are driven. Initiate nothing. Yet if an opening offered I think my prudence would prove frail against the temptation. Yesterday was the first really bad bile-attack since Xmas ; so I cannot complain ; it was due long ago and well deserved.

[1] *Life,* vol. ii. p. 407.

To Wm. Craig, Esq., Milton House, Alsaga, Cheshire

IVY HOUSE,
OLD TOWN, CLAPHAM, S.W.
December 2, 1906.

DEAR SIR,

I am afraid you say only what hundreds of thoughtful and earnest Catholics are saying and what thousands are thinking. The fact of so wide-spread a ferment ought to be a basis of hope, could one but visualise distinctly the shape and form of those changes of spirit and method that seem so desirable. But the whole system is so close-knit and coherent, and the root-fibres of tares and wheat so intertangled, that it is difficult to see what could be changed without changing all. One thing I am sure of—that, in spite of theory, the Church is ultimately taught and governed from below ; that the formation of the lay mind is the thing to trust in and to work for. All permanent and profitable reform has come that way—through God's spirit moving, as it is now moving, over the wide surface of the waters ; working in a million hearts and minds at once and independently.

If the Church is to maintain her monarchic form and live, she must interpret that monarchy after the English democratic type ; not after the Russian autocratic. That is a change that theology will never admit ; but which will be quickly and noiselessly imposed by the development of the lay mind, to which any other conception of authority will soon be obsolete and impossible. When folks will not listen, or will only listen to laugh, theologians will wisely lapse into silence, as they have done in so many other matters. So I think we must have faith and hope in those higher and more universal powers and laws to which ecclesiastical powers and laws are subject, for all their sense

of unlimited independence.   The Son of Man is Lord
even of the Church.

NOTE

The following letter was addressed to Bishop Vernon
Herford, who had founded " The Church of Divine
Love," hoping to make of it a nucleus of Christian
reunion.

To Bishop Vernon Herford

16 OLD TOWN, CLAPHAM,
April 14, 1907 ?

DEAR BISHOP HERFORD,

Much ill-health has put me in everybody's
black books, as an infamous correspondent.   My
lucid intervals are crowded to repletion with neglected
work, the struggle with which throws me again.   It
is a most vicious circle.   I wanted much to write to
you immediately after your pilgrimage to Storrington,
just to explain the fundamental question on which,
in spite of so much sympathy, I should find it hard
to agree with you.   All that I see of myself and others
in these troubled times has convinced me that the best
way to overcome the lamentable divisions of the
Church cannot be to create new divisions ; but for
all of us to stick fast—as far as honesty will stretch—
to our several communions, and work there for the
widening of the conception of Christianity according
to the particular exigencies of that communion, in the
face of the new enlightenment.   Thus it may come to
pass that these widening streams may at last debouche
in a common ocean.   I would not so much mind
passing from one of the existing Churches to another
as any attempt to add a fresh element to the universal
confusion.   Frankly, that is why I look a little bit
askance at the Church of Divine Love ; and would

so much rather see you working hand in hand with
the liberalism in some of the big communions. God
knows it is a slow, cramping, thankless task, but, as
a Roman Catholic, I feel that, though I am a small
atom, yet I belong to a well-knit universe where
everything tells on everything else—remotely, perhaps,
but far more surely and lastingly. Again, assuming
that the magical conception of priestly power is of the
past, I feel that the true repository and source of the
power of sacred order is the whole community, which
acts through and in its appointed organs; that the
difference between, say, a Wesleyan minister and
myself is that in him it is the Wesleyan, in me it is the
Roman, communion which acts and teaches, and blesses.
Whom do you stand for ? that is the question. Who
and how many would acknowledge you as their
representative ?   God's Spirit is immanent in every
Christian communion ;   but in different measure.
He is with two or three who are organised into a body ;
but still more with two or three millions ;   still more
with a continuous, world-wide, world-old organism
like the Catholic Churches of East and West. And
I feel sure that the spiritual power of a man is pro-
portioned to that of the body whose organ he is. For
that reason again I cannot sympathise with your
isolation so far as it is not the result of persecution
or necessity. I feel I ought to say this to you quite
openly. And indeed I do not speak dogmatically,
but as one who is groping after truth in so many
respects, and can readily make room for other points
of view. Only, you seemed from your conversation
to have got to somewhat of an *impasse* and to be
searching for some path of greater utility; and to me
that path seems to lie in the direction of aggregation
to some work already in process, rather than in the
inauguration of any new work. The most fruitful

workers all *feel* that they could do more alone, but surely this *feeling* is just what needs discipline and sacrifice. This comes ill from a rebel like me. Yet God knows how gladly I would keep quiet were I once convinced that to do so were *really* the interest of the body I serve. There are times when a soldier is *bound* to disobey—if he knows his officer is drunk or mad or misinformed. If his venture succeeds he is crowned; if not, he is shot. I shall probably be shot, " *aber ich kann nicht anders.*" [1]

To the Rev. Charles Osborne, Vicar of Wallsend-on-Tyne

16 OLD TOWN, CLAPHAM,
March 30, 1907.

MY DEAR OSBORNE,

I am an absolute pig for ingratitude. And it makes matters worse to say it is not forgetfulness but endless procrastination. In my lucid intervals I struggle with arrears of neglected pen-work, and whatever can possibly lie over to another day is rarely done. Your last kind letter rebukes me daily when I encounter it in my drawer. *Dimitte nobis et vobis dimittetur.* Truth to tell, since the *Much-abused Letter's* appearance I have attained a publicity I would fain dispense with, and which may place me beside Campbell in Madame Tussaud's Chamber of Horrors. While I admire C.'s undoubted courage and independence I regard his synthesis as far too cheap. It is not so easy as all that. Unlike liberal positions, which are philosophical and abstract, conservative positions are largely the resultant of life and experience and blind instinct; and until we have smelted out their hidden truth we cannot toss them away. The antinomy I wrestle with is that institutionalism,

---

[1] For continuation of this correspondence see *Autobiography and Life of George Tyrrell*, vol. ii. p. 409.

or externalism, is at once essential and fatal to religion. Every day I feel more of a Catholic (not Roman) and more of a Quaker than ever. It is not comfortable, but I feel I am more likely to be on the right track than if I saw something as clear as Campbell sees in his New Theology. I send you (please return it) an essay I read before a little society of twelve of your priests — all broad, more or less Catholic, and hard-working vicars and curates. A fine, noble-minded set of men, I thought. Hubert Handley is their pope. Also, I often attend meetings of a Society for study of religion made up of Jews, R.C.s, Anglicans, Methodists, Unitarians, Quakers, Congregationalists, and " unattached " members. All good men, strangely like-spirited amid all their mental differences.

Of course Campbell has been set on at once by the hounds of mediocrity, and so far I will stick up for him when I review him for the *Hibbert ;* but I wish he had more restraint, and would not let himself be drawn over to the counter-philistinism. For myself, I wonder daily why excommunication tarries. Undoubtedly Rome is a little frightened. Her non-understanding of the world of to-day is past credence. She is far too astute, too " worldly " in intention, not to accommodate herself if she knew how. But she simply doesn't. She has blocked up her windows so carefully that I don't see how the light is to get in till some one blows the roof off. I am getting ready a more purely " theological " work than hitherto, whose thesis is just the limitations of theology from and by revelation. I am weary of chatter about " development of doctrine," and believe it has been far more disastrous to liberalism than to dogmatism.

To an Italian Professor

April 23, 1908.

I quite hold to the idea of a large body of ex-communicates, making a standing protest against the papacy. But if they set up their own altars and churches and add one more to the existing crowd of sects, they will at once cease to be interesting, and may well become highly ridiculous and ineffectual. Besides, it would be to attach that exaggerated *unconditional* importance to symbols and sacraments which Modernism protests against. It would be to forget that, in case of need, the desire for external communion is all-sufficient. If ever I decide that the Modernist programme is impossible I may frankly pass over to Protestantism or Positivism or Anglicanism or Socialism—most likely to Nothingism ; but I will certainly have nothing to do with a new sect.

To the Same

April 27, 1908.

And now, as regards your objections in detail. I quite admit with Loisy that Christ believed firmly in the immediacy of the Parousia and that this belief was the stimulus of His own activity. But it is vain to pretend that belief in a near cataclysm is a permanent and essential part of Christianity. The Kingdom of God *for us* is the result of a slow and continuous progress. The psychological force of such an ideal is totally different from that of a near cataclysm. It is neither possible nor desirable that the world should live permanently in a state of hysterical apprehension, and be always expecting a violent revolution. Such apprehensions are periodic regenerating forces for society. But society cannot live in a chronic state

of disturbance. The state of the earliest Church was,
after all, fanatical and unhealthy, although this loss
was compensated by spiritual gain and reinforcement.
For this reason I dislike the view which makes the
feverish apocalyptic spirit *essential* to Christianity.
I regard the illusion of Christ and His Apostles—the
cataclysmic power and the Jewish content which they
gave to the idea of the Kingdom—as irrelevant to the
essence of the Gospel.

.   .   .   .   .

My objection to *pure* Pragmatism is drawn from
Balfour's *Foundations of Belief*. As far as I know
myself I sympathise with Pragmatism a great deal,
but I am not a pure Pragmatist—unless, indeed,
one takes Nature in the widest sense. I believe, not
that truth is subordinate to action, but that they are
co-equal, co-ordinate factors (or aspects) of life. Here,
too, I suspect we mean the same thing. But I protest
against identifying Modernism so much with any
evanescent philosophy. We have not escaped the
Scylla of scholasticism to fall into the Charybdis of
Pragmatism, or any other "ism."

Again, though the Kingdom of God is a kingdom
upon earth, to speak of it as "temporal" is *male
sonans*. It is eternal and spiritual just because the
highest life of man is an *eternal* life. The temporal
conditions of that life are essential, but not principal.
Quærite primum regnum Dei, etc. We have got beyond
the crude materialism of the Jewish Messianic hopes,
nor can we be satisfied with an economic paradise.
We cannot believe in animistic conceptions of immortality; but if humanity is not eternal and divine it
is not worth thinking about.

To the Same

June 30, 1908.

I am sorry you try to dissociate the mystical and social forms of Modernism. All dissociation is deplorable. They are complementary and mutually necessary. Every Messias is a mystic. Of course, I feel your impatience with *mere* dreamers and doctrinaires. But that is a different grievance. All great social reform is the work of powerful individualities. Else *non habet radices et exorto sole arrefacit.*

To the Same

August 24, 1908.

.   .   .   .   .

Looking all round after a year, or rather five years, I am inclined to think that this wave of Modernist resistance has spent its force and has done all that can be done for the present. We have learnt experimentally the great numerical strength, the great moral and intellectual weakness of our opponents. We have proved that no reform is possible at present ; that the rapidly ripening times are not yet ripe. I think we should now lull our adversaries into false security and let them believe, if they will, that in suppressing Modernists they have suppressed Modernism. The tension of the present active warfare hinders two processes : (1) the self-stultification of unchecked and uncriticised Medievalism ; (2) the quiet spread of correct historical information, put forward without any sort of practical or controversial application. The present wave of revolt was the product of these two processes. As I said, its strength is spent, and we now need a period of quiet to gather force for a greater and further effort. In eliciting *Lamentabili* and *Pascendi* and the mad decrees of the Biblical

Commission the present struggle has set the old system on a path of self-destruction from which there is no return.

:   ˙   ˙   ˙   ˙

To Arthur Boutwood, Esq.

16 OLD TOWN, CLAPHAM,
January 13, 1909.

DEAR MR. BOUTWOOD,[1]
I have just received and glanced over your book, and hope to read it carefully in a few days. I doubt if you will have said anything more to the disfavour of " Modernism " than I myself have thought and said. I feel that it is a dangerous and desperate remedy, and has come too late : *cum mala per longas invaluere moras.* Of course I think especially of the Roman Church, as more irretrievably tied to dead positions than her sister Churches. Possibly the Church of England may be able to accept the results of history, and yet retain the substance of her Catholicism, i.e. she may have room for Modernism. I *hope* so. But my growing impression is that the instinct of the Athelstane Riley, Spencer-Jones, and Halifax schools is like that of Pius X, wise in its generation. There is a rude philosophy in the folly of the anti-Modernist campaign. The principles that take the Pentateuch from Moses have ended, *because they must,* in taking the Fourth Gospel from John, etc. I notice Modernists (like W. Ward) are always crying for new bottles for new wine ; and forget that it is their avowed mission to save the old bottles. Modernism is a defiance of the parable. " The bottles will burst," says Christ. " They will not burst," says the Modernist. The best way to keep the old bottles is to stick to the

---

[1] Refers to Mr. Boutwood's book, *Father Tyrrell's Modernism,* written under the pseudonym of Hakluyt Egerton.

old wine.   Nor will the old cloth hold the new patch.
I am glad that external forces hold the opposing
tendencies and parties of your Church together at
present, for in their conflict they will learn to know
themselves and their opponents better.   Either they
will find a synthesis or will clearly establish the impossibility of a synthesis.   In the latter case there
will be a split when the external clamps are removed.
Spencer-Jones & Co. will join the Vatican *bloc* ; the
others will be merged in the nebulous religiosity that
seems destined to take the place of dogmatic religion
for the present.   My own sympathies are not with
Spencer-Jones but with those who seek an *entente*
with science on the one hand and with the historical
Catholicism of the East and the Alt-Katholicismus
on the other.   Even if the accord be impossible, the
quest of it is beneficial.   If Modernism fails in the
Church of England (and by Modernism I always mean
a synthesis of Catholicism and Science—not the
supremacy of the latter) it may be abandoned as a
noble dream.   In the Roman Church it has not a
fair chance because the other term of synthesis there
is not Catholicism, but Ultramontanism, which is
a species of Protestantism.   My own work—which
I regard as done—has been to raise a question which
I have failed to answer.   I am not so conceited as to
conclude that it is therefore unanswerable.   And I
think it may be the destiny of the Church of England
to answer it,

VI

TRUTH

To the Rev. W. G. Tarrant

16 OLD TOWN, CLAPHAM, S.W.
February 27, 1908.

MY DEAR TARRANT,

I see there is no ground for prosecution, and much for gratitude, in the synopsis of your sermon, for which Mrs. Shelley asks me to thank you. Your objection is the same that you put to me at Essex Hall. It turns on the question, as difficult as Pilate's and not unconnected, what is Truthfulness ? John Bull answers it in a rough-and-ready way which appeals to our *prima facie* moral sense. But is it so easy ? Two quite different ideas govern most minds in the matter. One is that of Augustine and the scholastic tradition with which we are all saturated—Truthfulness is the agreement of your words with your meaning. No matter what false impression your words make on others, you must say what you mean. A man alone in his room could tell a lie by saying : Queen Anne is not dead. The other view is that truthfulness is a duty to the minds of others ; that we must strive to say what will best serve to make them think right ; that Robinson Crusoe was incapable of a lie till Friday turned up. That seems to me the sensible view and cuts away all justifying of " equivocation " and restriction. I must consider my hearer and ask if what I say will, on the whole, rectify or

misguide his mind. " On the whole "—for the mind
is not an empty kettle, a passive receptacle, but reacts
to my speech according to its own powers of comprehension. A truthful man is one who does his best
to lead others to the truth. The words that express
my meaning to myself may express the opposite to
another ; and in that case I lie by saying to him what
I mean. Truths are not separate fragments to any
mind, but are knit up with one another—like the roots
of tares and wheat. Deal gingerly, or you will root
up wheat with the tares. I would not say to a Mussul-
man child or peasant : Mahomet is not God's prophet.
If he believed me he would conclude that there was
no God at all ; if he did not he would conclude I was
an atheist. Tell a simple Catholic that Christ was
not born of a Virgin and the result will be similar.
For him there is far more untruth than truth connected
with the statement. But all Catholics are not simple,
and for the unsimple it is necessary to say that what
is not true in history may stand for a faith-truth.
Gradually the simple will disappear and then the faith-
truth can be better expressed in the language of concepts
than in that of myths and images. But meantime one
must not uproot important and vital truths in the
interest of unimportant and negative truths. Will
children *ever* be able to receive religion except under
the form of myths and images ? Will God ever be
for them other than a great man, and heaven other
than a grand place ? Would you sweep away all this
imagery of ordinary religious language and keep to
mere concepts ? Well, your children would be little
atheists ; and I am not sure that our concepts would
be more stimulating to ourselves than skeletons
stripped of their flesh. No doubt there is less imagery
and symbolism in Unitarianism than Catholicism,
but I am not sure that it is all gain. You described

heaven to us the other Sunday afternoon as Wordsworth described the Lake Country.   It is a deal better
than the description in the Revelation of St. John.
It is truer in a sense; but is it true ?   Tell the young
men there is no such *place* and you will uproot their
belief in religion.   If they asked you straight you would
say : " Wait a bit, and let us begin at the beginning,
and talk it out, and I will show you it is true in a sense."
But the chances are you'd never get them to see eye to
eye with you ; and you would simply destroy their faith
for a matter of no real consequence.   And so I say
the truthful man follows God's method and stoops to
the infirmity of the infant mind ; he says what will
bring *most* truth to his hearers and does not make his
own mind the rule for others.   I wish truth were as
simple as John Bull thinks.   But it is not.   *Every*
statement is misleading in some way.   To mislead as
little as possible is the ideal.

I determined to heave this brick at your head before
going abroad for a couple of months.   When I come
back I must call on you and stand firm in my turn.

(Notebooks, 1908–1909.) *To C. D.*

. . . The case of H. raises a general question affecting not only the Roman Church, but every Church
whose ministers are implicitly contracted to teach
certain doctrines and not others.   There are, of course,
circumstances that render his case peculiarly difficult.
No complaint has been made of his official utterances
as preacher, catechist, etc.   He is condemned and
suspended on a garbled version of a private conversation.   I told him it would be idle to dispute about
these garblings ; for his true sentiments would be
just as heterodox from the bishop's point of view.
It suffices to deny the authenticity of the *Comma*

Johanneum to be a Modernist and heretic. The particular degree of his modernity is quite irrelevant : " He who offends in one point is guilty of all." The real question is whether the bishop has a right to require internal orthodoxy, or anything more than nonheterodoxy of official utterance. With us Romans the priest is more and more an *instrumentum mortuum ;* the delegate and messenger, not the representative of the bishop or Pope. An Anglican preacher gives us his views and opinions to some extent. If he asserts his Church's dogmas he gives us his own comment and interpretation. Our priests are supposed to give, not their own, but the current official interpretation. We know and hear nothing of Father So-and-So's " views," as we do of Liddon's, or Scott-Holland's, or Gore's, or Henson's views. As the grace of the sacraments is not injured by the sins of the minister, so, with us, the truth of the Church's message is not hurt by the doubt or unbelief of the messenger. All that our priests say in the pulpit or confessional or school is governed, expressly or tacitly, by the clause: " The Church says . . ." For this reason the unbelieving Catholic priest can continue to act as the Church's messenger more easily than the unbelieving Anglican or Protestant, whose pretence to speak his own mind makes him a liar and hypocrite. The former is the bishop's *employé,* contracted to deliver a certain message in the bishop's name—not in his own. If he breaks this contract the bishop can arraign him justly *in foro externo.* His inward sincerity as to faith and morals belongs to the *forum internum ;* to the tribunal of conscience, into which the bishop has no official right to intrude. There is an obligation of conscience that a priest should live worthily and believe rightly. But if H., or another, sincerely believes that Modernism is the true interpretation of Catholicism, that the bishop's interpretation is false, I can see no obliquity in his fulfilling his contract as the bishop's messenger, while holding his own view as to the form and substance of that message : *Lex non curat de internis*. A man who celebrates Mass in secret mortal sin breaks no contract with his bishop ; nor has the bishop any business to question him about his conscience. His guilt is his own concern. It may well be that he does not consider mortal what the bishop would consider mortal. Of course if his sin is public the bishop can interfere on grounds of scandal ; and if a Modernist talks promiscuously about his negations, the same holds good. In H.'s case the conversation was privileged, and the report garbled. If a man may not express his opinions at a clerical conference and discussion, what does a conference mean ?

But a more general question arises out of this : Is it just that our bishops should seduce young boys into a position of absolute financial dependence on the Church, and then, in later life, turn them adrift, on account of convictions that have been forced on them by irresistible evidence ?

The principle on which they justify themselves is that such convictions, being contrary to what they call " faith," must be false, culpable, and insincere ; that no priest can lose his orthodoxy but by a wilful and immoral act ; that if he can be suspended and beggared for crime, he can be so still more for heresy, i.e. heterodoxy. He is, in short, the wilful author of his own suspension, since he has broken a virtual contract.

The principle is, of course, monstrous, and derives from the confusion of faith with theological orthodoxy —of a moral with an intellectual attitude. A man may no more contract against future intellectual attitudes than against small-pox or heart-disease.

He can as easily control the winds and waves as the data of his experience and the laws of his mind.

These boys are, then, educated for the Church on the supposition that it is their duty never to see certain facts and their consequences. If they come to see them it is their own fault, and they must be punished by infamy and starvation. Thus the mind is sealed up, and intellectual insincerity made a sacred and heavily-sanctioned duty.

Unfortunately it is, nowadays, in many cases an impossible, and therefore non-existent duty. In Catholic countries and ages the probability of mischievous enlightenment was negligible, and the injustice of such episcopal procedure not so flagrant. To-day it is rare that a priest escapes a knowledge of facts, the admission of which is Modernism and heresy ; and the chances that he will be forced to admit them are appreciable—a crime punishable with starvation and infamy. Although the dogmatically destructive results of Biblical and historical criticism have not yet obtained universal acceptance, they are accepted widely enough to be a part of the public mind. In earlier times such tenets were the possession of a minute and negligible minority ; a man might be morally certain that he would always think with the practically unanimous bulk of general opinion. Now that opinion is fairly divided on these questions no prudent man can answer for what he may think later.

It cannot be pretended that the boy or young seminarist gives his life to the Church on the understanding that he may one day discover facts incompatible with his vocation ; that, therefore, the risk of destitution is one that he has foreseen or freely accepted—much as a workman in accepting a situation accepts the risk of being thrown out of work by sickness or accident ;

that the bishop is then no more bound to him than an employer to a disabled employee. For not only does the bishop deny the possibility of such disconcerting discoveries, but imposes this conviction on the juvenile and credulous mind of the seminarist. No employer ever assures the employee that he will never be thrown out of work by accidents. Were he to do so, were the employee accordingly to make no provision for such an emergency, the employer would be bound to support him in the event of such an accident. No, our bishop-employer assures the youth that no accident can ever happen but by his own fault, and therefore dismisses him without mercy when the accident happens.

Now the bishop is free to hold his view about the culpability of intellectual candour. But the sane world, which does not hold it, which sees young men seduced to destruction by it, is bound to take measures to protect those who are victims of this mischievous system.

As to the Church of England, matters are somewhat different. Her ministry is recruited mainly from the universities. Those who offer themselves for it do so with a certain measure of freedom. They are not captured in childhood and segregated and blinkered until it is too late to recede. When they accept ordination they no doubt believe that their theological convictions will not change, and that they will always be able to teach what their Church teaches and to fulfil their implicit contract with her. But neither they nor their bishops now hold that a sincere change of views is impossible, or is necessarily criminal. They know there is a risk of their being some day unable to teach the doctrines of their Church. They foresee the possibility of being thus thrown out of employment. Should such a crisis arise the preacher finds himself disabled in the exercise of his ministry by no fault of his own ; and as it were by an accident, whose possibility was faced when he undertook that ministry. Whether he or his Church should bear the temporal and financial consequences ought to have been a matter of explicit arrangement. Holy Orders being of their nature perpetual and indelible, it would seem that the Church, in ordaining, binds herself to the life-support of her minister. It cannot be denied, I think, that the existing officials of an hierarchic Church have a right to require that preachers shall not contravene that Church's teachings ; that while the preacher is bound to preach what he believes to be the true interpretation of Christianity, he has no business to preach it in the Church's name, if it contradicts what she believes to be the true interpretation. Within certain limits he is a delegate. If he contradicts the message entrusted to him by his Church he is dishonest. Of course he may honestly try to show that the Church's interpretation is wider or other than that of his bishop ; but eventually the verdict of the highest ecclesiastical tribunal must prevail in the interests of order.

All points to the anomaly in these days of a clergy paid to defend, not truth, but certain apprehensions of truth. Let those who agree with the Church's apprehensions of truth preach them and defend them freely, and not under the fear of temporal loss, the hope of temporal gain. Let them be so independent of the Church for their daily bread that the moment they can no longer defend these apprehensions of truth they can afford to be silent, or to preach other apprehensions in their own name, and not in the Church's name. But of that I have written at length elsewhere.[1]

[1] This remark is probably a reference to his article on " The Dearth of Clergy," published in *The Contemporary Review* of May 1909.

VII

ANGLICANISM

NOTE

The following letter, in some ways so different from Father Tyrrell's later writings, is of interest as showing the fundamental consistency of his earlier and later views.

To Viscount Halifax

BEAUMONT COLLEGE,
OLD WINDSOR,
July 24, 1897.

DEAR LORD HALIFAX,

I am pleased to think that my article [1] afforded your lordship a certain amount of consolation. At the same time, though it has met with warm approval from many Catholics whose opinion I value very justly, it would be a mistake to suppose that it in any way represented the sentiments of the majority, which with us, as with every other body of mortals, is made up of those who take narrow and short-sighted views of every question, and whose zeal and good-will are greater than their discretion. Were not God's foolishness wiser than the wisdom of men we might despair of any good ever being accomplished : but if we have eyes of faith we can see Him at work everywhere, moulding good out of evil. I am afraid the same acrimonious bitterness has characterised every

---

[1] " The Prospects of Reunion," *The Month,* July 1897.

quarrel recorded in the pages of Church history ; and one cannot pretend that the orthodox side has ever shown a too brilliant example of charity to the unorthodox. This, I think, is inevitable—taking human nature as it is in the many—wherever any difference of opinion creates *sides ;* for thousands, who care little about the truth, love controversy and contest for its own sake, and eagerly join the fray, not to heal the breach but to enlarge it ; not to reconcile differences but to accentuate them. Were it not for this class Church papers could not subsist. Frankly, however, I think your lordship has been far too sanguine all along as to the possibility of what could in any sense be called corporate reunion ; and that you very much overrate Cardinal Vaughan's influence and underrate the immutability of Rome with respect to judgments once uttered, if you think the decision on the Orders question ever could have been or ever can be other than it is. And this, looking at it merely as an outsider without any reference to papal infallibility. If Rome were to eat her words in this matter she would no longer be Rome ; she would soon lapse into dogmatic chaos, and cease to be worth uniting with.

Also, I do not think your lordship enters sufficiently into the intellectual position of those who have been born and reared as Catholics, and to whom the Anglican position—which surely is, even to yourselves, most complex and difficult to state clearly—must necessarily be far more unintelligible even than ours is to you. And therefore, altogether, I think you are expecting too much. Speaking as a Catholic, it seems to me that God delays reaping till all the harvest is ripe ; and that then the need of being with Peter will be felt and recognised among thousands as easily and quickly as other Catholic truths, which no one would have listened to fifty years ago.

9

Meantime the process is here and there completed in individual souls, for whom submission then becomes imperative ; but this I believe is rarer than commonly supposed. Many come to Rome simply because they find Anglicanism impossible, and suppose that there is no alternative ; whereas it may well be that as yet they have not light enough for the step, but must remain in some twilight limbo till God delivers them. God often deprives men of the full light and of sacramental grace, yet supplies in other ways. I think you will understand that it is at no sacrifice of my position as an implicit believer in the claims of Peter that I pray that your lordship may be instrumental in God's hands for the spread of Catholic truth in the English Church ; nor have I the least doubt that, if God sees good to torment you with fuller light, no human consideration will deter you from abandoning that great work to other hands and becoming an *abjectus in domo Domini.*

To the Same

RICHMOND, YORKS,
November 19, 1903.

MY DEAR LORD HALIFAX,

Oil and Wine (not *and Honey*) was to have been the title of the untitled grey book which you have already got. I have told Longmans to send you a copy of *Lex Orandi*, which has got the new Archbishop's imprimatur ; some things in it may please you, but on the whole it is heavy, owing to the need of obscurities and circumlocutions in order to evade the snares of the Philistine. Still, I hope it will tell slowly, and with a few. I trust *The Tablet's* prediction of Loisy's speedy annihilation is only an expression of its wishes, and has so far received no confirmation. Certainly

an authoritative condemnation would come very ill
in the face of the existence of a commission appointed
to deal with criticism on its own grounds, and by its
own methods; it would almost be a confession of
failure and of panic. Given the commission, I think
that a condemnation should be preceded by a refutation; or, if not, should be withheld. We must face
the fact that criticism has come to stay; that it is as
much a science as astronomy, and will go its own way
irresistibly—*eppure si muove*. A repetition in this de-
partment of the Galileo blunder would be immediately
most disastrous—though perhaps eventually most
profitable as bringing out the limits of ecclesiastical
inerrancy. I am too little versed in the subject to
say how far Loisy may be right or wrong, but I cannot
help seeing that there are not, as might appear at first
blush, two parties in the Church taking opposite views
of the same mass of evidence. That would be comparatively satisfactory. But, speaking in the rough,
what I see is that, just in the measure that men acquaint
themselves with the evidence, they approximate,
with a sort of moral unanimity, to Loisy's positions.
The dissentients are only those who have not seen,
who will not look. That is very serious. To show the
theological inconveniences and impossibilities of Loisy's
admissions as a critic brings out the difficulty into
high relief, but does nothing to solve it. "So much
the worse for theology," say the critics. "So much
the worse for criticism," say the theologians. Loisy's
is the signal merit of having at least tried, with a
master's knowledge of both interests, to effect a mediation between Catholicism and criticism. If he has
failed in so complex an undertaking, with none to help
him, surely it will be a most ungracious act if the
cause he most cared for should be the one to stone him.

I sometimes *feel*—rather than *know* definitely—

that, in this matter of criticism, our leanings are not quite in the same direction. For in the English Church the interests of reunion demand an insistence on the dogmatic principle and a protest against the licence of criticism ; with us, the same interest demands a limitation of exaggerated dogmatism and a defence of the rights of enquiry. Hence your broad church-men are the least, ours are the most, favourable to reunion. It is our narrow men and your broad men who will hear of no compromise whatever. But I hope that the Catholicism in which we may eventually unite will be one in which all that is good and true in Modernism will be saved and sanctified ; and for this reason the extreme " ecclesiasticism " of some of your priests, more Roman than Rome herself, fills me with dismay. I say to myself : " These men would burn me at the stake for an evangelical." To that sort of Catholicism may England never be converted. In you, on the contrary, I feel there is deeper sympathy, a truer appreciation of the genuine religious force contained in Protestantism and Nonconformity—a force that only needs to be run into the Catholic mould and not to be discounted as valueless. Infinite though the problem be of bringing all these vagrant forces back again into one organism, yet it is a sort of pole-star which we cannot reach, but towards which we can steer.

To William Scott-Palmer (Mrs. Dowson)

August 29, 1907.

My attention has only just been called to your article in *The Church Times* (" Towards the New Beginning ") and the correspondence it has evoked. It would be superfluous and impertinent for me to speak of my sympathy with the former. It is principally about the not very uncommon point of view represented by Mr. Rickard's letter that I would offer a few remarks.

He seems to assume that, as the champion of Catholic principles, *The Church Times* is bound to champion that most uncatholic and sectarian attitude towards enlightenment, which has ever been the ruin of Catholicism, and has played straight into the hands of " Protestantism." He evidently belongs to that school of Anglicans who cling to (and imitate) all that is most perishable, moribund, and impossible in the Roman system ; to all its " uncatholicism " ; to sacerdotalism ; to sacramental materialism ; to moral and ritualistic casuistry and rabbinism ; to theological obscurantism ; to every " dead and beggarly element " against which the living and fruitful elements are struggling ; to just that section or sect of Roman Catholicism which in secret entertains the most profound contempt for " the so-called Anglo-Catholic " and " his sham sacraments ! " Such are the men who so often " go over to Rome " and add to the diseased elements of her constitution—" converts " of the most violently ultramontane type.

The compatibility of freedom and authority, of science and revelation, is surely a most essential and fundamental Catholic principle. Its application is the perennial problem. The Church which solves it first will sweep the world into its net. So far as, without attempting a logical synthesis, the Church of England has always preached, ultimately, respect for tradition and respect for conscience (moral and intellectual), it is perhaps she who seems more likely to win the race. But, on the other hand, the problem presses more urgently at Rome, where the principle of authority has been driven to such an extremity. " Liberalism " cannot be suppressed any longer.

Under the futile and ill-judged repressions of Pius X
it has advanced by leaps and bounds ; it has learnt
its own strength ; and that its adversaries have no
trust except in " segregation " and almost physical
repression ; that they are silent in the face of facts.
Pius has only driven the moderates over to the ex-
tremes ; alienated the sympathies of the non-catholic
conservative spectators ; and made his own cause
ridiculous.

Mr. Rickard would have the Church of England
enter on the same fatal path. I am not sure but in
that case she would drive her own liberals to throw
in their lot with their struggling, but surely invincible,
Romanist brethren. *The Church Times* could not
be truer to its own programme than by asserting the
principles of free enquiry and discussion as against
Romanism, and those of Catholic tradition as against
pure Protestantism. No reasonable person will demand
a premature synthesis at its hands. It certainly
ought to welcome every effort, however feeble, towards
the reconciliation of Catholicism and the new learning,
and to take an object-lesson from the failures of Rome.

Their " *unus* (*Athanasius*) *contra mundum* " is
necessarily the fate of the pioneers of truth. The
formula of Athanasius was a novelty that eventually
prevailed in the world of orthodoxy. But when one
is alone against the world in adhering to an outgoing
formula, and in opposing what has at last *won* the
seal of general consent, then surely to be alone is to
be wrong. The *first* adherent of an eventually prevalent school is right ; the *last*, who stands out against
a newer school, is wrong. The reaction and intransigence of the Rickard school is only of the latter sort.
They will resist the universal march of the world's
intelligence, and the world will ignore them and pass
on. That is a curious conception of the functions

of a Church that professes to be the light of the world
and the salt of the earth.

" Nobody " seems to think that to become as a
child means to accept *bad* philosophy, science, and
history ; that the error of the wise and prudent is in
departing from scholastic realism. I take it that
Christ meant that which " saves " a man and makes
him a Christian is not science and theology and history ;
but a spirit and temper. The notion that in so blessing
babes and ignorant persons he blessed ignorance and
error and fallacy is very convenient for an uneducated
clergy, who have reason to fear the criticism of the
educated. . . .

It would be well to confine such discussions as
you propose to formal *conferences* and lectures. For
occasions of public worship I think it would be
better to preach in the style of Christ as much as
possible ; to avoid all problems, historic, philosophic,
and otherwise. It is not so much the absence of
knowledge and intelligence, as the presence of ignorance and unintelligence, that empties our churches.
It is because St. Thomas Aquinas is imposed on us,
rather than because Kant is ignored. It is the parade
of competency and erudition where none exist. Still
I am not sure that preaching is not much overdone,
and that where (as in ninety-nine out of a hundred
cases) the true gift is lacking, some kind of appointed
lessons would not be vastly more profitable and
tolerable. To oblige an ordinary man to preach fifty
sermons a year is to oblige him to talk a deal of flatu-
lant nonsense.

As to what you call the present " upheaval " in
the Roman Church, it is easier to understand its nature
and causes than to predict its consequences. " Reform " was possible when the Church was less centralised than now. It was less easy then to exclude

and frustrate the reformer. To-day nothing can be done till the Roman Curia is converted to Christianity. There is more hope of the Jews. I had intended to address a letter to *The Church Times* on these points; but I have been too unwell to get them into literary shape, or to think them out properly. But I thought you would be patient and indulgent with my ramblings.

I feel more and more that I have wasted my life dabbling in shallow waters instead of pushing out into the deep. I suppose it is easier to make a splash that way. Now I seem to be drifting in a tub to the middle of the Atlantic—feeling very small and helpless and lonely. To the *most* religious people in the world; to the few *absolutely* honest souls who presuppose nothing and will not formulate deceits to themselves, one has nothing to say except " I understand."

VIII

POSITIVISM

NOTE

In the following correspondence I have included one long letter that has already appeared in the *Autobiography and Life*. Mr. Malcolm Quin was at that time a Positivist minister at Newcastle-on-Tyne ; [1] he had been much impressed by some of Tyrrell's work, though they disagreed profoundly on many points. In a letter, which Father Tyrrell did not live to receive, Mr. Quin indicates one point of divergence : " Your experiences of the Catholic Church lead you to emphasise most the things of freedom ; my experiences of the Revolution incline me to insist chiefly on the things of order."

To the Rev. Malcolm Quin

STORRINGTON, SUSSEX,
January 2, 1907.

MY DEAR SIR,

You will, I am afraid, think me very discourteous in not having long since acknowledged your very kind and helpful letter of November 8. The relation between Catholicism and religious Positivism has been a matter of deep interest to me ever since my acquaintance with the late Mr. Kegan Paul, who had passed

---

[1] Author of *Aids to Worship, Catholicism and the Modern Mind, The Problem of Human Peace, The Politics of the Proletariat,* etc. He has since abandoned the ministry.

from you to us. I have long wished and even intended to put together my reflections on this head, and much that you say in your letter and in the papers you so kindly sent me will help to clear my thoughts. But at present I am too overwhelmed with correspondence and sundry literary engagements to be able to give the subject its requisite care and leisure ; and it is not one to be dealt with at odd moments and interstices. As to the *Much-abused Letter*, I suppose it can be read two ways : (1) As Protestant concessions in the interests of Catholicism, or (2) As Catholic concessions in the interests of Protestantism. It is most difficult to judge it without the context of the addressee and his outlook. My own position in this and other brochures is that, however great the havoc criticism may play with our current theology, the religion it makes for is most certainly not of the Protestant but of the Catholic type ; that individualism is a lost cause ; that in religion as in civilisation it is through society that we live and move and have our being. But even the best-informed outsider cannot realise the conditions and dangers which have roused us liberal Catholics to make a stand against the reactionary and anti-progressive principles which at present bid fair to wreck the Roman Church altogether, or to render her as little a living influence as Cleopatra's Needle by the Thames Embankment.

To the Same

STORRINGTON,
August 8, 1907.[1]

I have just read your circular with keen interest and sympathy, and feel inspired to inflict upon you some of my reflections. There can be no doubt about it that we are both governed by the same idea of the

[1] See *Life*, etc., vol. ii.

value and significance of religion and of the principles
of its interpretation ; in other words, that we (i.e. you
and I ; *not* our co-religionists) are making for the
same Catholicism from opposite approaches. I am
very ignorant about Positivism as a concrete society.
But I suppose that what you consider the deeper,
truer, and higher developments of Comte's thought
and spirit would be viewed by his revolutionary
followers as the weaker, inconsistent, decadent side
of his philosophy ; and that the clearer recognition
of this cleft in the unity of your great master's spirit
is like to cleave his followers into two camps. I gather
from the more domestic part of your circular that the
depression from which all institutional religion is
suffering at present extends to your little body. I
suppose it is idle to deny that the deepest root of this
depression is confusion, uncertainty, lack of faith in
ideals and. spiritual values. It seems to me that
" popular " Christianity has based its faith on sand,
and that Positivism is still seeking but has not yet
found a rock solid enough to reassure the waverings
of average humanity. I ask myself : Is not your
movement, like that of the liberal Catholics, too aca-
demic, too philosophical to be ever a power with average
humanity ? But we liberal Catholics only ask liberty
for our own as well as for the popular reading of
Catholicism. We recognise that an universal Church
should cater for every level. We only protest that
the lower and more general should not be privileged
at the expense of the higher ; and that men of science
should not be driven out of the Church—(for all this
you might look at chap. ii. of my recent book *Scylla
and Charybdis*)—that there should be some place for
those who have outgrown the childhood forms of
religion. Well then, here we part company—so far,
namely, as you would impose on all what must always

and inevitably be " meat for the strong " ; that you are guilty of the same un-Catholic sectarianism as Rome is, when she would diet the strong on what is milk for babes. Positivism is an almost purely rational religion. But the most rational men will always be a minority ; and even they are rational only by fits and starts.

Then I ask whether recent epistomology or science-theories ; whether the work of some of the Pragmatists, and that of philosophers like Volkelt, James Ward, Poincaré, Adhémar, above all of Bergson, has not ruined the very foundation of Comte's trust in science ; whether that trust itself has not been a passing stage and not the final stage of man's growth ; whether finality is possible.   What, I imagine, is the permanent value of Positivism is its spirit of fearless criticism, its refusal of any arbitrary dogmatism in things of the spirit.   If Bergson is as right as I imagine, the scientific construction of the world possesses a purely practical value, but is the very furthest possible remove from theoretical truth.   At all events Comte's " first principle " is now in the crucible of discussion, and can no longer guarantee the rest and stability which it was designed to secure.

When you speak of " revolution " I am not quite clear as to your meaning.   There is surely a sense in which revolution is the *sine qua non* of spiritual and social progress—understanding by " revolution " a change affecting the fundamental categories and methods of science, the fundamental laws and institutions of society.   There comes a day when gathering experience, when the growing fulness of life naturally and rightly calls for radical reconstruction ; when new bottles must be found for the new wine.   It is not too much to say that revolution is a law of life— individual and social.   If, however, by revolution you mean a wholly or partly destructive and negative synthesis—one that misses and drops the values of the old, that does not explain and include them all in a higher unity—then, of course, I share your fear of revolution. There I would agree (to speak in figures) that the abrupt secularisation of the Church of Ste. Geneviève in Paris and its transformation into the Panthéon was a pseudo-revolution ; a violation of the law of life. And the same is to be said of the whole secularisation of France. But here the blame attaches not only to the State but to the Church, which has opposed the right and necessary sorts of revolution and thereby provoked the morbid sort.

I will join you against revolution if you will join me against reaction and petrifaction. So much so that my objection against the actual concrete Positivism (as a religion) is that it is a revolution in the bad sense—a schismatic breaking away of what should be and remain the more forward part of a general process. If Comte had remained (or become) a Catholic, if he had pushed his religious ideas as a deeper interpretation of the same Catholicism of which official Catholicism is the only possible form for the backward multitudes, the immediate results might have been quite inconspicuous, but he would have sown seed in a soil where, in the long run, it would have borne far more abundant and lasting fruit. May I again refer to chap. ii. of *Scylla and Charybdis*? It is as united to, not as cut off from, the savourless mass that the leaven does its work. You have cut yourselves off and you are helpless. Why don't you come in and help us? You, at least, who are beginning to see that the Christ and God of Christianity cannot without suicidal inconsistency be excluded from the " value-interpretation " which Comte applied to all the secondary and subordinate ideas of Catholicism.

To the Same

16 OLD TOWN, CLAPHAM,

1909.

I have been reading your book with great sympathy and interest and trying to make out where we diverge. I suppose you would think me too much of a revolutionary ; and this because the very synthesis you aim at (Catholicism and Science) implies a revolution, and cannot be effected by any process of continuous development. On the other hand, I see more and more the need of faith in life and thought ; and that a rigorous Positivism is as fatal to the natural as to the religious interests of humanity. I believe in the progressive *tendency*, but I do not see a scrap of reason for thinking that the said tendency is bound to actuate itself, or that life's balance of good and evil will ever be different from what it is now. If humanity perishes with its planet, can it signify ultimately ?

You see I am puzzled still about a very rudimentary point : Is this life all—for me, and for humanity—or do we look for a better ?

But I mean to read your book again and may be able to bring my ideas to a point.

To the Same

16 OLD TOWN, CLAPHAM,

June 8, 1909.

You quite mistake if you suppose I demand eternal life as a reward. So to seek it were to love it. " Though He slay me, yet will I hope in Him " is the cry of one who had no hope in eternal life. The Psalms were written without any such hope. But to put the question, and then deny it dogmatically and explicitly, is another affair. Our later age has put the question : Does mankind signify absolutely ? If absolutely, must we not also say eternally ? Is not this the very implication of the law that dictates disinterested goodness ? Deny it dogmatically, and the law is but a trick of Nature's to get more work out of us (cf. Balfour's *Foundations of Belief*).

You repudiate metaphysic, and yet you imply that were the world but three days off annihilation you would find the moral effort supremely worthful and imperative. Of course you would ; and so would every man who had not violated his nature. But how to justify it on strictly Positivist grounds, and excluding metaphysics, I do not see. I cannot make the simplest affirmation without an act of faith in the unprovable. I wish I had leisure to go through your book and show you how saturated it is with metaphysical conceptions from cover to cover. I *feel* it in every line of your letter. I quite understand Comte's revolt against a dogmatic metaphysic and all its idols ; but without a sane, modest metaphysic we cannot breathe or think. We must have God or His equivalent. But it is stupid to say this crudely in a few words. I feel that at root we mean the same thing.

PS.—I mean : Is God more of a metaphysicality than " the law of our own higher nature " ? Are not both, fictions founded in fact, i.e. there is a given experience from which faith leaps to an interpretative hypothesis that works out well ? Do we know the existence of other personalities than our own otherwise ? or that of what we call the external world ? Is not our world of so-called experience nearly nine-tenths a construction of faith in the not-experienced ; I think Volkelt's critique of Kant's *Erkenntniss theorie* has demonstrated this conclusively. What we need is a metaphysic that is not *a priori* but is suggested and verified by experience at every step.

Do you know E. Boutroux's *Science et Religion*, which has a good critique of Comte's merits and demerits ?

IX

PRAYER

To Mrs. Stracey

RICHMOND, YORKS,
November 27, 1905.

I do not *know ;* and that is the simple truth. As to my practice, I have gradually grown dumb, partly from a sense of the fictitious character of all our notions of the divine and a desire to keep clear of unreality, partly from a conviction that the verbal " externation " of our desires, however profitable when possible, is not the essence of prayer. Overmuch reflection on religious problems is bound to produce this paralysis. To use forms helpfully one must be able to forget that they are forms ; to approach God as " Our Father " one must not be too conscious of the hopeless inadequacy of the appellation. But this is a subjective defect and has little bearing on your case.

The instinct to pray is too spontaneous, too universal among religious people not to be well founded in the laws that govern the world to which our spirits belong. The outward form, in which that instinctive impulse embodies itself, depends on the form in which we present that mysterious world to ourselves. Christ has taught us to picture the divine as a heavenly Father whose children we all are. Taking things that way, what can we do, how can we embody our love for one another better than by lifting up our eyes to the skies to ask help in our needs ? Our Lord

would not have been (as He certainly was) " true man "
and a man of His *milieu* had He departed from the
current religious ideas of his day as to prayer ; had
He not taught and practised intercessory prayer of
the simplest and directest form—prayer not only
for the meat that endureth, but also for the meat that
perisheth. His *human* mind was that of a little child
in simplicity and freedom from our weary modern
sophistication. It was in His heart and spirit that
He rose beyond the limits of humanity. Yet the
inadequacy of the " Father and Child" scheme is
proved nowhere more abundantly than in the seeming
inefficacy of prayer, its barrenness of all *demonstrable*
fruit. We ask and do not receive ; seek and do not
find ; knock and are left knocking. Masses of evidence
of answers (mostly temporal) to prayer might be
collected ; as has been done by the P.R.S. for the existence of ghosts. But I think, if properly sifted and
criticised, little would be proved beyond (and this
I greatly doubt) an occasional and exceptional efficacy
in the way of an interruption of the natural course of
events. This would be a most lame and impotent
conclusion ; since, according to common religious
teaching, failure should be the exception and not the
rule. Moreover, prayers for grace should never fail,
whereas our experience tells us they nearly always
do when we pray for others ; so that if it seems otherwise when we pray for ourselves this must be put down
to the subjective reaction of desire. It is no theory
of the responsibility of physical or moral miracles,
but simply the uniform testimony of experience, that
stands against the literal truth of the common doctrine
as to the efficacy of prayer. In each case there are
always a thousand reasons to give why the prayer
failed ; but for the failure of the vast bulk there is
no adequate reason forthcoming except that prayer

is not an efficacious means. And yet I feel sure that the instinct of Christ and His saints, however incapable of analysis, is a right one, and that underneath the literal sense of the prayer-doctrine there is a sacramental sense. I think we shall find that there is an organic connection between every member of the spiritual world ; and that, however circuitously and remotely, every sincere and selfless desire for the welfare of others in general or in particular will tell in the long run, and that the bread cast on the waters will return after many days—and this, not by an inversion of law, but in strict conformity to the laws of Providence that nothing evades, not even an involuntary sigh. This, of course, is faith and not knowledge ; and will probably be a poor consolation to you in your embarrassment. But its practical upshot is that they do well who can practise the prayer-doctrine in its crude simplicity untroubled by the contradiction of experience ; that they do better, perhaps, who take it at its sacramental value and can pray with a blind trust that the instinct is not an idle one ; that they do not ill who are content to believe that love is a potent force in the working out of God's schemes and that our desires are causal. In answer to your question :

1. I honestly believe (I don't know, but have faith) that the good desire uttered in every prayer tells for the good of the individual prayed for, and that, no doubt, *in reference to* the particular case ; for *this case determines the desire.* 2. Except when the effect is produced by the expectancy of the recipient I do not see that faith in the efficacy of good desires conditions their efficacy as a *sine qua non* (the Gospel insistence on faith as a condition of prayer-efficacy refers mostly to prayer for bodily or psychic *cures*). 3. We cannot " *make* ourselves believe " in the sense of trying to violate our intellectual conscience. But

then should one *want* to believe the literal sense of the prayer-doctrine ? Isn't that the childish form of a maturer faith that needs no forcing ?

To P.

Date uncertain.

It seems to me that the problem of prayer can only be solved in its connection with that of conscience and the whole spirit world. As you know, I do not regard my conscience—your conscience—as an isolated spiritual judge seated in my soul or your soul. Conscience is, in each one of us, both private and particular and universal. I alone can hear what my conscience tells me, and yet its message would be of little import did it not express to me the wider and more absolute message of the universal conscience.

I must obey my own conscience against the whole world—and yet I owe it this obedience, not because it is mine, but because it is the representative, in my own soul, of the universal conscience.

Thus the true martyr of conscience is the martyr alike of a personal and a universal command. So of prayer. In it we have another manifestation of this double law. We pray, but God prays in us. We pray to what is without, but to what is also within us. Thus the answer to prayer is, in some matters, and to some extent, the product of prayer itself—prayer is always creative as well as impetrative.

Hence the first and most essential characteristic of true prayer is *reality*—a characteristic on which little enough insistence is made in the routine teaching on the matter.

Of course, in so far as prayer is purely mechanical, it cannot be classed as a religious exercise ; it is more akin to the practices of magic. Yet it were too rigorously dogmatic thus to condemn all prayer that is infected with this taint—much of it may be saved by a core of spirituality hidden under these trappings of materialism and externality.

Yet it remains a fact, and a regrettable one, that the true doctrine of prayer is not more generally insisted on ; that only those who explore the mystical writers, and not those taught by the ordinary manuals of religious piety, are helped to a deeper and more vital conception of its character.

What we want to develop in all these matters is a sense of spiritual responsibility. We do not, perhaps, pray, like the Italian brigand, for assistance in the prosecution of a crime ; but we do pray, at times, with little reference to the higher dicta of conscience. We cast all the responsibility on an outside factor; yet only in so far as we think and speak—otherwise pray—in union with that factor, can we expect to be heard.

To V.

May 14, 1901.

I have always felt as you do about retreats ; probably because our temperaments are as alike in some points as they are unlike in others.

The whole notion of fixing the Holy Ghost to times and seasons and forms of prayer is only defensible if these performances of ours be viewed simply as a sort of impetration, to be answered in God's own queer way, at the time and through the medium we least expect. The idea of making *acts of the will* has always been perplexing to me ; the mere verbal act being voluntary in a sense, and expressing, perhaps, a desire for the reality uttered, but certainly not identical with it. To say *Credo* may freely express my desire to believe ; but a real act of faith is as much *given* to me as is joy or sorrow or any other state of soul. I am sure many feel this as regards " acts of contrition." We can assert the proper ideas and motives by free control of the mind, but the response of the heart is not in our power ; nor is it of the mere *feeling* this is true, but of the *being* contrite ; i.e. the practical attitude of the soul in relation to sin.

Druzbickis' fallacy, that *Volo velle* is the same as *Volo*, has eaten deep into modern theology. I want to will means I do *not* will ; that there is a contrary will in possession, albeit in disputed possession. St. Augustine and the Dominicans are nearer the truth in this matter.

FREIBURG,
April 2, 1906;

I quite understand your desire for a life of prayer— the nostalgia for the old days " when His lamp shone about my head." God knows I feel it. But I think they will return for us all in some better form. I find the Breviary lives for me again after a long transition period of death. One has to pass through atheism to faith ; the old God must be quite pulverised and forgotten before the new can reveal Himself to us. Patchings and mendings have an end ; and revolutions are normal in all true developments. But revolutions are heralded by periods of chaos. I feel sure you are not far from your Easter—*Adhuc sum tecum*—even still, and after all.

To Miss Dora Williams

RICHMOND, YORKS,.
June 22, 1904.

DEAR MISS WILLIAMS,

(1) I see you harbour resentment, and therefore take your charge of " inconsequence " at its true worth, a mere " *tu quoque* " or " you're another." I will leave you the last word since it is really my own reverberated.

(2) "How do I know the flowers don't pray?" I am quite sure they do. They pray for rain when they droop; and for light when they struggle upwards and fight one another for the best place; and sing *Te Deum* when they lift up their heads and open their mouths and stretch out their arms. And so, too, I pray by being hungry and give praise by being well and happy; just as the young ravens cry out "Caw! caw!" which, being interpreted, is *Pater Noster*. As usual we are quite agreed. I only wanted to deprecate your atheistical notion of a godless world that demanded interventions from outside, as though the winds and waves had a will of their own to oppose to the will of God and needed to be kept in order. It is He who makes the spider catch the fly and who makes the fly struggle to get away. The fly prays by struggling; the spider by pouncing. Both prayers buzz in His ear at once; and the issue is the answer.

(3) I am sorry I called Fichte "tough"; I meant "stringy," which is quite a different idea—like treacle, sealing-wax, or glue, which never come away neat, but streel a comet's tail behind them.

(4) I have just such a string or stringiness of visitors up here at present, and no prospect of nipping it off clean for some time, and therewithal a sudden burst of literary fertility whose fruits must be garnered quickly and surely; for life is very short, and *nox venit*, with its candle-extinguisher and eternal night-cap.

To the Same

May 30, 1905.

DEAR MISS WILLIAMS,

You were elbow-deep in flour when you last wrote ; and my imagination sees you so yet and tells me not to interrupt you in the great business of life which has made the word " lady " a title of honour— if etymology is right. A vision of elbows reminds me of a " vigil of arms," which is the night of wakeful prayer spent by the candidate previous to his dubbing. With a soldier's instinct Ignatius of Loyola spent such a night prior to consecrating himself by vow to the service of Our Lady (or some one). Could I, his follower, do less ?

As to prayers of petition —if you have been answered there's an end of it. From fact to possibility the argument is irresistible. Not that I ever questioned the possibility. Only I, personally, have never had direct experience of any undeniable consequences of prayer other than the natural ; at all events nothing of greater weight than the usual S.P.R. evidences of the preternatural. But I do not see a bit how that should affect one's faith in, hope in, or love of God. On the contrary, I think the miracle-view of prayer is really a need of an imperfect faith ; not at all the best. To believe that this terrible machine-world is really from God, in God and unto God, that through it and in spite of its blind fatality all works together for good, that is faith in long trousers ; the other is faith in knickerbockers. Consider the lilies, they toil not, neither do they spin, *neither do they pray.* To pray is to take thought for the morrow, what you shall eat, etc., etc. (i.e. to pray for miraculous anthropomorphic interventions). I love Heine's essays so far. I take ten pages for a night-cap. He is far nearer the heart of things than Fichte, and takes the whole of life, and not only a few tough slices of it, into his philosophy. I think you love toughness *as such ;* you think it will make you strong. Tender things may be, often are, more nutritious. I can fancy myself tugging with my teeth at the leathery crust of your bread.

To Dr. Israel Abrahams [1]

16 OLD TOWN, CLAPHAM,
January 22, 1909.

DEAR DR. ABRAHAMS,

That is a splendid paper, and I am in profound sympathy with it. It makes evident what one expected, namely, that the *genuine* utterances of Christ about prayer merely echoed the better spirit of his own religion. The Rabbinical position of that day—though not quite steady—represented a very high stage of religious evolution. The conception of prayer had advanced hand in hand with the conception of God. For the pagan, as for many crypto-pagans, God is one of the major factors of Nature, to be studied, used, and subjected to man's needs like the rest. Conjuring and magic is the earliest form of prayer. The *mens naturaliter pagana* is always with us ; always at war with the *mens naturaliter Christiana ;* not only in the same community, but in the same soul. Christianity, in its endeavour to absorb, was largely absorbed by the Greco-Roman, and later by the Germanic paganism, and its conceptions of God and prayer have fallen far below those of Christ and His religion. It seems to me that, carefully examined, the Rabbinical prayer of petition is reducible to the prayer of confidence, resignation, conformity, abandonment to the Will of a Father who " knows that we have need of

[1] Reader in Talmudic of Cambridge University.

these things " and does not require to be informed or
importuned or conjured ; who desires prayer as a sort
of praise or confession of dependence and trust.   The
" unsteadiness " of the position—a survival of earlier
conceptions—is the contention that, though we don't
get because we pray, yet if we don't pray we shan't get.
For the latter admission implies a power to alter God's
plans and bend His will (negatively) to our own.
I would hardly call the prayer of petition, with which
my paper dealt, " religious," except in the lowest and
most universal sense of the term.   It is undoubtedly
an appeal to the gods.   It implies at least a belief
in the invisible ; and perhaps some not unworthy sort
of trust and confidence.   But so far as it *uses* the
gods, it treats them as factors of Nature.   Yet as
immanent and co-operant with all the forces of Nature,
God does put Himself at our service and lets us yoke
Him to our car ; and I think we might very well allow
petitionary prayer to be the application of a natural
law—a control exercised by the human will on the
Divine Will, not as transcendent but as immanent and
identified with Nature viewed as a free and intelligent
process ; quite analogous to the other controls we exercise over Nature through obedience to her laws.   It
is all a question of facts—whether in the vast mountains
of alleged evidence there be any little deposit of truth.
I could find it in my heart to say : I hope not.   For
the exaggerated trust in such prayer is no friend to
moral effort or to true faith.   Yet I suspect the evidence cannot all be criticised away ; and were such
prayer recognised as in no true sense religious, but as
a gift or faculty like faith-healing, it would be robbed
of its mischievous and demoralising influence.

PART II

I

PERSONAL

To Laurence Housman, Esq.

CATHOLIC CHURCH,
RICHMOND, YORKS,
June 23, 1900.

MY DEAR " LAURENCE,"

[1] Your letter deals with what is to me the most interesting of all subjects—myself ; and though your analysis is grievously at fault in some points, it is sufficiently sagacious in others to merit consideration. There is no egoism in my self-interest ; for it is based on the fact that I have no other specimen of humanity submitted to my direct inspection ; and only from my knowledge of this particular can I pass to the universal, and thence to rash judgments about my fellow particulars. I am for you a modified Housman ; you, for me, are a modified Tyrrell ; and if we know so little of ourselves we must know far less of one another. Yet the desire to break through our eremitical cells and to get inside other souls is as irresistible as it is hopeless ; though I cherish a vague hope that the corporal " *commixtio* " which is the term of animal love (*duo in carne una*) may hint a spiritual interpenetration of mind with mind, and feeling with feeling, to be realised in that merging of souls in God which the Catholic religion dreams about in her doctrine of the Communion of Saints and other

[1] *Life,* vol. ii. pp. 26–27.

adjacent and dependent mysteries. As to your analysis, I never claimed to be more than indifferent honest. As the nearest that man can come to wisdom is to realise his folly; so none is further removed from honesty than he who brags himself honest. I know I am but as a skein of silk that has been touzled by a kitten; still, in that I freely admit it, and also do heartily dislike the state of tangle, I am, at least in aspiration, honest as *any man of my experience* can be. For surely the shorter the thread the less its capacity of implication; and it is easy for these Yorkshire ploughboys to be simple and straight, but very difficult for a *fin-de-siècle* Jesuit with all my circumstances and antecedents. If in any sense I hunt with the hounds and run with the hare it is certainly and frankly because I genuinely sympathise both with the eager excitement of the chase and with the agonising terror of the victim. Not a minor but the major part of my composition has and always will have doubts; for the highest reason which yields to faith is the feeblest element in most lives, a still small voice rarely heard, more rarely obeyed. My lower rationalism, my imagination, my senses and passions are all singularly sympathetic with doubt and even denial. But I do not "fight down" my doubts, as I should in some cases advise others to do. Rather I go deliberately in search of every difficulty in that line lest I be haunted by the thought that new revelations might rob me of my faith, or that those who deny have reasons for their denial that I have not *felt*. Hence I really do go through stages of spiritual depression and blankness to the extent of being pressed by the great fear; but not of admitting it. This faith of mine is very different from the tranquil belief of those who have faith in the faith of others; who are borne up easily by education, custom, and example,

and blandly attribute their firmness to their own free
choice, forgetful of the corks and bladders under their
armpits. That is impossible for me ; for there is no
man or body of men on earth whose belief would have
the least influence on mine ; and so whatever seeming
buoyancy I have is due to my own continued and
conscious exertion. You cannot then expect me to
be as reposeful as Frank Urquhart in my faith. My
whole life is a continual process of adjusting and re-
adjusting ; for the very reason that I am too miserably
honest to stick my head in the sand and be comfortable.
Still I cannot but feel that the process has been one
of growth and development and of a deeper rooting
of faith, and I have ceased to anticipate a catastrophe,
being too well accustomed to breakers ahead to be
scared by them. I am not one bit afraid of my sentiments and emotions getting the better of me ; first,
they are more than half worn out ; secondly, because
my whole danger is from rationalism and from an
undue depreciation of the legitimate part played by
sentiment in the choice of beliefs. There I think we
are really contrary, and that I am your complement
and you mine. I called you " Laurence " because
I think of you once a day under that title when your
patron's name occurs in the Canon of the Mass, and I
make a slight inclination at the name which means
that he is to look after his namesake, for that I am weary
of him. Also because it is a musical name, pleasant
to utter—as I might inadvertently call a lady of the
name " Florence," not meaning to be tender. My
nonchalance is on the whole very genuine. Death
is awful to children, but nothing to the old ; and so
I have seen too many spiritual catastrophes to be much
interested in " one among so many," and I have failed
too often in my interpretation of people to be much
mortified by another failure. As to affection, I never

know myself till some crisis reveals that the last are first, and the first last. One of my strongest is for a dead person whom when alive I rather disliked, but who grows nicer on reflection.

Now put all this into your philosophical pipe and smoke it. If you ever want *absolute* solitude, paradisaical scenery, and bracing air, come to this deserted village in Swaledale, where I shall remain as long as I possibly can.

To the Same

S. LAURENTII. M.,
August 10, 1903.

DEAR ST. LAURENCE,

I am grieved you should question my qualifications for Westminster ; I cannot agree with you at all. But the death of my friend Leo and the accession of Pius has damaged my prospects irretrievably. The ten days interim, when there was no infallible authority on earth, were the happiest of my life ; I went through a perfect encyclopædia of heresies and am now suffering from an acute orthodox reaction in consequence. For very other reasons I too, like yourself, feel sterilised mentally and morally, an " at-the-end-of-everything " sort of feeling. I think one does work out certain veins at last and come to the inevitable " *vanitas vanitatum*," even in regard to the highest values. What is God for ? What good is He ? was the question of my early years ; and it comes up again at times. I feel that He, too, is a vanity ; and that I want something bigger and better—less in the bush, more in the hand. East wind and a greasy diet and flesh and blood reveal this truth to me from time to time ; but they, too, are vanity, and have their time. The truth is, we only touch the infinite and absolute in such moments of disgust and disillusionment ;

and forthwith we begin to put bands and hoops round it, and to cut blocks out of it, and shape them into gargoyles, and dress them up in rags and tinsel, till our very soul loathes the result. And then the Guy Fawkes bursts up and we say, " There is no God," and lo ! there He is, and the process begins over again.

" When thou thinkest me farthest from thee, then am I nearest." So, of the Roman Church ; so beware.

To the Same

LADY PLACE, STORRINGTON,
December 6, 1906.

" I sleep, but my heart waketh." The storms and tossings of the last couple of years induced a lethargic indifference to one's normal interests and affections, comparable only to that of extreme sea-sickness. One knows it is morbid and superficial, and that one still cares in one's sub-stomachic consciousness. I was in London, for some vile November days, into which I foolishly plunged from the warmth and brightness of Southern France ; and went from migraine to migraine with a day or two in between. So I retreated hither a few days ago to the bosom of Mother Nature, who strokes away all my irritation with her cool hand. In January (towards the end) I *must* come up again for a few days, and I swear a great oath that I will look you up. I did not see a quantity of my friends this time—only the indispensables.

It is pleasant hearing that you have got a happy corner in your life just now. It is only fair that we should reap a pearl now and then for so many tears sown in the hard earth.

I hope we shall soon have a nice profane talk such as my soul loveth. Don't ever believe that I forget old friends. It was only a few weeks ago that I burnt your letter of May two years past, which I kept and

11

kept waiting for appetite to answer. You know the
feeling—for you know all feelings, good and bad.

To the Same

16 OLD TOWN, CLAPHAM,
March 15, 1909.

MY DEAR HOUSMAN,

Fear not ! There's many a slip.[1] The advertisement surprised me more than anyone ; for things
had not gone beyond the vaguest talk between me and
the mercurial Thorp, who was smitten with my jingles,
and went off to Elkin Matthews and fixed the thing up
while I was asleep. I don't say that I shan't venture
something, for I'm a-weary of my grave reputation
and of letters addressed " Venerable Sir " or (as to-day)
" *Vaillant Champion de la Verité, de la Liberté, de la
Charité.*" The only cure is to cut capers in my skin,
and to scrabble at the city gates like David.

How on earth am I to see *The Englishwoman* and
your proud poem ? I'll see if she lives at our library.
" Jonah in London " is a lovely theme. I can fancy
the rabble at his heels and the grip of Constable X
on his coat-collar. Still, be my soul with the prophets,
with the men who are fools to the wise and to whom
the wise are fools.

Do you know, I possess an old aunt curiously of the
type you describe. We called her the Steel Nib, and
voted her hard and spiky. Long years brought out
a quiet heroism and trueness of heart we never dreamt
of ; and now she is the best friend I have left. I have
learnt to trust steel nibs more than quills.

I perceive that the Christ will not leave you alone,
but continues to torment you before your time. There
is *some* mystery about that figure, even should our

---

[1] Question of publishing some translations of German and Italian
poems (eventually published by Elkin Matthews).

Christologies be blown to atoms by the d—— critics. There my Pragmatism helps me. Our Christologies are only attempts to formulate what He has been, and is, for the experience of so many. They may break down ; but the experience remains. God (if I may use an obsolete term) seems to draw us through Him, however we kick against the goad. In short, He is God for our experience, whatever He be for our theories, and we may as well give in—at least, you and I, who are incurable mystics with Voltairean minds. I am in town till April. Tell me where you are. Mrs. Burke (née Bishop) was speaking of you the other day with great affection to my accompaniment on the bass viol.

To the Rev. T. MacClelland,[1] Rector of Little Torrington

MULBERRY HOUSE, STORRINGTON,
December 6, 1907.
MY DEAR MACCLELLAND,
How very kind of you ! I had great hopes that a prior engagement was going to fall through ; but it has recovered its legs and so I cannot accept your kind invitation, which would have given me great joy. From Eastbourne I shall probably cross to Paris and not return here till about April. But I trust we shall meet then.

I was a Dantemaniac for about four years, but a troubled and busy life has starved my literary soul for so long now that I hardly hope to recover. I actually collaborated a little in my friend Edmund Gardner's book on *Dante's Twelve Heavens*. But now I am a perfect dunce. Perhaps some day I shall be allowed to live my own life again ; but I have got so entangled with other people's troubles, and with subjects which really bore me to death, that I despair

[1] Died in 1917.

of freedom. My only salvation is that I try to live away from my tormentors in communion with Nature, and have done so pretty continuously for eight years. In my regular and solitary afternoon rambles I forget men and their miseries in communion with that which was before Abraham and before Adam.

I have a very pleasant picture of you in your rectory with your wife and your little girl. You would not be mortal if no shadows tempered your sunshine. But they do not enter my picture, and I pray God to make Little Torrington all I dream it.

To M. Loyson (Père Hyacinthe)

STORRINGTON, SUSSEX,
April 25, 1907 or 1908.

DEAR M. LOYSON,
You will forgive my long delay in replying to your letter of February 5.

I think you credit me with more courage than I really possess. The most timid animals will fight when they are driven into a corner—it is desperation rather than courage. I have slowly learnt by experience that courage is the very rarest of all virtues and has almost innumerable counterfeits. It all but failed in Christ, and failed entirely in His Apostles and in their successors. In the mass Modernists are cowards ; but so are all men in the mass. But even sheep take courage when they are in numbers, and I have some hope that as Modernists multiply they may become bolder. I am afraid that the courage of isolated individuals is not very effectual in history unless it is backed up by a large public sympathy. For this reason I am content that Modernists should not be more heroic than other men who feel themselves unsupported. Greatly as I admire those who stand out alone, I expect more wide and lasting results from a

strong body of men of quite ordinary courage. No
doubt they will want a leader ; but such a leader will
be found whenever there are large forces to lead.

To the Rev. A. Dickinson

MY DEAR SIR,

You are by no means the only Wesleyan
minister that I can number among my kind well-
wishers. Thank God differences of theology, too long
identified with differences of faiths, are getting thrust
out to their proper level of significance, and unity of
spirit is fast triumphing over the schismatic results
of scholastic discussions. Diversities of manifestation
will always remain, but they will be estimated at their
true purport and value. As a matter of fact I have
never faced a camera ; and now that I have so unwillingly become notorious, I rejoice in the liberty of
not being known to the public by appearance. I like
to be able to slip into churches and chapels at my ease,
without reading next day in *The Daily Mail* that I
have joined this or that body. So you will forgive me
if I cling to my last remnants of privacy. My friends
say I am not such a fool as I look—from which I infer
that you would be disappointed in my appearance
and had better paint me as your fancy dictates. Please
pray for me, for I have hardly time now to pray for
myself.

To Miss Florence Bishop [1]

March 7, 1904.

I think your soul-ache is a weather-ache. And
that's the real misery, that our souls are part-and-parcel
of this earth-machine. To-day is a regular " snuffler,"
and I have a handkerchief laundry going on before my

[1] Now Mrs. Hubert Burke.

fire. No, I ain't Lilley ; he is the Vicar of St. Mary's,
Paddington, my friend and the Baron's, though not
a Roaming Cawthlic, nor likely to be. No, they are
rather frightened now at the squamash that has been
kicked up over Loisy and hesitate about pulling his
nose. Cardinal Richard tells the Pope that the
Ultramontanes will secede if Rome doesn't anathematise Loisy ; and others tell him that if he does a third
of the French clergy will be lost. So there you are,
but it don't matter.

Your poam is neat, but wants finish ; besides, it is
borrowed from my well-known oad on the same theme :

> Tho' povertee my porshun be
>   And tho' I walk in tatters,
> Exposed and bare to wintry air,
>   I know that nothing matters.
>
> When in disgrace I hide my face
>   And Fame no longer flatters,
> My eyes I'll wipe and smoke my pipe,
>   And think that nothing matters.
>
> And when with pain that racks my brain
>   I'm mad as twenty hatters,
> I'll just pretend it suits my end
>   And say that nothing matters.
>
> And if the wife who plagues my life
>   For ever nags and chatters,
> When at my Club or in my pub
>   I feel that nothing matters.
>
> When problems deep do murder sleep
>   And doubt my portal batters,
> I say, oh well, just go to H——,
>   For nothing really matters.
>   Etc., etc.

It is hard to believe you had not seen this some time
or other. Still, I dare say you forgot, and were unconsciously influenced by it.

If you want a walk on the moor with me to-day,
you must put on bloomers and jack-boots or boot-
jacks or whatever it is. The animal in my last was an

heraldic monster, the real *totem* and progenitor of the O'Tyrrells (or Thnoirraihls) of Castle Tyrrell, Co. Kerry. It is feroshus in the extreme when rubbed up the wrong way; but when gently stroked emits an angelic smile. His food is priests' goar. The motto is *Cave ne irascatur*, or " Mind your eye." Ask the Green Dragon, Everard Rouge, if this is not so. I reproduce the same here on a larger scale.

To Miss Dora Williams

December 1, 1904.

Yesterday I learnt from K. C. that you were in bed, and I realised what a beast I was to have delayed writing ; but things have been going crookeder and crookeder with me, and the tax on my nervous energy leaves no margin. Oddly enough, three other close friends besides yourself have chosen this season to plunge into calamity ; and I have got to that semi-hysterical stage in which I can sit down and laugh as each post brings its contribution to the general mess. " The devil d—— thee black, thou cream-faced loon ; where got'st thou that goose-look ? " is my greeting nowadays to the postman. Your friends are playing the same drowning-game, it seems.

What is all this pother about Fogazzaro (I hear his *Il Santo* is on the Index) and me ? When did I write a letter to a Professor of Anthropology ? Do you know there are actions for libel and defamation even in these days of most free speech ? Take care, I am as warlike as Tweedledum (or Dee ?) at present, and there will not be a tree left standing for miles around as soon as I buckle on my coal-scuttle and bolsters.

Here now is your Willie going to wreck the *Demain* and get himself excommunicated. Look at the enclosed from Professor Stockley of Cork, who will *not* have his dogmas re-cooked. I have now to sit down and define W. J. Williams. There's a nice job !

But, even if it is not true, tell me that you are much better—quite well ; and that the world is full of light and hope ; and that the Celestial Puss has been a vegetarian and purrs smilingly on the heavenly hearthrug.

This is an allegory. He has been through the flame
and must crawl. I don't know why I gave him a tail.

To the Same

December 15, 1904.

DEAR MISS WILLIAMS,

How kind of you ! I am afraid I always give
an exaggerated idea of my woes, to judge by the
commiseration I excite. My present headaches are
really the result of surfeit. I was told my migraines
would never go till I got fat, and that I must accustom
my inside to greater burdens than it will bear kindly
at first. So I ache that I may not ache. It is a piggish
cure ; but honesty compels me to give the doctor his
due. I will try the Nux Vomica in my next distress.
Why from Cambridge ? Is it a university product ?

To-day I will say no more, though as usual your note
provokes me to loquacity and self-justification.

To the Same

December 22, 1904.

DEAR MISS WILLIAMS,

How kind of you ! I see it deals with the real
realities and true truths. I shall have much to say
about it and the *Bestimmung* [1] when I have read them,

[1] Fichte.

To-day my mind is whirled round like a plum-pudding in " process of becoming ! " Presently it will be solidified and each deleterious element will have found its fixture. Still I must not close this note without perplexing your friendly little devil by the assurance that in such matters as are of no consequence whatever, like medicine, food, sleep, etc., I am a very Puritan for method, prudence, regularity—for the simple reason that it is the best way of banishing them to the region of the sub-conscious and habitual, and this, though I am Irish ! Let him make what he can of that ! " What fool prescribed that stuff for you ? " a doctor once said to me. " You yourself, seven years ago," I was able to say triumphantly. Believe me, I am full of clockwork. Greek freedom rested on a basis of slavery. One of my helot devils shall be entrusted with the Nux Vomica, so that his betters may be free for peripatetic gossip. You are partly right about " The Devil and his Angels " [1]—the mystic Pt. I was by M. P. ; the rationalistic Pt. II was by me ; *et sic de cœteris.*

Give my best Xmas greeting to the person you speak of as " Will."

To the Same

February 22, 1905.

As to what I may do in the event of the Roman Church leaving me (*sic*), it is hard to say. But I am not at all sure whether to be stranded on the beach might not have many *human* compensations. Of course I agree with your doctrine that to be battling with the waves, and choking with gulps of brine, and knocking one's skull against the rocks, is morally invigorating, and the 'very essence of the spiritual life,

[1] See *The Soul's Orbit*, written by M. D. Petre in collaboration with G. T.

and that my present environment leaves nothing to
be desired in that respect; still, if the tide left me on
some sunny strand, destitute of all but a copy of
Pickwick, I am not sure that I should feel " bitter,"
however bruised. But really there are reasons still
for being a Romanist *provided* one is allowed to breathe
and live in peace. Yet the Church is but a *means*
to the great end of living ; not that end itself. Should
membership obstruct the end, it defeats its purpose.

To the Same

August 8, 1905.

Thought I *had* answered ; but I see I haven't. I
have had a lot to do, and Bremond has been here,
and others ; and much migraine and waste days.
My philosophy of the Cat-God *ought* not to depress
you if you understand it ; but you don't or won't.
At all events I believe equivalently all that you do
and a great deal more. You see, here is a cat :

And now I add a few strokes so as to include it in a
higher synthesis, and it is a cat no longer, though the
cat-truth is saved and transcended. What it is I

cannot quite say ; but it certainly smiles, and probably
won't scratch or bite. But the truth is I am a harder
sort of animal than you, and can put up more patiently
with the grim aspect of things.

I suppose Willie is something of a Jesuit out of

amiability rather than out of malice.   There is some
truth in everyone's view, and one can always honestly
agree up to a certain point with opponents, especially
as they always only state the strong part of their case.
It needs energy and aggressiveness to argufy and go
into the *whole* question root and branch.   Thus, e.g.,
Fawkes[1] and Wilfrid Ward both came back from Paris
convinced that Loisy agrees *exactly* with them, i.e.
with contradictory positions.

Personally I think it is ridiculous for one who takes
the ultra-liberal view of Romanism to be " received "
ceremoniously into the Church, and to upset all his
friends and relations for a matter so very indifferent.
Not so for one who accepts official Romanism and
believes it a matter of life and death to fly from
the City of Destruction.   I always tell aspirants that
I will not let them in by a private back-door of my own ;
if they can't come up by the public drive there is not
sufficient reason for an *outward* change ;   they can be
Catholics *in petto*.   Were I outside I should not come
in under the present *régime* ;   but should remain outside as a Catholic *in spe*, waiting and looking for the
redemption of Israel.   Here W. does not agree.

I do sympathise *in general ;*   when I know *in particular* I shall sympathise *in particular*.   You write
sadly and lonelily (what a horrid word !) ;   but I know
you have dozens of friends.

To the Same

September 20, 1905.

As you did not say what your " proposal " was I
cannot express an opinion.   In connection with the
first part of your letter, it might be a very serious one
indeed, and certainly I do not want to be pinned down
to anything, be it an oak or what not ;   be it by the

[1] The Rev. Alfred Fawkes.

wing or what not. Still let us hear. Now is the time for proposals ; for your Ariel may be taking to wing very soon, getting past all pinning whatsoever. If you are my age in years you must be long ways my junior in experience if you feel life is before you and not behind you. I could ring the curtain down gladly enough on so poor a performance, without waiting for the last act. But the manager is inexorable ; and I don't even know if refreshments await me in the green-room, or if they will be to my taste. But the grand thing is to go on grimly. " Life consists in standing by one's past mistakes—and making fresh ones."

What is a " flirt " ? I thought it was always a she. But you know so much better than I ; I only ask for information. Isn't it so really ?

PS.—This note, through mishap, only gets posted to-day, September 22, 1905.

To the Same

RICHMOND, YORKS,
October 20, 1905.

EMA. SIGNORINA,

As I live, you never once breathed a hint of Rome till you got there. I have all your letters inscribed on my heart with microscopic accuracy. Once you said you were packing—that was all.

Are you really so volcanic and furious as you say ?
Believe an expert, it is most wearing for the soul and
body. And what good does it do ? Will you change
Nature ? Besides, is there not likely to be some right
and reason even in her piggeries ? Granted the lower
often only apes the higher love out of a sort of instinctive diplomacy (in which case one has a right to be
angry), does it not as often merely supervene and
complement ? And then is it so dreadful that our
whole nature should be brought into captivity in the
train of its better part ? Of course I write *a priori*,
as a pure spirit, incapable of love and only able to
flit about like a sparrow and peck here and peck there
—and there is that much truth in your likening me to
Christ.

Genocchi is a " dear " ; the Pope not such a " dear "
as you think. I am too old to be taken in by the
Pontifical smile. It reminds me too much of the
Almighty Puss—about whom we are not going to
fight any more, since I know it is only pride prevents
your giving in.

Tivoli is most seductive as a proposal, though of
course it falls short of all I had hoped. Still it is not
workable for me in the immediate future. My " call "
is to London for at least a year—a little bachelor's
ménage of two rooms, an ill-tempered Mrs. Raddle, and
a slavey or Marchioness. I must repair the broken
arc of my shattered connection and restore it to a
perfect round.

I wish you and W. did not read each other's letters,
or leave your correspondence on the mantelpiece
and between the pages of books. It necessitates a
studiosity on my part that is most costly—for I have
a different language for each person and have no skill
in Volupuk or Esperanto. For the same reason
I abhor general conversation, and love head-to-head

under-four-eyes interviews most of all. For which
reason I am the stupidest person you could ask on a
visit. Besides, I have not lived out of presbyteries
and colleges for twenty-five years, and have forgotten
all civilised conventions and manners. You will have
to apologise for me as a *homo sylvaticus*, a sort of
Mowgli or Troglodyte or Rip Van Winkle.

To the Same

October 29, 1905.

" Why tarry the wheels of my Chariot ? "   Well,
because the chariots in front won't get on and the
police are inefficient ;   and because a chauffeur who
ought to be in London is in Crete, and his substitute
is ranging through Italy ;   and because nothing ever
went straight with me since I was born.

You must think me quite *passioné* for Gregory's
powders if you write your most important PSS.
inside their wrapping, which I only unfolded this
morning to see how small a matter could produce so
voluminous and weighty a perfume as fills my room
these several days.   But why should I in my mature
years take Gregory's powder, which was the bane of
my early years ere even I had a head to ache or a
brain to weary ?   Surely it is medieval to have recourse to bleeding and cathartics for every ailment now

that we cease to believe that all ills are from little
devils that we have swallowed in unblessed lettuce,
and that must be driven out by fair means or foul.
As governed by my friends, I should wear only woollen
and only cotton ; should sleep with my window wide
open and tight shut ; should take moderate and
immoderate exercise ; eat plenty and no vegetables,
no meat and plenty ; smoke and not smoke, drink and
not drink, and browse on all the medicines in the
pharmacopæia. As it is, I do a little of everything
by turns and will take a tabloid or two presently—for
peace' sake.

As for the Plasmon Cocoa, etc., I will pray over it.
But my general rule is to take whatever is going and
side with the triumphant majority against the weak
and unfortunate.

I will write and tell you when the block seems to
be clearing.

To the Same

November 12, 1905.

It is not winged but webbed feet I'd need to cover
space in this clime. I am perfectly sick with delays
and disappointments, and things go from bad to worse
with me. I am most disgusted with your Giulio,
who must know better, and is plainly sold to the
Jesuits and the devil. I don't say Pius isn't a *Saint*
—far from it—I say he isn't a " dear "—which was
your word. He would roast Willie and me over a
slow fire and chuckle softly to himself as he plied the
basting spoon. Of course he will go to heaven because
he *means* well, just as the cat *means* well when she claws

the mouse. Cats love cats. I am too angry and tired
and cross and sick and mimsy to say any more.

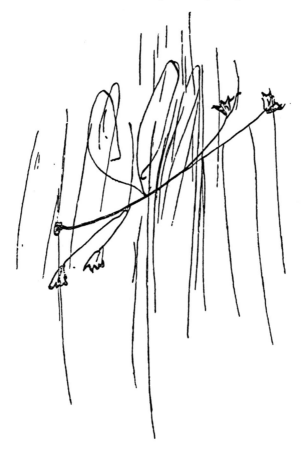

To the Same

December 6, 1905.

When your friends get sick *you* go to bed and groan
and thump your pillow while *they* run about and crack
jokes. This is a recrudescence of savagery—of the
" couvade " custom which puts the husband to bed
when the child is born and visits and pities and coddles
him, while the wife runs about in attendance on him.

I believe it originated in the revolt of outraged hus-
bands against the ignominious neglect and contempt
to which they are subjected at these interesting crises.
But I haven't time to write an article on it. No,
I'll not tell you anything about my gyroscopic fortune ;
only that it is more likely to bring me swooping down
on you just when you have settled into a sense of
security. I'll give you time to get over your neuralgia
and no more.

You should not praise my art, for it has made me
self-conscious and killed the free play of inspiration.
Mere talent needs praise, but genius thrives best under
neglect and persecution ; at least *I* have always found
it so. Madam, you say that which is not when you
persist in crediting me with what I have disowned.
Criticism has left me little to swear by ; but if there
be a sound verse in the four gospels, then with my hand
or finger-tip on that verse or part of a verse I do swear,
honest Injun, and as sure as there's cats above, that
never in my whole life have I written a letter to a
professor of anthropology ; no more than I have
known or corresponded with a professor of anthropology. As for your brother's remark, it is just what
a nasty tricky Jesuitical Roman Catholic would say—
if he himself were the author ; though I am sorry to
sow dissension between brother and sister.

Had I been full of anger, what you tell me about
Demain [1] and W.'s articles would have burst me.
But as I bursted last week, it did me no harm, but
passed through a sieve. This anæsthesia is a fatal
symptom; we must fight against it, and pray back
our faculty of anger. Then as Dum and Dee we shall
go forth conquering and to conquer. It is *most* dis-
gusting that the one solitary outlet should be blocked
up so promptly with wooden heads. We must, must,

---

[1] A French weekly organ of liberal Catholicism.

must have a good anti-clerical organ for the defence of religion against clothes-screens.

This is an inscrutable allegory.

To the Same

16 OLD TOWN, CLAPHAM,
October 26, 1906.

MADAM,

If you value those tokens of regard which are extorted under threats of assassination you resemble a lady of my acquaintance who affects scarlet and dyes her hair.   It is not a dumb but a loquacious devil who possesses me ;   and my silence is a triumph of self-conquest.   It is so long since I have been in love that I cannot prescribe.   If you were in hate with somebody I could help you to conduct your hate artistically.   Love is a stupid, banal, blundering force that does not lend itself to such delicate chiselling ; moreover, it is relaxing ;   whereas hate is astringent, tonic, teeth-setting, nerve-knotting, fist-clenching, biceps-bracing.   Give up syrup and take to bitters, and you'll be well in no time.

To the Same

IVY HOUSE,
OLD TOWN, CLAPHAM, S.W.,
December 2, 1906.

ILLUSTRISSIMA,

I am like Balaam's ass between two equidistant bundles of hay ;   paralysed.   Again, you and Signora your mother discharge your guns simultaneously one at each ear of me ; so that I know not whether to turn to—right or left. The Williams pigeon-hole contains at present three letters from your ladyship ; two from your ladyship's mother ; two p.c.'s from W. J. W. ; one minute but precious *billet-doux* from Miss Lewis, which she speaks of disparagingly as a farthing-dip or nightlight, but which was as welcome as the best patent incandescent. Say but this much to her and she will understand. And then you must run off and tell Mrs. Williams that I simply could not face Eastbourne with my skin off when they had seen me with it on. You have never been skinned, so you cannot understand. On Monday or Tuesday I go to Miss Urquhart at Storrington (c/o Wm. Tyrrell, Esq., will always find me there) to found a hermitage there ; and above all to pull up the appalling arrears of literary work which have accumulated all these idle months and which are absolutely necessary to keep my little pot boiling. I shall not emerge till something is accomplished and something done. As to W.'s book,[1] I have only just got it ; and I hope to re-read it as soon as I get to Storrington. I shall do so very carefully ; for I know it is the best plea for the " liberal " reading of Newman, about which I grow more and more sceptical.

I think the book will slowly make its way and spread out to wider circles from the centre of W.'s personal friends and sympathisers ; that it will be better known and understood afterwards than now. We have no right to expect a work of such compressed thought on so special a subject to take like a novel or a book of piety.

I have been sick again and again in this odious, foggy, noisy London, and shall be delighted to get out of it.

[1] *Newman, Pascal, Loisy and the Catholic Church,* by W. J. Williams.

To his cousin Sylvia

RICHMOND, YORKS,
Christmas, 1905.

Dear Sylvia, when I think of you
I fain would be a poet too.
Two poets in the family
Would grace our noble pedigree,
Which, as by this time well you know,
Dates from two thousand years ago
Through Pepin " of Burgundy "—so named
As partial to that vintage famed ;
Whose radiant nose while time shall last
Looms through the darkness of the past,
A warning light that we may shun
The rock our forebears split upon :
It's good to warn folk off from ill,
But there is something better still ;
'Tis easier to cry out Don't than Do,
That is of many, this of few.
That is the light of Pepin's nose,
This in the poet's spirit glows.
Oh, let this far more sacred flame
Shine back on beery Pepin's name,
And shed on shades of ancestry
The glory of posterity.
Make other people feel as you,
That is the work you've got to do :
To make them love the fair and true,
Sun, Moon, and Stars, the Flowers, the Dew,
Clear summer nights, and mighty storms,
Majestic movement, noble forms,
And God revealed in Nature's plan,
From little microbes up to man ;
Breathing in every creature's breath,
Fighting with Darkness and with Death,

Shooting His arrows far and wide—
The poets all are on His side,
And all the little children too.
For though they can't find words like you
They see the world just as it looks,
And not as talked about in books :
For prose puts everything askew,
Inverts the poet's point of view,
Insists, with scientific frown,
That babies see things upside-down,
And only by experience learn
Head-over-heels the world to turn.
Now who is likelier to know
Than God, who made the babies so ?
He is the Chief of poets, too,
And knows that upside-down is true.
What with our follies and our faults
We cut preposterous somersaults,
And twist our natures back before,
And can't see fairies any more.
The poets are the truly wise
Who keep till death their baby-eyes,
Or, if they make another pair,
Yet keep the old for Sunday wear :
Certain that God's eyes are the best
And sit in judgment on the rest.
Would you a poet *be*, not *seem*,
Lie in your Garden still and dream,
See what is shown you, do not try
To conjure visions from the eye.
Not unto such is vision given,
Not unto such the poet's heaven,
But to the little one who takes
The world as on his sight it breaks,
And undeterred by wisdom's frown,
Sees, feels and says it's upside-down.

And now I see I must resign
Pretensions to the art divine ;
For prose cut into equal bits
The definition badly fits
Of poetry ; of which 'tis said
The poet's born, but is not made.

Your affectionate Cousin,

G. TYRRELL.

To Sister M.

February 26, 1906.

I was silent only because I did not know what to
say or where to begin. It is all very sad, more for
mine, than for me who have broad shoulders. I don't
think *you* will be troubled or think that I am other
than you knew me. These are difficult times, and one
pitches anything to drowning men and women, without
stopping to think whose property it is or how much
it may cost. At the worst I have stretched true
principles unduly in my desperation to find a *modus
vivendi* for the stifled ; and the medicine prepared
for a few has been judged as though it were bread
for all. But there is little blame to be attached to
persons—if any at all. Minds and countries that are
poles asunder must irresistibly clash. I have been
as a man at the wickets for years—determined to
score all I can, but certain that sooner or later I should
be stumped out, or caught out, or run out. The last
has happened ; for I volunteered to stay on at Richmond and give up writing altogether ; but it was
decreed otherwise.

I will *always* remember and pray for you ; and you
for me ; and when the dust settles and I come back
to London I may venture to see you.

To the Same

VANNES,
June 25, 1906.

I am not ungrateful; nor forgetful of so true a friend—only very, very tired; and now wandering anywhere to get away and be at rest. But I mean to settle in England as soon as I get back my brain—and my mass. I am much tempted to shut myself up in a monastery and sing office through my nose for the rest of my days. I have never known till lately what a temptation "spiritual comfort" can be—as inviting as a warm bed to one who stands at night in his nightshirt on a bleak mountain-top—as I do, spiritually. "Foxes have dens, etc.," one may be in good company after all.

To the Same

BOUTRE VINON, VAR,
September 1906.

I wonder if the crab of August 29 got you after all ? I hope not. You are too old for such tricks and should leave them to me. I have almost got to like them—which is a great degree of perfection. How kind of Fr. D. ! Indeed, one is so overwhelmed with kindness from nearly every quarter. But my programme is perfectly obscure at present—I can hardly see a week in advance. At any rate it would not be right to trespass on his kindness and let him risk having a black mark put against his name. One of my great troubles is protecting my quixotic friends who are thirsting to share my infamy. The verse you are trying to recall ran, I think, as follows :

> Fierce was the wild billow,
> Dark was the night,
> Oars laboured heavily,
> Foam glimmered white,

Trembled the mariners,
    Peril was nigh :
Then said the God of God,
    Peace, it is I.

Ridge of the mountain-wave,
    Lower thy crest ;
Wail of Enroclydon,
    Be thou at rest :
Sorrow can never be,
    Darkness must fly,
When saith the Light of Light,
    Peace, it is I.

Jesu Deliverer,
    Come Thou to me ;
Smoothe Thou my voyaging
    Over life's sea :
And when the storm of Death
    Roars, sweeping by,
Whisper, O Truth of Truth,
    Peace, it is I.

But it is thirty years since I have seen or heard it ;
so it may be all wrong.

Pray always for me.

To M. D. P. (on the death of a little nephew)

                              June 24, 1908.

That was surely quite unexpected—just as there
was some reason to hope for better things.

I am very sorry for the father and mother ; but it
is best to say nothing on these occasions except that
one knows the fact.

For the little chap himself one who knows life can
hardly be sorry. He has had his peep into the world
and seen just its sunniest hour before the shadows
begin to lengthen. Well for most of us if we had been
put to bed then.

I am not sure but Arthur is the person most to be
pitied at present ; he has but small store of faith or

philosophy to stifle facts with. Still there is the narcotic of excitement ; the interest of grief as a new experience ; and a quick healing power that we have lost.

Poor Billy's little account with eternity is rather a puzzle, to which the *Dies Iræ* is hardly a satisfactory answer. Holy Church has no sense of humour. "*Accepit eos in ulnas suas*" would be a better gospel for such Requiems. Indeed it is hard to believe that God takes the oldest and worst of us so seriously as we take one another. "Dost Thou hunt down a flea ? " says poor old Job.

To R. M. S.

December 25, 1904.

It is all very fine, but I'm not so green as not to see that your quack has put my nose out of joint. [1] However, I am content to take a back seat for the present. I don't think he will wear well, and you'll probably tire of him soon. I don't see much reason to credit him, rather than Nature, with your tardy recovery. At all events he does not work miracles. I dare say the hypnotist would have done it all in one go. However, if you can "dress yourself and do your hair" you have got all that any woman really cares about. Aren't you afraid to trust your giddy daughter down here all alone ? I confess I don't like being left at her mercy unprotected. For my sake, if not for her own, you ought to be more careful. You know how she used to pursue me over the hills and dales and lay traps for me like Kathleen and St. Kevin. Your patent goloshes are most flattering ; but you forgot that, like the rest of me, my feet are "sizable."

---

[1] This correspondent was a martyr to neuritis, for which she tried many different cures.

They (the goloshes) are just big enough to keep my great toe out of the mud. Besides, it is the *mud* and *dirt* I object to, and not the wet. So if N. swoops down on her victim I will send them back by her, for some poor bare-footed person ; if not they will return by post. Poor dear old Jack, there is no one whose photo I need less. Still it is always pleasant to be reminded of him ; though I confess " Tim " (Miss Lyall's dog, whom I appropriate) runs him close. I actually called on Mrs. B. to-day (the second time), and she told me all I knew about you already, and I affected the utmost astonishment and interest, as my way is.

I am sorry that I cannot number the gift of healing and of sympathetic touch among my charms, but the spirit is given in different measure to all. Love me for what I am and forgive me for what I am not.

Ever yours,

No. 2.

To N. S.

August 1900.

It is rather rough on me to have two correspondents from the same establishment, who write simultaneously and naturally expect independent answers. So I can only cope with my debtors by paying about 6*d*; in the pound all round. This 6*d*. is for you, who as being in bed are in a more extreme case than your mother, who is only disabled.

But first tell your mother how really sorry I am for the bad news about N. She seems to be fated to trouble upon trouble, and those who pretend to know say it is a sign of predestination—anyway it is the sign of the cross, which ought to come to the same thing;

All your fears as to my transportation are groundless. Many unpleasant things are likely enough to happen, but that will not. If they leave me alone quietly, things may mend themselves, but I am determined they shall never have my scalp to add to the number that decorate their wigwam.

As to your criticism on the love letters,[1] please remember that you have never been *in love ;* and also that you have always lived with boys and profess to have no knowledge of your own sex. I do not like the effusiveness, the bare-nakedness ; but even I know from experience that most women are like that. Men may be less pure, but they are more modest and reserved in their affection. . . . Wait till you yourself get the disease, which for your own sake I hope you never may, and then we shall see how you behave under it. You can no more tell from a person's character how they will act in the crisis than you can foretell what they will say when they are drunk.

Yours parentally and sagely,

G. T.

To the Same

April 1903.

I was annoyed with *Allah*[1] because the author *seems* to enlist sympathy with fanaticism. What we admire in an Indian widow going to the Suttee is the sense of duty, not the Suttee. Hichens covers the Suttee itself with the halo of romance. A greater tragedy is the dutiful self-immolation of one who surely disbelieves in that particular form of duty !

> Ah, but the word, if I could have said it,
>   I, by no terrors of hell perplext ;
> Hard to be silent and have no credit
>   From man in this world, nor in the next,
> None to bear witness and reckon the cost
>   Of the name that is saved by the life that is lost.[3]

[1] *An Englishwoman's Love Letters.*
[2] *The Garden of Allah,* Robert Hichens.
[3] Lyall, *Verses in India,* p. 86.

These are the words of an agnostic who dies rather than yield his " Christianity " to Mahometan violence ; who suffers the loss of all for a cause he doesn't believe in except so far as it has become the symbol of duty in general.

To the Same

June 8, 1905.

I think you must believe in *aut pati aut mori*, if you believe in " oughts." It only means that to live in the highest sense (the ought life), is always to suffer ; that the painless life is not worth living. Still it may have a fanatical meaning ; and perhaps had in St. Teresa's mind. One should seek the " ought " but not the pain. That will come for sure. But there are joys as well as sorrows, roses with the thorns ; to shun the roses or to seek the thorns is to follow as false a path as they do who seek the roses and shun the thorns. The woe for the many is that, in seeking thorns, they have not only missed the roses but missed the right path. Their temptation is to seek the roses while they last, since the path is lost beyond hope.

To the Same

BOUTRE VINON, VAR,
August 14, 1907.

This is the wildest place I have seen—a triangular plain of about one hundred acres and an old fourteenth-century house in the middle; furniture seventeenth-century ; hill on three sides ; no house in sight. From top of the hills, in every direction, mountains beyond mountains, the spurs of the Alps, all carpeted with oak and box and juniper. Grass burnt up ; yet fire-proof herbage in great abundance, i.e. lavender, thyme, sage, verbena, and a whole flora unknown to me, chiefly blues and purples, the wild carnation being the only red. The air is heavy with scents ; swarming with

butterflies of great variety and colour ; buzzes all day
with bees, flies, and cicali, and twitters all night with
millions of field crickets. Twice a day a strong, fresh
breeze ; and then the torpor of the blazing fire fore
and afternoon. One walks out in shirt and trousers
and white umbrella ; and sits in, in—considerably less.
A true wilderness. The change is good. Still I seem
permanently damaged one way or other. I can do
well if I do nothing ; but anything whatever costs me
a migraine.

To the Same

AIX EN PROVENCE,
March 24, 1908.

Please thank your " ma "[1] for her letter. The
spring will bring up her children one after another,
and she will find some solace in that—little words and
messages straight from God, not transmitted through
the Pope nor marked *Imprimatur*. There is no Bible
like a garden and no revelation like spring. Much love
to her and to everybody.

To an Italian Professor

December 31, 1907

CARISSIME,

First of all as to your address, let me say *Amico,
si ; maestro, non* ; I have learnt too much from you not
to feel how absurd it would be to let you view me as
maestro. In point of education and scholarship I am
far, far behind you. If I have any gift it is a sort of
woman's power of leaping to conclusions without the
aid of premises ; of guessing what history ought to
say ; of forging hypotheses and syntheses. Of course
I read a great deal in my own desultory, unsystematic
way, and so probably have, in my subconsciousness,
the premisses of which I can give no clear account.

[1] A great lover of the garden.

And then circumstances and difficulties have pushed me unwillingly into prominence, and made me seem a leader of a movement of which I am only a student and disciple. It should be characteristic of our group to "call no man master," and to keep jealously that personal independence for which we are fighting. How deadly the greatest servants of truth become as soon as they are made *masters*—e.g. St. Augustine, St. Thomas, Newman, etc., etc., not to speak of the " *servus servorum Dei*."

To D.

STORRINGTON, SUSSEX,
May 30, 1907.

MON TRÈS CHER AMI,

It was delightful to hear of and from you again. In the ecclesiastical whirlwind our ships seem to get scattered and blown apart—and perhaps they are safer so. But I wish we could all meet in some quiet port and brag over our adventures as over past history. What scope for decorative lying ! for the pen of a B. ! He must live to biographise us all. But where is he, *le perfide?* and why this subterranean latency ? I am quite nervous. Such a man may turn up again either as bishop or co-respondent, or as conspirator monarchic or anarchic. I wrote to him yesterday c/o *Malebranche.* He seemed much corrupted by Rome, and found favour in the eyes of the crafty and ungodly. I even suspected him of having received thirty pieces of silver to get the bit into my mouth again, so suddenly anxious was he that I should lay down my pen and put on my stole. But I said I could not negotiate with Babylon till I had said my full say, and got out the volume just sent to press and called (after its last chapter—the reply to Lebreton) *Theologism.* If it is not the most perplexingly urbane, irritating, rational, irrational, orthodox, heterodox book in the market, it is not my fault. That done, I devote myself to the *Nation* (late *Speaker*) as reviewer, critic, middle-article-monger, etc.; and hanging up my wet garments to Neptune watch the storm-tossed ark of Noah from the safe shore as she lifts herself on the towering wave to crash down on the sharp-pointed acroceraunian rocks of criticism. (That is the *National* style at 3*d*. a line.) I may also become a monk—but I am not sure. I think I shall finish the summer here; then cross the *manche* for another Wanderjahr, for

> I'm fevered with the sunset,
> I'm fretful with the bay;
> And the wander-thirst is on me
> And my soul is in Cathay—

and the devil of unrest has got into my toes.

Vain, ambitious man! and so you still aspire to the Index! *Disce obtemperari, pulvis! Ama nescire et nesciri.* With so simple a headpiece as now sticks on the Church's shoulders your vanity may be gratified. Were I Pope you should be extinguished with a mitre *sic*, and we should have no more of you but the

pipings and pastorals to your bleating flock; and appeals for the *denier de culte.*

To K.

16 PITT STREET,
January 1909.

Please don't give me a martyr's halo, which becomes me as little as a Quaker's hat. Like the White Queen I got the screaming done years ago. It was coming up to the climax that cost pangs. Now the travail is over and the child born and my feeling is simply one of great relief. I have purged my soul and have no further need of concealments and equivocations. That is what I mean by the unleavened bread of sincerity and truth; and I assure you it is excellent fare compared with hosts soured by equivocation. I have never been better in mind or body. Not but I would rather have hosts and sincerity if it could be had. But Rome is out of that sort of diet as far as I am concerned.

VERSES ON A PICTURE POSTCARD, "THE RICHMOND AND DARLINGTON EXPRESS"

The Rome Express

Good People, here a symbol you may see
  Of things that have been, are, and are to be.
Behold the train that bears us to our bourne,
  All tickets single, since there's no return.
No other way, unless to walk you choose
  And in the wilderness your path to lose,
A task so hopeless as to make it plain
  Your legs were meant to bear you to the train—
No further. So be wise and stay at home
  Or patronise the Grand Express of Rome.
'Tis true its progress seems a little slow,
  But " slow is sure," as hare and tortoise know.
'Tis true the furnace needs a little blowing,
  But after all the train is really going.
'Tis true the engine is of type antique—
  Piston or cylinder in vain we seek;
And since the gradient is a little steep
  All it can do is just its place to keep,
And to this end it needs the aid combined
  Of kindly passengers with porters joined.
Deem not the officials worthy of your blame
  Who in the foreground play a little game,

13

And occupy themselves defending wickets
  Other than those at which they take the tickets.
Full well they know that there is time to spare,
  At any time the train will still be there,
That nothing can be done to mend its pace, .
  But just enough to keep it in its place ;
While cricket-victories must redound, they see,
  To the great credit of the Company ;
Its batsmen, not its drivers, are its fame ;
  Its bowlers lend a lustre to its name.
The signal-man, who works the semaphore,
  Doth in his little nest serenely snore,
From points perplexing keeps himself aloof ;
  But see, upon the hindmost carriage roof,
Indifferent to all that lies behind,
  The official guard, on belly prone reclined,
Backwards on Richmond bends his steady stare :
  His hope, his joy, his wife, his beer, is there.
Behind him range a goodly company,
  The oldest patrons of the R.R.C.
Full well inured to all its ancient ways,
  Their conduct is deserving of all praise.
Not theirs to growl at what their fathers bore :
  They read their papers, wait, and ask no more.
Within, alas ! far other spirits reign
  Who d—— and stamp and bitterly complain,
New customers as yet not broken in,
  And restless under Roman discipline.
They say " they paid to get to Darlington
  And not to look at matches going on."
With other observations out of season,
  And vain appeals to common-sense and reason.
And some presumptuous, zealous for their neighbours,
  Descend to help the porters at their labours,
And others, from the windows stretching out,
  Impatient urge them on and wave and shout.

THE ROME EXPRESS; OR, A VALENTINE TO THE MEDIATING LIBERAL.

Lo, in the rear an Amazon who shoves,
  And murmurs to herself " I feel it moves ; "
Herself immobile, nothing can defeat her :
  Rock versus Rock and Petre versus Peter.
Lo, in the front, upon his lowly mount,
  A man whom some a prophet do account,
Or true or false I hardly like to say ;
  But see the Angel standing in the way,
All pregnant with a message from the Lord :
  " Why smitest thou thy moke exceeding hard ? "
With gaze seraphic fixed upon the Past,
  With ruby banner blazoned " Not so fast,"
Mid-tracks he stands, an unofficial guard,
  His name, in Hebrew, " Israel's Watch and Ward."
" I smite," quoth Balaam, " for the brute is slow,
  And we would fain be where we want to go."
" Tut ! " saith the Angel, " all this practicality
  Is close akin to dangerous rationality.
The end of ends, as all good folk agree,
  Is to support this railway Company.
This zeal for getting on is well enough,
  But getting on too fast means getting off.
Do we not learn from records of the Past
  The dangers due to getting on too fast ?
Progress, indeed, but ah ! at what a cost !
  How many limbs were maimed and lives were lost !
It is not negligence but deep design
  That guides the managers of this here line :
To keep us safe is their sole aim and will,
  And nothing is so safe as standing still.
Tug, Balaam, tug, but do not snap the rope ;
  Blow, stoker, blow, but do not blow us up.
Shove, ladies, shove, but don't forget your places—
  To vie with experts adds not to your graces.
Grudge not the officers their game of cricket ;
  Their notions neither worldly are, nor wicked ;

Nor strive to compass with inexpert brains
   How cricket experts are expert at trains ;
That is a mystery wholly superhuman,
   To fathom which you'd need to be a *new man*.
To mortal minds they merely seem to play,
   Like Nero fiddling while Rome burned away.
And yet not all, for it is plain to see
   That some of them are working valiantly.
See how the stoker stokes, the driver drives,
   How others shove at peril of their lives.
And then, perpend what evils would ensue
   To the contented paper-reading crew
If, with unwonted rush and dust and wind,
   Their brains were addled and their eyes made blind.
These are the Company's long-trained elect,
   To whom we owe the most profound respect,
Who know no duty but to pay their fare,
   And to be borne the Company knows where,
And to arrive the Company knows when,
   The mysteries of Bradshaw past their ken.
For sake of these (and there are millions such)
   We experts must put up with very much."
He spake and vanished ; Balaam smote the moke
   In unrepentant wrath ; the rope it broke.
Forward the prophet falls and cracks his head ;
   Backward the train slips towards the station shed ;
Over the shovers go, their heels in air,
   The welkin rings with shrieks of wild despair ;
Quicker and quicker rush the fated wheels —
   Then shock, and clamour, as of thunder-peals.

    .   .   .   .   .

The officials calmly see the wickets down,
   Then hands-in-pockets saunter towards the town,
Inspect the ghastly scene of wreck and woe,
   Record their comment by a simple " Oh ! "

    .   .   .   .   .

Angel of Israel, faithful Watch-and-Ward,
  The pointsman's pointer and the Guardian's Guard,
Tell me, oh tell me how it came to pass
  You did not come to terms with Balaam's ass ?
Far more to that slow-footed, steadfast menial
  Than to his rider had it been congenial
To learn that virtue usually lies
  In tacking, backing, and in compromise ;
To him with legs outplanted had come home
  The truth of the Rigidity of Rome.

II

ETHICAL QUESTIONS

To F. H. (*Notebooks*)

. . . I find something frigidly Anglican and respectable in Matthew Arnold's "righteousness" as the characteristic of the Divinity. It is a bloodless sort of attribute; and so comprehensible, even when qualified by "eternal," as to starve the mystical sense. It gives me a sort of university God, a personification of the Nicomachean ethics. It was the culmination of Jewish religious development to pass from an all-powerful to an all-wise, and finally to an all-righteous God. God must be righteous, but He must be more. Even the Jesus of criticism is more than righteous or sweetly reasonable; though He is that inclusively. He was an inspired enthusiast, a passionate lover. It was His "sweet reasonableness" that saved Him from being a fanatic or a Mahdi. The specifically Christo-Pauline God is the God of grace (or love) who is worshipped by faith; who includes but transcends that God of righteousness, or the law, who is worshipped by works. As intuition, or the "illative sense," is to explicit reasoning, so is love to righteousness, and so is faith to ethical goodness. Love, or grace, is inclusively righteousness; mercy is a deeper kind of justice, mysterious and impossible to analyse. The Father in heaven, the Father of the returning prodigal, transcends the just judge of the higher prophets, as the latter transcends the God who delights in the fat of rams and is touchy on points of ceremonial. Similarly, what St. Paul means by faith (i.e. the trust evoked by the revelation of God's grace and mercy and fatherhood, the spirit of sonship as against servitude, of love as against fear) transcends the worship of ethical perfection as much as the latter does that of ceremonial observance. It is the spirit that makes alive ; that discerns, or rather feels, the Divine Will intuitively—spirit answering to spirit, God within us to God without us—that is above the law, since the law is but its tentative analysis and expression. " God is Charity," " God is Love," are higher categories than " God is Righteousness." Of course they have led to antinomian abuse, to the neglect of righteousness. Catholics have inclined to sacrifice God's righteousness to His love ; Protestants conversely. The " *Bon Dieu* " of the Latins is morally lax and easy-going. Our love-lorn nuns and emasculated priests have debased eternal love into eternal sentimentality. Their " faith " has not taken up and transfused the law of righteousness. It has not seen the divine love and grace resting on and enhanced by the divine justice. The long-haired, languishing Jesus, with His bleeding heart, is their symbol of God—not the man who fought and died for the Kingdom of Righteousness.

Yet the ideas of love and grace, just because they stand for what is superrational and mysterious, and evoke a response from the deeper and more hidden springs of spiritual life, are more fit to depict the superhumanity of God. For it is surely in acts of self-giving love and mercy and gratuitousness that man most exceeds himself—in acts for which he can give no ethical reason beyond the compulsion of something divine in himself.

To V.

May 31, 1901.

. . . In your letter of the 17th you are wondrously
heretical, and quite in agreement with a recent correspondent, who complains that if Christianity had its
way it would be as bad as Socialism for levelling life
down to dull monotony ; that neither tragedy nor
comedy would survive ; that it is to sin and the devil
that we owe all that is greatest and best, even in the
saints. If *all* were saints they would be of the John
Berchmans' type, heroically mediocre and regular-
featured. Perhaps Christianity, like other elemental
forces, was never meant to exist in that free and
" abstract " state, but only in combination with the
powers of evil ; in which case we should speak more
civilly of the harmful, but necessary and helpful devil.
But I cannot see my way to admit that it is better
to be capable of defying one's conscience than to be,
like Father Hunter,[1] the slave of righteousness. This
" slavery " is the goal of all moral effort and self-
training, and is the property of the blessed and of
God Himself. That *non posse peccare* is compatible
with liberty, and is its highest achievement, is the
doctrine of Augustine and all theologians. If you
object, *Qui potuit transgredi et non est transgressus*,
they explain this of a tempted, but unshaken and
unshakable will ; of an appeal felt by the senses, but
not even listened to by the reason. The will is still
free because it is bound only by its own act, by its
own vehement love of goodness. I think what you
dislike is a self-interested love of righteousness as of
one's own personal advantage, which often keeps men
straight who have no disinterested love of good for
its own sake. Those who sin badly are often less

[1] An early Jesuit friend.

selfish than these. And there are those who love the
good disinterestedly yet not purely, and who will do
ill and destroy themselves for its sake ; or who are
simply indifferent to their own share in the Kingdom of
God. You feel about Satan and Michael as I do about
Esau and Jacob—each needed the good elements
of the other. Timid, effeminate characters, *as such*,
choose God's cause as the safer, while the stronger
and more serviceable go to the devil. Christianity,
owing to the circumstances of its birth, laid so much
stress on sweetness that strength, physical, mental,
and, in some sense, moral, has been at a discount ever
since. Did I refer you to Yeats's poem " Oisin and St.
Patrick " in this connection, where one's sympathies are
enlisted on the side of the old pagan warrior, perplexed
by the new milk-and-water religion of the saint, and
choosing hell as offering more scope for his prowess ?
Though I dislike Kingsley, and allow Newman the
dialectical victory, I feel the former had a truth,
which the latter ignored, in his plea for a male Christianity.

To the Same

June 24, 1901.

As to your first assumption, I agree with you, if
your determinism extends to our will ; if we are but
conscious wheels in a machine in which we are moved
passively, and move nothing. I had rather be a free
agent in a devil-created world than that. But give
me my freedom, and I would rather battle with, and
despise, the brute machinery of the godless *non-ego*
outside me than feel that I was the slave of another
free agency which I hated and despised. Is it not
easier to bear unintended injuries than those that are
intended ? i.e. the fated and determined, than what
another could have prevented and would not ? I

once found Spencer's conception of life, so far as it
removed most evil from the realm of freedom human
and divine, altogether restful and tranquillising, and
I still can bear many discords better when I reflect
how much more circumstances than persons are to
blame. And surely the Mahometans find a certain
repose and peace in their fatalism ; as did the Stoics.
Yet I allow that this rest depends on an *implicit*
theism and belief in liberty ; and could hardly survive
the *implicit* rejection of such convictions. On the
other hand, of course, were there no determinism, no
fixed laws of divine action in the world, were all immediately dependent on divine caprice, we should go
mad as surely as in a world of mere chance and fortuity.
I assume, therefore, that for the development of our
personality by self-government and self-direction,
stable laws and uniformity are absolutely necessary.
A father who listened to every cry ; who gave his children everything for asking ; who laid down no laws or
rules or conditions by which, as far as possible, they
should help themselves to what they needed, would
destroy their characters. In crises unforeseen he might
come to their aid, but he would make such crises as
rare as possible, and would be inexorable in exacting
the normal and universal conditions. In fact he would
put them *en rapport* with a certain " determinism,"
or set of laws, to which he would bind his own will
no less than theirs. Often they would cry out
to him against this ruthless machinery, but he who
saw further and deeper would turn a deaf ear and let
the mill grind on. Is it not in virtue of nature's uniformity (i.e. the stable determinism which God has
set between us and Himself as a bridge) that, in material
matters, the race has risen to a control over nature and
to a high degree of self-government and independence?
And is it not the same in higher matters ? and in regard

to individuals ?   As a fish needs the water, so a free
agent must swim in an ocean of determinism. It is
to our freedom what air is to the bird's wings. But
as our freedom on this side of the wall of determinism
does not detract from uniformity, so neither God's
freedom on the other side.   Without altering the
structure or mechanism of nature He and we can, by
knowledge of it, play upon it, and hold commerce
through it ; nor does the answer to prayer ordinarily
mean a miracle or an interference with uniformity
any more than where a father gives bread to his child.
I think the mischief of superstitious prayer lies in its
contempt of natural means and co-operation ; in its
ignorance of the dignity of law ; in its expectation of
a *miraculous* answer involving a breach of uniformity ;
in not remembering that God has, for our good, freely
bound Himself to respect His own laws and therefore
to work within limitations.   To deal with us at all
personally He must take on Himself limits like our
own.   I think as we understand things better we pray
less and less for temporal benefits or even for miraculous
providences of any sort, and trust ourselves rather
to the " determinism " which, harsh and ruthless
though it seem, is but the will of Him whose wisdom
reaches from end to end and disposes of all things
sweetly.   We begin with : " If it be possible, let the
chalice pass," and end with " Since it may not pass,
Thy will be done."   Though God condescends to the
simpler faith, I cannot doubt but that the stronger
pleases Him better, the faith of Job or of Christ's
Calicem quem dedit mihi Pater nonne bibam ex illo.

To the Same

March 2, 1902.

As to your All-in-One and One-in-All problem,
I should like to know in what sense you understand it.

Is it an antithesis ?   For myself everything converges
to the conviction that the difference between you and
me is only that of severed tracts of experience in the
same personality, such as exists between my sleeping
and waking self ; save that here there are a few con-
necting links that make the personal identity evident,
but there, there are none such owing to the perfect
physical discontinuity of our brains.   Read Pierre
Janet in the light of that hypothesis and you will see
how many mysteries disappear.   But how this squares
with theology God only knows ;   though I am not
sure but I learnt the idea first from St. Paul.

To the Same

May 30, 1902.

I see more clearly where we split in our view of the
subconscious self.   With you, as with F. W. Myers,
it is the fuller, realer self of the future, forcing itself
up into the light.   With me it is the accumulation of
past life, the formed or dead matter which gets pushed
behind and congested as life goes on.   It is just possible
that it is both—that the subconscious is the " not-
present," and therefore the past and the future, both
of which characterise our present choice ; the one by
way of obscure memories, the other by way of obscure
anticipations.   We both agree, though you sometimes
have denied it, that full consciousness is the higher
state ; for you say truly that we tend towards a state
in which what is now obscure anticipation will become
distinct fruition.   Your feeling that the subconscious
self is often the realer and better self leads you, I
fancy, to underrate the free conscious self in favour of
the buried self, without distinguishing between the
buried *past* self, which is automatic and mechanical,
and the buried *future* self, which has not yet been

fully appropriated at all. *Habits* and *ideals* are alike subconscious ; they represent what a man *was* and *tends to be*, rather than what he is. I think you have given to habits the honour due to ideals, which latter are in *some* respects higher than our attainments (i.e. in the ideal order), but, as lacking reality and act, are, as yet, lower. Our good habits have no such superiority.

Had you seen my articles on " Zoophily " in *The Month* and *The Contemporary* about Miss Frances Cobbe, you would not call me a zoophilist without qualification. Both my religion as a Christian and my philosophy have since then gone far to fortify my natural instincts in the matter. If God cares for the sparrows and the lilies, it is because they are part of that same life which I live, whose severed expression will one day be the common possession of all ; and I shall at last know what is going on behind Jack's grave-looking eyes and realise both the joy of rabbit-hunting and the terror of a hunted rabbit ; and shall feel what sunshine and rain mean to the roses.[1] A propos of Zakopani,[2] you will find in *The Soul of a People* that the Burmese have anticipated Mdme. Z; by centuries. Everyone must be a monk for a bit ; and temporary vocations are well recognised. Were it not for its pessimism, its despair of the world, its contempt of *l'avenir*, I should say Buddhism was better than our fussy, strenuous, struggling, reforming Christianity, which crucifies God and men in the belief that the world can be made better and conquered to God. It is only that wild yet irresistible fanaticism that saves me from à Kempis and the Buddha. At all events I think the world, like the flesh, is intended to be struggled with and not fled from, and that in the grip of conflict the muscles of the soul are developed

---

[1] *Life*, vol. ii. p. 14.   [2] A Polish institute is here referred to.

and our personality brought out in a way which mere arriving at tranquillity could never effect. There is great energy in the crucifix as contrasted with the slumberous Buddha-images. And yet—

To the Same

Summer 1904.

. . . There are so many unwritten letters, articles, etc., accumulated, and then N.'s MS. dumped down on me, and a request from L. that I should get another sort of tract ready by August 15, etc., etc., that I have lost heart and am fairly in the blues; *spiritus promptus, caro autem infirma.* . . .

For the present I will stick to Richmond. I sometimes feel that to die, not only in, but through, one's work, is the right thing to desire ; though to court such extinction needlessly would be fanaticism.

Have re-read Jones [1] very carefully. That perhaps did much to exhaust me, for it is endlessly suggestive and has, *inter alia*, brought me nearer than ever to a conviction as to the view of our seemingly separate life as a distraction in our fuller and universal life, to which death restores us. " Before Abraham was I am " is true of every man's " I." And that this is free from Pantheism and saves our distinct personality I think I can show—a great relief, surely, from the fabulous animistic view of sprites born with our bodies and carrying on a similar life *post mortem ;* and an answer to a thousand sad questions. In this view the sub-conscious is not the automatic hand that writes while its owner converses, etc. Rather it is an inverse relationship ; my present self is related to my fully conscious self as that hand is to that agent ; and enjoys a similarly limited power of vision and

[1] Professor Henry Jones (probably his work on Browning).

choice. The *ego* or self that is conscious in both ways (fully and partially) is one and the same. The " I " that writes automatically (i.e. automatically with respect to the full self, yet not without a limited thought and freedom) does not perish with the automatic state but abides as identical with the fuller " I," who is the heir of its experience, or rather the true subject of that experience.

I find a good solid reason for all this in the nature of *habit, heredity,* etc., and " *I feel it moves,*" as Galileo said. That is the best news I have got so far.

Father F. is suffering from acute peritonitis complicated by pancreatic hypertrophy and cerebral desiccation, and the rest of the community are equally well. I treat you to this excellent writing because it is the kind that costs least labour, and it makes me quits with you for your locust-leg script.

To G.

December 14, 1904.

I believe there is much illusion and empty spiritual ambition in our early desires of *universal* utility ; that in aiming at all we lose everything, and miss the very best values of life. For most there is far more heroism, unselfishness, and strenuous virtue demanded and evoked by the married life, with all its disappointments and difficulties, than by the self-centred life of the cloister, with its artificial protection and its negative sanctity. Apostolic work for individuals on a large scale makes celibacy desirable and furnishes an equivalent education of the affections ; but with the mere ascetical, self-regarding celibacy, I confess I have lost all patience, through observing its detrimental effect on the character.

To the Same

RICHMOND,
November 2, 1904.

I am glad I may defer my treatise *De Matrimonio* till it is more urgently needed—a good job, seeing my notions get wider and more elastic on the subject the more I reflect. I doubt the competence of any man to deal with the matter who has not been married two or three times ; our moralists are, unfortunately, all celibates, or at least unmarried, whence the airy and *a priori* character of their rulings. Provisionally, I would make a few remarks just to give you something to disagree with. I think that the austere view of Augustine is at root very fallacious and mischievous. Converts are apt to be fanatics, and a loose life often corrects itself in some form of rigorism. As I once said before, the attempt to enforce Augustinianism on human nature made necessary concessions and compromisings of principle which resulted in those degradations of the ideal of which we now complain—just as Augustine's doctrine of truthfulness was so impossibly severe that we had to invent a doctrine of equivocation, by which the flood-gates of mendacity were thrown open wider than ever. We must then look for some temperate middle-way. One or two principles seem very clear to me :

(1) It is a patent fallacy to say that in " the intention of Nature " every single use of matrimony is directed to progeny, and that our intentions should be directed in the same way. Nature's way is somewhat prodigal ; she calculates that by sowing a million she may reap one. If she reaped all she sowed there would be no standing-room on the earth in twenty years. All we can say is that the *habitual* use of matrimony is directed to the maintenance of the race.

14

(2) But in itself it is the utterance or exercise of love between husband and wife—and that I think is all that they need " intend." It is pedantry to say that we may never eat or drink except with an intention of nutrition. *That* is Nature's intention, no doubt ; but it is not necessarily ours. She has given us feelings of hunger and thirst, and to satisfy these *reasonably* is the truest way of obeying Nature. It is a mere accident that we have discovered medicine hidden in the jam. Not to promote nutrition, but simply to satisfy healthy hunger, is the healthiest intention. There is, of course, an artificial, cultivated, unhealthy hunger, and " depraved appetites " of all sorts, due to the pursuit of table-pleasures as an end in themselves. Men provoke thirst artificially for the pleasure of satisfying it. The parallels are obvious.

(3) Then I think there is a very childish old-world dualism, which splits the connubial relationship into a purely spiritual, non-sexual friendship *plus* a purely animal affection ; and, calling the first the " higher " factor and the second the " lower," tries to strengthen the *soul* of the relationship by starving and killing its *body* or embodiment. Here again the parallel is obvious. We have learned a truer idea of the dependence of soul on body, and the perils of oriental asceticism. The friendship between husband and wife is often just that between persons of the same sex ; but then it is mere friendship and not conjugal love. Again, it is often merely an animal affection, which, too, fails of being conjugal in the human sense. As friendship is a chronic affection that shows itself on certain conditions in certain ways (services, gifts, sympathy, etc.), so the conjugal sentiment has its proper and natural manifestation.

(4) That manifestation is stupidly described as " animal." It would be as just to call speech animal,

because it is the braying, or neighing, or roaring, or
barking of a human being. Even at its very lowest
in man it is not animal, for no animal is " impure "
or " sensual " ; it needs an element of degraded reason
and conscience to make sin out of animality. The
nature of the act depends precisely on the nature and
character of the agent, and on the love of which it is
the expression.

(5) I think there should be two elements in right
conjugal love—desire and affection ; desire, which
craves to possess the other ; affection, which subjects
and postpones that desire to the happiness and desires
of the other. It is, therefore, a continual triumph of
selfless love, and needs *both* loves as factors. From
this it is easy to see how the use of matrimony would
be instinctively regulated by such a mutual love,
without any hard and fast rules. If *each* was always
ready to sacrifice their desire (or repugnance) to the
repugnance (or desire) of the other, there would be
no room for friction or reproach. And that will be
the case where there is real reverential love and real
desire on both sides. These cases are rare ; and so
are happy marriages of the best sort. Amen.

To one who had asked advice

August 27, 1900.

As to the matter of which you write, I am *so* sorry
for you, for I know the amount of suffering involved ;
yet I can hardly say I am surprised, for it seems to be
the necessary price of every natural grace that it is
an occasion of difficulty and trial ; and the power
of loving is identical with the power of loving amiss.
I have been a curious observer of this tendency in
nearly all the great saints, in spite of the ingenuity of
their horrified biographers to interpret and explain

away—the three Francises, St. Ignatius, St. Paul, St. Jerome, and many others of both sexes ; all have had the difficulty and learnt how to profit by it. There is an unity if not an oneness in our affections. We cannot, as some talk, pull out one stop and push in another at will. That is one of those endless fallacies of analytic psychology, which treats every new aspect of affection as a new and separate affection. It seems to me then (and I have applied the view in several altogether similar cases with good effect) that an affection such as you speak of may be either *in resurrectionem* or *in ruinam*, according as it is managed or mismanaged ; that it may be the greatest of helps or the greatest of hindrances. It is, however, so difficult to keep well in hand, and at the best involves so much pain, that in many cases one would recommend its extinction in an early stage ere it has taken deep root. But often there is no early stage and the thing is created mature and ineradicable ; nor would I ever advise total abstinence to anyone capable of temperance—even remotely. It is plainly a difficult case for the Ignatian rule of the use of creatures ; nor should one hastily conclude that, because one is too preoccupied by the affection, or distracted, or even impassioned at odd times, therefore it must be uprooted. There is something to be set off on the other side against these *cons ;* and a balance to be struck. There are inordinations to be fought against with more or less success ; and never to be acquiesced in. What I always advise is to leave nothing to the inclination of the moment ; not to speak or act through pressure of present emotion ; but, as Ignatius says about food, in your quiet and reasonable moments make up your mind definitely as to what you will say or do ; draw a line of propriety and resolve that you will never cross that. Thus we fashion the rough material of feeling according to the image of right reason ; and we mix God with our affection and give Him the first place. And if, moreover, we at all realise that it is God that draws us in all that is good, and that the love and the object are both expressions of His will—so long namely as both are worthy and not perverse—it is plain that such an affection must bring us nearer to Him ; and that it is purged by the pain and sacrifice needed to keep it well in hand. Frankly, I don't think a soul has fully lived till there has been such an experience ; but I should not say that save of the higher kind of human love. I do not think that where the lower and merely emotional element predominates unduly (it can never be wholly absent, since our nature is one) the experience is of much spiritual profit. Just because higher and lower are necessarily mingled, and the predominance ·of the former depends on conscious action and watchfulness (whereas the latter asserts itself as soon as we let the affection drift us along), one needs to be perpetually striving upwards lest so delicate an adjustment should be spoiled.

To A. S. R. (Notebooks)

1908–1909.

. . . The appeal to Nature against existing forms of sex-morality is in many ways a dangerous one. It puts a hard and fast line between two stages of man's upward growth, and calls the lower " natural," the higher " artificial." Because the lower is formed, stable, customary, it contrasts with what is in process of experiment and therefore as yet unstable. But the lower was once as artificial and unnatural. Gravitation is the law of the moral as of the physical world. Everything is tempted back to the earth in search of rest. All that has been combined and built up painfully longs to fall asunder—" earth to earth, ashes to ashes, and dust to dust." Society, laws, customs are not more, or less, artificial than beehives or anthills, except so far as they are less stable, more modifiable. It is no argument against civilisation that, when released from it, men quickly return to brutality and savagery. For civilisation has become the natural medium of the civilised man. He needs to be buttressed up by public opinion and sentiment. He is, in one way, more dependent than the savage. But it is because the necessities of a higher life are numerous and complex and can only be supplied by co-operation and tradition. Society holds him in position, and only to some extent does he gradually grow to it. Take a bee from its hive and it is no longer in a state of nature. If we appeal to sexual instinct as " natural," we should also appeal to the murder instinct, which is quite as natural. We forget that anger is just a murder-instinct. Dogs fight with a wish to murder. Murder is Nature's device for eliminating the unfit. Society has restrained the murder-instinct of the individual and submitted it to the collective judgment. Individuals become *members* of the social organism, and it is for the organism to regulate the number of its own limbs. They now belong to it and not to one another. Hence, too, it is for society to regulate the instinct of reproduction and, indirectly, to forbid all arbitrary and private use of that instinct. Her regulations may be absurd, and she only gropes her way experimentally to a system that will compensate the individual for the sacrifices she exacts. She must secure him against violence if she forbids him to strike for himself. She must make marriage possible for all if she forbids promiscuity.

To E. D. (*Notebooks*)

1908–1909.

I cannot find the passage in which Shakespeare contrasts the characteristics of love and lust. Those of the latter are set forth with terrible discernment in the *Sonnet* (cxxix), " The expense of spirit in a waste of shame." That love should have been applied, and applied even *par excellence*, to sexual desire is the more curious as, in its more elemental and unqualified manifestations, lust is not merely selfish, but cruel ; a sacrifice of the other, not of self. Yet it is rarely untempered by love as it rises with the type of animal life in which it is set. The blind, imperious appetite is the device by which Nature takes the care of the species out of the free jurisdiction of the individual. It expresses her love of the unborn ; her advocacy of their rights. Lust is one of the great Nature-forces which, like tempest or earthquake, play havoc with human life, except in so far as man learns in some little measure to understand, control and direct it. Man proposes, lust disposes. The best-steered life commonly splits on that rock. The first differentiation of the germ is into a somatic and a spermatic cell. The former develops into the organism ; the latter lies quiescent till puberty, when it simply begins to multiply in its own kind. This physiological doubleness of the individual life and the sex life permeates our character, and is never more than slightly overcome. For other vices and divisions of our personality we are largely responsible ; for this, Nature herself is mostly to blame. Hence no vice tells less directly on the self-formed character, or consists so easily with general integrity. When it seems otherwise, it is because lust is the servant and instrument rather than the cause of immorality. Never is a man more passive and less himself than under its narcotic influence ; never does he awake to resume his true self more entirely than from its spell. For the moment his field of vision is contracted, his reasonings are cunningly sophisticated. But on recovery the whole system of illusion vanishes utterly, without any permanent warp to his normal judgment : " Whereas I was blind, now I see." Lust, like drink, is literally a brain-poison. It makes a man worse than insensible ; it makes him mad. For that reason alone it should be used like chloroform—in cases of necessity ; not otherwise. Its control, by prevention,[1] is one of the first duties of self-government, the first condition of freedom. Such *power* of control seems to be an almost indisputable duty for all men, single or married. Unfortunately marriage has come to be viewed as an exemption from that duty, to the prejudice not only of married, but of unmarried, continence. For the unmarried view the duty of continence as one incumbent on them only in virtue of outward, and often unwelcome, circumstances. Christianity has perhaps raised the standard, but has not raised the level of purity. It has to some extent made society more consciously and reflexly impure, by adding the piquancy of sin and sacrilege to much that was else mere social offence.

Given the power of control, when is it to be used ? Say what we will, man's development is a war with Nature so far as man is taken out of Nature. The fuller Nature that includes man and human society is a harmony of warring and struggling elements. There is everywhere an upward thrust and a downward drag. The organic is dragged down by the inorganic,

---

[1] The word *prevention* has been almost deprived of its true meaning by careless use. Father Tyrrell never lost the habits implanted by scholastic training, and used words in their defined sense. Thus prevention would have signified for him, in this place, a control based on prevision ; an action taken in preparation for the event.

the animal by the vegetal, the human by the animal. Everything gravitates to the bottom; everything struggles to the top : *Mors et vita duello conflixere mirando.* Rest passes into sleep, sleep into death and decay. Pain, vigilance, conflict are the condition of life. The first judgment—that lust is natural, universal, and therefore not to be restrained by the narrower laws of society and religion—is a fallacy. The scope of lust is not the rational and social being, but the mere animal species—the raw material of humanity. Nature's eugenic has multitude and brute strength as its ideal. To raise the kind, society must limit and select the material ; must subject the end and law of lust to a higher, less general end and law. Reproduction is a social concern, although every individual is equipped for the business. Every man can fight and defend himself, but society determines his use of the natural right, and selects soldiers for the general defence. It is, then, not a grievance that society should prescribe the conditions of legitimate reproduction, but only that she should do so foolishly or unjustly. Her marriage laws are frankly a war against Nature. When she does not war wisely (and she seldom if ever does) Nature drives men to violate her conventions. All religion has got to do with it is to teach men self-control and continence and respect for the prevailing social conventions.

But the great problem remains as to the licitness of sterile gratification, of the permission, excitation, and satisfaction of sexual desire as an end in itself. Here the orthodox and traditional reasonings are so ignorant and fantastic as to create a revolt of common sense against the restraint they enjoin. Yet, as in so many other ethical questions, this bad advocacy may be damaging a good cause ; and there may be a true moral instinct which these worthless arguments fail to explain and justify. By permitting sterile gratification *inter conjuges*, under certain circumstances, the Roman Church has yielded the whole point as far as her arguments are concerned, and her *contra naturam* pleas fall to the ground. If she allows it *ad concupiscentiam sedandam* to the married, why not to the unmarried ? The Augustinian standard may have been impossible, but at least it was consistent ; and impossible, perhaps, only because Christianity has done little or nothing to strengthen the will, except in the morbid and profitless direction of monastic asceticism. Grace, we are told by the Jesuits, has nothing to do with *mere* ethical perfection. Strong wills and strong personalities are at a discount under a despotic *régime ;* lean on the priest and the sacraments and *pecca fortiter.* The Church does not raise men from the gutter ; she blesses the gutter and leaves them there. The essence of Jesuitism, as Pascal saw, is the sanctification of the gutter ; the astute accommodation of the ideal to the actual : " Peace, peace," where there is no peace. These tactics are a confession of the Church's failure. She cannot raise men to the Christian standard ; so she lowers it to their level. The Augustinian sex-morality would not work. But it was easier to open the sluice than to close it. Perhaps the best we can say is that, if the principle of sterile gratification were admitted in any instance, it would be impossible to limit it ; and that, generally permitted, it would be fatal both to matrimony and to the power of self-control, i.e. to society and to the individual. It might also be contended that, as lust is directed to the species-interest, it is an element of man's life that belongs to the jurisdiction of society, and not of the social individual. But, in truth, we do best to trust to the traditional instinct, lest bad reasons destroy our confidence in it. I will think about it.

To the Same

. . . I plead guilty to taking refuge in a fog towards the end of my last letter. It is the modern fashion of ethical, as well as of religious apologists, in their flight from the spears and darts of critical assault. Hence a general tendency to defend and glorify fogginess marks the decadence of every *Weltanschauung* as surely as does the tendency to resolve mythical absurdities into mystical symbols. It means that theology is raising a smoke to cover its own retreat. All Newman's apologetic, and that of his disciples, is of this kind— an apologetic for no apologetic—pleas for intuition, for reasons of the heart, for Pragmatism, for the illative sense, for all sorts of unreasoned reasons. But quite apart from my very slight and decidedly unfriendly interest in theology, I am a sincere believer in un- reasoned reasons and a profound sceptic as to the possibility of demonstration where concrete truth is in question. St. Anselm perhaps constructs God as inevitably as Euclid constructs his equilateral triangle ; but the constructions are equally bloodless. Who cares about this three-cornered equilateral God ? These demonstrations make millions of infidels and never a single believer. Taught to rest their belief on an argument, men drop the belief with the argument ; and at best it rests on ideas, not on experiences ; in the air, not on the earth. Even when the belief is con- firmed and quickened by experience, they have been taught to ascribe its substance and strength to the argument, and when the argument goes they consider their surviving faith the result of illusion and habit. Only when it is too late, and when their intellectual card-house is toppling over, do theologians come to the rescue with their fog-theories. As soon as the intellectual revolution is accomplished they rear up another Eiffel-tower of syllogisms *à la mode* and, un-taught by history, prepare another disaster for posterity.

Theology and ethics seem here to be in the same case, and vitiated by the same tendency. So completely, moreover, is our moral tradition bound up with Christianity, and our ethical theory with Christian theology, that they cannot long escape the fate of the system with which they are entangled. That they linger on, after their support is gone, is due to the fact that, while theological ideas are rooted only in the mind, morality has been rooted by practice in the habits of the individual, and in the institutions of society ; so that the field of the moral interest is far more extensive than that of the religious. We may say that a religion is not wholly dead as long as its moral influence survives, and clamours for its other half.

But speaking of ethical theory in general, and apart from theology, I feel it endangers morality in just the same way that theology endangers faith ; namely, by confusing itself with what it explains, and exposing experience to the vicissitudes of theory. I think the attempt to define the beautiful, and to deduce rules and criteria of art from that definition, is not more hopeless or baneful than the attempt to define the good, and to deduce an ethical code from the definition. It is also akin to the attempts to explain society by a social contract. Society is the work of instinct, striking out with its tendrils in all directions, till it stumbles on something to grip and utilise. We keep no record of the thousand futile experiments through which utilities have been discovered ; and the whole result as it stands seems the work of reason and pre-meditated design. It is so with the moral instinct and its findings. Experimentally man gropes his way to the sort of conduct that best furthers the expansion and elevation of his spiritual nature. He is tempted to explain why this food agrees and that disagrees with his constitution. His reason is sure to be partly, perhaps wholly, wrong ; yet the fact remains true. Unfortunately he deduces other prescriptions and recipes from his imperfect analysis, which do not agree with him at all. In other words, I think we find out what is right in conduct much as we find out what is right in food. The temptation to explain the resulting code by rational principles, to reduce it to unity, to extend it to new or imaginary " cases," may be and is mischievous if we imagine that explicit reason (as opposed to the implicit reason of moral instinct) is the supreme arbiter of right and wrong ; if we imagine that the breakdown of our ethical theory robs the traditional code of its authority ; if we imagine that the code has been reached through an application of principles, and not instinctively and by experiment ; if we mistake our rationalisation of the code for more than a working hypothesis, like our astronomical or physical unifications and our " laws of nature "— an hypothesis which must at once yield to the actual data of the moral sense.

Like theology, ethics has its use, so long as it rests on and returns to moral experience ; so long as it deduces ideas from facts and not from other ideas. Intellectualism in theology is an acknowledged danger. Intellectualism in ethics is rampant, universal, unchecked.

What M. Arnold says of poetical criticism is applicable no less to ethical. We cannot really define or explain what it is that makes a good lyric, or makes one better than another. We make our anthology of lyrics that are admitted by all to be first-class, and we use it as a standard of judgment. So neither can we tell

what it is that commends a certain character or action
as heroic and ideal, or why it rebukes and inspires us.
It is no real explanation to say that it reveals to us
our better potential self ; what we would be and are
not.   That is only another statement of the fact that
it does rebuke and inspire us ; and that, with a power
wholly lacking to ethical prescriptions and moral
exhortations.   The infinite complexity of a human act,
expressive of the whole personality of the doer, is past
all analysis.   It is there, and we like it or leave it ;
its motive power is as mysterious as the charm of
music.   An ethical anthology would be a safer guide
than any ethical theology, and would be a source
not only of light but of heat.   It would speak to
the head through the heart, and not conversely.   The
personality of Jesus has done more for us than the
Sermon on the Mount.   The personality of Socrates
helps me more than the Nicomachean Ethics.   You
will say : This makes morality a matter of taste, and
leaves no objective criterion.   I answer that good
taste, whether in art or conduct, is something quite
objective, and that human nature is an excellent,
permanent, and independent criterion.   There is a
difference between taste and good taste ; between
what *does* please us and what *ought* to please us.   There
is room for education and criticism of taste ; and
society is our school and compiles our moral anthology
for us.   To a child or an adult of vitiated taste it is
dull reading ; but if we set ourselves to school, our
taste is developed and mended ; we learn new delights
and finally acquire a power of independent criticism.
We learn to feel that the better things answer more
truly to the exigencies of our spiritual nature and
unfold its higher potentialities.   No doubt the collective taste needs endless purifying and elevation.
Moreover the play of intellectualism has given us an

ethical code which is in many ways artificial, and elicits no response from our moral sense. It needs endless sifting to eliminate what is merely conventional and *a priori* from the true utterances of the spirit. In such criticism we may not trust to our individual judgment, which may be subjective and peculiar. We must try to find out how far the general judgment is really spontaneous, and not merely traditional and customary. There may be cases where we do not merely *not see* the utility or justification of the general rule, but where we positively see its hurtfulness and understand and repudiate the basis on which it rests —cases where our own judgment is no longer individual or subjective, but objective and universal.

And now perhaps I have said enough to explain the words you object to as being an evasion of critical reason. The feeling against " sterile gratification " may be impossible to defend by any explicit reasoning ; yet, for all that, may rest on more than convention, or primitive taboo, or fallacious *a priori* ethical deduction. Even if one's own moral taste be not dead against it, the fact that it is condemned by the best and highest types of character, that it is condoned only by the decadent, should make us enquire whether its prohibition be not the utterance of a keener moral sense than our own. I do not say it is evidently so ; for the best and highest do not always judge by their own inward light, but often accept the current moral code without criticism. Hence I have not solved the problem, but only determined the conditions of its solution.

To Laurence Housman, Esq.

February 17, 1901.

DEAR ST. LAURENCE,

I will begin with your end. Lust, like the maternal affection, has its altruistic side, it is the beginning of better things, the rude and grotesque embryo of the most spiritual and even divine love. The materialist and the idealist may agree as to the continuity of the process ; they differ as to the end from which it sets out. If the world is only mud worked-up and pinched into pretty shapes, then too the love of Calvary is but lust grimacing. I, beginning at the other end, and holding the whole process to be governed and effected by the Idea, by the divine thought and love striving for even fuller utterance, through the limits of the finite, see in the lower un-finished essays but the analysis and elements of the higher. But the elements of the fair are not all fair, and torn from their context may be horrible and grotesque. Would you allow your perfect work to be interpreted by your first daubs and dashes, or would you have these explained and justified by that ? May we not say, *pace* St. James[1] : " Lust when it is finished bringeth forth life and love. Do not err, my beloved brethren."

To F. M. (Notebooks)

1908–1909.

. . . But is it so very clear and " of course " that there is nothing left of the old sense of sin, with its attendant duties of contrition, confession, penitence, reparation, humility ? There is a great truth in Luther's view that a new life is the best and only repentance. But was it new where true ? Was it true where new ? As a protest against perfunctory confessions and facile absolutions ; against the sys-tematic and periodical " slate-wipings " of those who view sacramental grace as a substitute for ethical conquests ; against a morbid turning back on the past and turning away from the present and future ;

[1] " Sin when it is completed begetteth death " (James i. 15).

against crying over spilt milk in the idea that mere crying and flesh-cutting, and penances as such, will repair matters, or that the real damage is heaven lost or hell gained, or a humanesque God hurt or infuriated—as such a protest Luther's view was true but not very new. As an encouragement to forget the seamy past altogether ; to live and feel as though we were every bit as good as the unfallen ; as though we had no such past behind us ; as though we had only to think of the future, as if we had been born to-day, and not of the future as related to our past, correcting it as well as corrected by it—all this was new but not true. It was too crude a corollary from the metaphorical idea of a new birth and regenerating grace. There is peace and relief in finding the right path again ; in getting into line with God ; in being reconciled with conscience. But our past is part of us *for ever ;* every moment of bygone experience enters into and determines my present action. One behind another, foreshortened to an invisible point, all my former deeds are there, each characterised by all its predecessors and characterising them in turn, making with them a new and original resultant, which itself is to be transformed by my present decision. However little I may be explicitly aware of them, " my sins are ever over against me." It is because in imagination we string our past deeds out on a line called Time, that it seems easy to " cleave it in twain, to throw away the worser part of it and live the purer with the other half." No such " new birth " is possible. There is no redeeming blood that can delete the record of what has been, and therefore is, and always will be. Yet it is just because the past is eternal, is built into the very substance of our spirit, it is just because it is irreversible, that it is reparable. It has not escaped our hands, or run like water through our fingers. It

15

is always there to be moulded and manipulated, to be filled up and levelled down and straightened out and turned to good account. We have no business to forget it any more than the workman has to forget the matter he is dealing with. There is a salvation by works—by works that are themselves the work of redeeming grace, of the divine life that springs up in us as a well of living water from the foundations of our spiritual being. I do not mean a compensating balance of merits and demerits. That were again to space out our experiences in a line, and to forget the unity and simplicity of the spirit at any given moment. I mean that the very act which, implicitly or explicitly, reprobates and detests my past sins neutralises them in the resultant, and takes them into its own substance. The act that makes me a son of God is characterised and constituted by the sins it pardons. They are the mould, the cracks and crannies into which the stream of divine mercy is poured. They are taken away, not by a subtraction, but by an addition that turns them from a curse to a blessing. The rock of offence becomes the pedestal of triumphal grace and love.

Are you so sure that the fear that cowered before the angry almighty Man in the clouds did not, like the doctrine of hell, stand for the childish apprehension of a truth that seems only deeper and greater when stripped of its short-clothes ?

Of course, if free-will is an illusion, if vice is but disease, and sin but an accident, I allow that it is a simple blessing to have done with the old mythology. But if I am a self-building, self-determining spirit ; if I have the making or marring of myself in my own hands ; if I bear with me always, as part of my personality, not merely the vices, traces, and tendencies of my past misdeeds, but the very misdeeds themselves ; if my conscience, the deepest and highest law of my

life, is the immanent will of the source and end of all
being, striving in me, as everywhere, to bring the
actual into accord with the ideal, it seems to me that
I have but a fuller expression of the substance of the
old mythology. A righteous indignation, a hatred
of injustice is an attribute of my own conscience,
when I judge my neighbour ; and that I am more
lenient to myself is not simply that I know all the
excuses and temptations in my own case, it is also
mere self-love and favouritism. Except on the
determinist hypothesis I cannot believe that such anger
and indignation is mere folly and ignorance ; that
it is not something divine or godlike—a clash of forces,
an uprising of the universal love and order against
individualist pride and selfishness ; I cannot but
think that this anger is an attribute of the universal
conscience, and that my own sins incur that anger.
The sort of moral tone and temper induced by the
practical (though not avowed) determinism of the
New Theology strikes me as poor and shallow, compared
with that of Paul or Augustine or Pascal or Newman,
weighed down with the sense of sin and paralysed
with the fear of the divine wrath. We are in so little
danger of sharing the exaggeration, crudities and
anthropomorphisms of that depressing theology that
we can well afford to redeem and save its true values.
Of course it is responsible for the smug, shallow
optimism of the New Theology ; for the decay of the
spirit of repentance and humility. Protestantism
obeyed a juster instinct when it struck the burden
of sin off Christian's shoulders by faith in the redeeming
blood. Yet a truer synthesis leaves the burden there,
but turns sorrow into joy. Our sins are of our very
substance, eternal and imperishable ; but divine grace
can transmute our shame into glory.

I do not believe that determinism has a leg to stand

on, except in so far as the defenders of liberty are constrained by the very nature of our understanding to talk of liberty in terms of mechanism. Determinism contradicts our constant and universal inward experience ; and that is its doom as a philosophy.

I saw it argued lately that we do not take less care of our health because it is governed by strict physiological laws ; therefore determinism would not lead to fatalistic apathy in regard to our moral health. What nonsense ! It is just because our health does not depend on external causes alone, but also on our free action, that we take care of it. We do not deny that the formation of our character depends on psychological laws, or that we work within strict limitations and can never make a silk purse out of a sow's ear ; we only affirm that we are free to apply and use those laws just as we do the laws of bodily growth and health.

To L. H. (Notebooks)

1908–1909.

. . . I own that, for me, religion stands or falls with the divine character of conscience. If I have learnt this from Newman I have verified it by my own experience and reflection ; and it is a conviction that grows stronger every day. For a time I was staggered by the undeniable fact that what blames or approves my conduct is the voice of society within me ; the thought of what others would say if they knew ; the imaginative realisation of social rewards and punishments, or even the sense of spiritual communion or excommunication in regard to others. But the truth of all this confirms, instead of weakening, the fuller inclusive truth.

For it is evident that the social conscience expands and develops. And this, only because certain individual consciences rise above, criticise, and improve the social conscience ; because they see and feel that it would be wrong to conform to it. This means that, as in matters of truth, so in those of " ought," the public mind is but the repository of the best individual experiences, and is so far an educative instrument ; a rule, but not the sovereign rule of right. It is but the delegate or deputy of universal conscience ; the first court of appeal, not the last.

Moreover, what moves us is not the praise and blame, the rewards and punishments of men, but of *good* men, i.e. of men who are embodiments of conscience and whom our own conscience approves as such.

Indeed, on closer reflection, the distinction between my conscience and theirs is illusory ; so that what really moves me is simply the praise and blame of conscience generally. For as it is not my private opinion, but the verdict of reason in general, that $2 + 2 = 4$; as general consent could add nothing to my certainty ; as the appeal, in less evident matters, to general consent is only a means of eliminating private opinion and getting at what is universally and objectively true, of securing the verdict of that reason which is nobody's private property but is common to all ; so it is with conscience. Conscience is something absolute. Present to me : yet not myself. The clamour of my subjective opinions, my passions and wishes, would often drown its voice. But it is also outside me ; it speaks to my fellowmen as to me ; to those who are not biased, as to my case, by my immediate prejudices. Through them it speaks to me clearly, when its voice within me is muffled. That is why it seems to come from society rather than from myself. Yet I am clear that even to the best of my fellowmen I owe no such absolute obedience as conscience claims ; that I should obey them only so far as they are presumably true to conscience ; that

I must disobey them when the presumption is
untenable.

You ask : Do I pray to my conscience—as it were
to a little sprite that sits in my soul ? As I have
just said I do not believe in " one man, one conscience."
There is but one conscience in us all ; one creative
will that urges every creature to its proper perfection ;
man, to a moral and spiritual perfection. Man's
consciousness of it, as an impulse and a guide, is his
conscience. It is his awareness of the divine will
in regard to himself. Conscience (like science) is
used both of the knowing and of the thing known.
The thing known is the divine will ; God, as willing
my perfection. *That* I can worship and pray to ;
not to my knowledge or awareness of it. It is in my
own conscience that I know God immediately. The
social conscience serves only to waken, stimulate, and
educate this knowledge. Through the social conscience
God speaks to me indirectly. There He is embodied,
incarnate. Within me He is pure spirit. In the
Christ, in the Ideal Man or in the Ideal Church, the
incarnation of conscience is absolute, all-pervading,
continuous. Such a man is wholly a manifestation
of righteousness. The transparency is perfect. " He
that hath seen Me hath seen conscience " ; his actions
are the actions of God.

When you ask : What is my relation to conscience ?
is it identity or diversity ? be sure that you are not
thinking of the spirit as " a thing," an encased atom
of some sort. Agreement of opinion, agreement of
will, of sentiment, of conviction, is not to be conceived
as the correspondence of two pictures in which every
feature is doubled ; but rather as the flowing of different streams into one and the same channel, to separate
again at a further point. The distinctness of such
alternately converging and diverging streams is never

perfect ; neither is their identity. When we pass to
the spiritual order the sum of experiences, that in
its totality constitutes and characterises myself, is
imagined, for purposes of thought and language, as
a stream, or as a string of beads that can be cut up
into mutually exclusive parts. But, in reality, it is
foreshortened and compressed, so that every moment
of its past lives in and qualifies every present moment.
Virtually multiple, it is actually one and simple.
Of these virtual parts of its truth-process and will-
process and love-process many are coincident with
(and indistinct from) those of other spirits and with
the moments of the divine life. These various lives
are distinct in their totality, but fused in various
moments of their totality. Each is a distinct history,
a distinct stream ; but all have certain common chan-
nels in their course. The stream of Christ's life ran
all the way in the divine channel. In Him the divine
played a human *rôle* throughout, with the best of us,
only at moments and seasons. Our totality constitutes a distinct stream. Union with God or conscience is then something very literal, and no mere
correspondence of two processes. It is a temporary
fusion of two life-streams in one bed. " I live,
yet not I, but Christ liveth in me " is sober fact when
my will is merged with that of God, which was that
of Christ. For distinctness in the spiritual order is
qualitative or nothing. Qualitative identity is simply
identity.

Of course I am not dogmatising, but only saying
how I take things. It comes to this ; man is not God,
because his life as a whole is not divine, but moments
of his life coincide with moments of the divine life.
Even were every moment to coincide, yet the totality
of the divine life, while including, must infinitely exceed
that of the coincident human life.

To Sr. B. (Notebooks)

January 5, 1909.

. . . True, the mere simultaneity of deaths impresses us irrationally. Every one in Messina had to die someway, some time or other ; and many more lingeringly, painfully, with added pains of anticipation. Much future joy and pleasure was extinguished ; but just as much pain, sorrow, and sin. What may more rationally impress us is the collective or public injury. The *respublica* goes on unmoved by individual births and deaths, by which its whole population is surreptitiously destroyed and renewed ; but a simultaneous dying of multitudes puts the machinery out of gear. Still more when whole towns and cities disappear. But a deeper problem is raised. It is perplexing enough to our belief in Providence when a life of great promise is nipped in the bud, and long years of preparation are frustrated. But we are used to that ; and are armed with consecrated platitudes. The only real " explanation " is to bring the case under a general law which intensifies the mystery. Everywhere Nature or God fashions the seed and fills it with a desire to grow and expand and take possession of the whole world. He is to each as though it were His sole care. Yet, except in a minute percentage of cases, all this care and tendency is for naught, as far as the individual is concerned. Worse still, this very perversity seems a necessity for the world in general, since it cannot possibly be occupied by one kind of life ; and each kind depends on the other kinds. Nothing is more frightening than this blind waste of a million seeds, on the chance that one may grow. When we see stars and planets flung like dust over the floor of heaven, can we resist the feeling that God deals with suns and worlds as with seeds ? Is it likely that He cares more

for species and peoples and nations and religions ?
We can toil and work in the faith that the cause of
progress and civilisation is His. Does He care ?
Did He care about the future civic development of
Messina, which was the religion, the ideal, the faith
of its best citizens ? Is a European earthquake
impossible ? Nay, is a world-wide disaster impossible ?
Will He wait till man has reached his Utopia ? Will
He never plant a careless heel on our toilsome anthill
of a world ? Is He not manifestly as indifferent
to the collective as to the individual career ? We are
driven back on Kant's : Nothing is absolutely good
but good will. It is not man's accomplishments,
but his endeavours, his ideals, his obedience to his
best, that really matter. To every weed and insect
God says : " Grow your best; be your best ; do your
best ; leave the issues to Me. You want Me ; I do
not want you ; by faith you are saved, not by works."
Yet the prospect of ultimate futility is unnerving.
We only attempt the best because we believe it possible
—because we feel God is with us, and wants it and will
carry it through. Perhaps that which strives in us,
which is thwarted and disheartened, and still strives
blindly, is just God Himself at war with the limited ;
breaking forth from His prison-house at every chink
and crevice—one and the same in all His manifestations.
Je n'en sais rien.

To K.

November 15, 1907.

That is miserable news.[1] I am so sorry for your
unfortunate mother, " whom not having seen " I
seem to understand. As for the poor thing herself,
I cannot wish a prolongation of such weary suffering.
Certainly the God of our childhood, who planned

[1] On the death of an invalid sister.

things out like an *économe*, was a vain idol, and the attempt to square things with such a simple view drives many into atheism. The book of Job (shorn of its prosaic and banal head and tail added by a Jewish hand) is perhaps the highest of expressions of faith. We do not know ; we cannot understand ; we have no reason to call good luck God's favour, or ill luck His curse. We must give up the idea that the universe has been planned principally for man. It evidently works for other ends than ours. All we can believe is that He who has given us our sense of its seeming cruelty, coldness, and injustice, is behind all and above all ; and works for the eventual good of all. If we were not taught to thank God for our good luck we should not be so scandalised at our ill-luck. Best to thank Him for all equally, and not pretend to discuss which is which.

To Lady Low

PENSION BELLEVUE,
FREIBURG I. BR.,
April 8, 1906.

DEAR LADY LOW,

Your words of sympathy and encouragement were very precious at a time of much trouble and misunderstanding. Certainly one realises every day how much closer is the spiritual bond between those who agree in the *fact* of faith than between those who agree merely in the *form*. Truly we should all be glad —I do not say if all agreed in form : for I doubt if that were either possible or desirable, and whether differences of form are not the condition of competition and development of spirits—but we should be glad if differences of form were valued rightly and not mistaken for differences of faith. But we can be very much more patient about the seeming chaos of religion when

we realise how much inward unity may be hidden
under all this outward diversity.

I wonder if there has ever been any *real* spiritual
personality which has not been wakened and developed
under the influence of some other spiritual personality ;
whether spiritual, like bodily life, is not a torch
kindled from hand to hand ; whether God does not
always incarnate Himself in some one soul in order to
reveal Himself to us ? I doubt much if secret communion with Him be possible till we have given Him
some shape in our mind ; necessarily a more or less
human shape. The most abstract mystics seem to
me always to converse with a Man after all. For less
definite religion the dim figure of the historic Jesus
fulfils the function ; but I am sure it is always a gain
in strength and definiteness when the Divine has
been shaped for us in some great love of spouse, friend,
parent or child. After all, we can only know it in
its manifestations ; what it is in itself we can never
know. A false prudery, an " edifying " vulgarity
makes pious hagiographers hide the evidence for this
truth which is to be found in the lives of the great
saints and mystics. We are all idolaters ; the best
idolaters are those who worship God in the form of
man and not in the form of an idea or abstraction,
or of something less than human. We have much to
learn yet. Religion is as much in its infancy as science
was till a few generations back.

I hear to-day that three of my friends have been
condemned by Rome. It is most sad in many ways ;
but it is a sign of panic on the part of the perishable
and perishing section of the Roman communion.
They realise, all too late, that a new spirit is stirring
among the dead bones—a spirit which they cannot
understand or control, and which they fondly hope
to extinguish by some sort of violence. Still many

of us must go on the bayonets for the sake of those
who follow us up ; and bayonets hurt.   ·

To Miss Dora Williams

RICHMOND, YORKS,
October 7, 1904.

To-day, after a considerable interval, enough in all
conscience, I took up the *Communio Sanctorum* (for
so it is rendered in the *Credo*) once more. It did not
need that " trial by ordeal " to which Dante subjected
his sonnets and which would convict so many sonnets
of meaning absolutely nothing. Of the mystical
psychology implied I could write volumes just at
present. All I read and hear seems to point, of late
years, to the truth that our separateness is largely
illusory and our sameness not merely that of similarity
but of identity. I know, at first stating, this sounds
like Pantheism, like a denial of a persistence *post
mortem* of self-consciousness, like a subversion of
fundamental religious beliefs and ethical postulates.
I can only say here that reflection disposes of these
objections to a very great extent, while it discerns an
enormous relief from some of our deepest doubts and
problems as a consequence of the new standpoint. I
was groping in this direction in some of the later
sections of *Oil and Wine.* Just now I have been
reading Schopenhauer, who so nearly says just what
I want, and yet tumbles into paradox and pessimism
for want of " the little more." As yet we are but tad-
poles in metaphysics,· but there are signs of budding
limbs and deciduous tails. That the dead look us
through and through seems to me now not merely a
faith, but, of many hypotheses, far in a way the one
nearest certainty. If, as you say (in your prose comment), it is a consolation to the racked soul to feel

that other souls are in sunshine (I met the same thought in Mrs. Holland's letters lately), and that their vigour may later derive to us by a sort of transfusion, may there not be even greater consolation in recognising the cause of this in the fact that the self or subject of all human experience is really one and the same ; that I may wake from a distraction to find that what I call my life and experience is but an episode in that wider life that I led, shall lead, and *am now* leading in the depths of what is stupidly called my sub-consciousness ? " I in thee," says Christ, " and thou in Me, that we all may be perfect in one." I much like your amendment of the Gospel figure. Instead of greedy children and neglected dogs, you give us a prettier picture of the relations that obtain between heaven and earth, and, I have no doubt, a truer one.

To the Same

RICHMOND, YORKS,
November 3, 1904.

Die Bestimmung[1] will be very acceptable indeed and I thank you for the kind thought. As to the *Orbit*[2] there is a horrible ambiguity in the sentence which you quote, " . . . we find God and we find ourselves. For these are two aspects of the same thing " ; " these " refers, not to *God* and *self*, but to the *finding God* and *finding self*. I mean that we cannot know either properly till we know it in relation to the other. It is the " flower in the crannied wall " idea, in another application. The other sentence, " We *become* something that we can feel, etc.," is an echo of Laberthonnière. He means, in the words of à Kempis, " He who cleaveth to the creature shall

---

[1] Fichte, *Die Bestimmung des Menschen*.
[2] *The Soul's Orbit*, M. D. Petre.

fail with the fallible, or vanish with the evanescent—
cadet cum labili ; he who embraceth Jesus shall abide
solid for ever." A man in the surf, who grasps a
floating stick, would not feel his own strength and
reality as he would were he to lay hold of a rock ;
and so the soul which clings to and lives for something
as mobile and yielding as itself has no sense of solidity
and substance, but only of evanescence and emptiness
and aimlessness. In appropriating God's ends and
making itself an instrument of the (immanent) divine
will it gains the strength and solidity which a tool
gains in the strong hand of the workman. Only
so does the soul " *become* its true self and feel and love
and possess itself," and this love is the same *act* by
which it loves God, though there are two related objects
of that act—God as in the soul ; the soul as in God ;
or God as the principal, the soul as the instrumental
agent of one and the same action, will and end. This
in no way interferes with the " I and you " relationship,
without which " love " is not conceivable in spirits
like ours; though one dare not say that there may not
be something better than the love of finite spirits which,
as finite, are poor and need one another ; and in whom,
for the same reason perhaps, self-love is a blemish that
it might not be in an infinite spirit—if such there be.
Still, I feel that to " *tutoyer* " God, though a necessity
for us, is no adequate way of expressing a relationship
which is *sui generis* and like no other ; that it is, after
all, a fiction such as that by which little girls carry on
dialogues with their dolls. Here it is that I find the
Incarnation such a relief to our poor imaginations.
God wills we should picture Him, speak of Him, come
to Him as made manifest in the most perfect humanity
of Jesus Christ.

To the Same

RICHMOND, YORKS,
December 8, 1904.

DEAR MISS WILLIAMS,

Your note-paper was as interesting as your note, and I studied it carefully. I observe you entered my name under the heading of Nourishment, rather than Stimulant or Medicine, and perhaps I should be content. Better supply a constant than an occasional need ; better create than merely repair. I should hardly have singled you out for so severe a charity as sick-nursing, but, as à Kempis says of affection, *onus non sentit ; plus affectat quam valet ; de impossibilitate non curat,* and in other ways bids defiance to common-sense.

But I am writing partly because I am feebly convalescent from some days of stupidity and headache, and cannot work ; also to answer " Will's " perversions of my meaning. Of his letter to me I made but little. No, although Protestant, I am also very Catholic in the non-sectarian sense, which is more or less the Matthew-Arnoldian, but not at all the Wilfrid-Wardian sense. That, however, is a big question which I have dealt with in a little work which he has never seen and is now extinct. For the other matter : *I* do not say that " sanctity and morality are irreducibly distinct," but the theologians, with their preposterous definitions of natural and supernatural virtue. They do not canonise saints for *natural* virtue (i.e. for morality), but for supernatural virtues. " Love " itself is said to be of two kinds, natural and supernatural, and the *natural* love of God which a Plato might have had is said to be quite worthless in order to " supernatural " salvation. This is monstrous ; still it is said. Neither Wilfrid Ward nor your brother are likely to be aware

of these esoteric mysteries of the schools. What I
object to is the appeal to the sanctity of the *canonised*
saints rather than to the collective morality of the
Church as a whole. Because the saints are not (now)
canonised by saints (as it were, experts judged by
experts), but by theologians and worldly ecclesiastics,
and at great cost, and by such crude external tests
as miracles, eccentricities, departures from the normal,
etc., etc., I refuse to accept the catalogued saints as
the fruit and verification of Catholicism, but demand
a proof in the general moral tone of the faithful at
large. It is said, we should judge it by those only
who *practise* as well as profess it. But an educative
institution is judged by its power to educate those
submitted to it. At a good school, boys are *made*
to study; a naturally studious boy will do well at
the poorest school. If only those who practise are
the test, would not almost any religion stand the test?
And one rightly asks, Were the saints holy because
they used the helps of their religion, or did they use
those helps because they were holy and believed such
usage a part of their duty? Ward's attempt to make
a parallel between the saints of Catholicism and the
experts of science is futile.

I did not see Sirius; but it matters not which change
represents his inmost self so long as under all his
changes he was "quite lovely." Perhaps he *is*
essentially a kaleidoscopic process and has no other
selfhood than that. Better so than have some dull,
cold, cloddy, central core masked with a mere semblance
of brilliance.

Oh, please don't trust to my prayers. I never got
anything for anyone yet. If the patient recovers it
must be due either to your faith in my faith—or (if it
is not too extravagant an hypothesis) to the ministra-
tions of the doctor and the nurses.

*To the Rev. A. L. Lilley (now Canon of Hereford
Cathedral and Archdeacon of Ludlow)*

June 1909.

MY DEAR LILLEY,

The substance seems to me most important ;
but it does strike me as written painfully and without
your usual limpidity up to p. 3.[1] I suspect my own
philosophy is too cut-and-dried. I refer immanence
and transcendence to the quasi-mechanisms or auto-
matisms created by spirit or life for its own service
and self-expression--to Nature. The uniformities of
Nature are but relative and practically sufficient.
" Law " is a subjective category under which we
apprehend those uniformities as necessary and determined. " Determinism " is the projection of this
working hypothesis from the subjective into the objective order ; and either denies the possibility of a
breach of uniformity or describes it as an interference
of an alien force. Pure immanentism limits spirit
and confines it within its self-made mechanisms as
the motor power—as a world-soul and no more. When
it identifies world-soul and world-body as one person,
it is Pantheism pure and simple. Were man a pure
automatism of habits and uniformities he could not
think of a transcendent or desire to relate himself to
it. He does so because, in his own creative liberty and
conscience, he has an experience of the transcendent
and desires to increase his transcendence and spirituality. He knows himself as creating and modifying
the habits and mechanisms of his own activity—as
transcending Nature ; as not merely a product of his
surroundings but as their master to some extent.
Hence his first vague idea of a God over Nature and
his ambition to be himself a God over Nature as far

[1] A proposed preface to one of Mr. Lilley's works.

16

as possible, co-operating in the progressive formation and arrangement of Nature within him and without ; getting inside Nature by his reason and so mastering her, and freeing himself from subjection to her " laws " which are for his service. This, I fancy, is the Pauline idea of liberty. *Quis me liberabit !* is a cry for grace ; for an infusion of the creative spirit over which his wit and work has no direct control. God works on Nature through the co-operation and instrumentality of His spirit in man, and by such co-operation man's personality, or reproduction of God is formed. But there are two factors—God's gift and man's use of it. The trend of Eastern theology is to make man a part in a mechanism or organism ; that of Western is to make him a Son of God and free, sympathetic partner in the divine work. That is what, with my own categories, I should read out of your Preface. If I only read it into it, then, of course, I have missed its point and you will discount accordingly. It may be quite clear to one free from my cut-and-dried preconceptions.

III

LETTERS OF ADVICE

To Miss W.

31 FARM STREET, W.,
February 14, 1900.

DEAR MISS W.,

I observe this "formality" with everyone as a protest against the "*Ma chère enfant*" style, which I abominate. Outside my duties as confessor I do not see that I have any commission to "direct" or drive people's souls. If I advise, it is always on a footing of perfect equality, to help people to see and decide for themselves or to read more clearly what their own conscience tells them : but not to dictate or stand to them in place of conscience. There are some things I should consult you about as being better informed . or experienced ; and there are other things you consult me about for a like reason ; but there is no parental relationship created in either case. Outside sacramental matter your priest is not your superior in any way, but only your adviser, whom you choose and listen to or leave, *on your own judgment,* and to whom you have no debt of obedience. For some souls the unauthorised tyranny of the "*Père directeur*" may be the less of two evils ; for you it will be very hurtful, and lead to violent reaction. My advice to you would be to go often to communion and seldom to confession ; to confess your faults and get absolution, but not to ask advice or direction unless you can find a priest whom you feel to be in sympathy with your character.

and cast of mind. You will rarely find such an one ; but better far to do without a " director " (for it is not an essential) than to have one who tries to force your mind into the mould of his own—a mould in this case far too narrow. As to prayer difficulty, of course we cannot cage the Holy Ghost or bind Him to come at our prayer hours ; He " bloweth where He listeth." It is often at meals, or in company, or at the most incongruous moments that the good thoughts come. And the best habit is that of being on the alert, and registering the inspiration for after-rumination. Else the " birds of the air come," etc. But no doubt you have stifled yourself with methods and routines instead of following the lead of your good inclinations. Like many converts you revolt blindly against everything Protestant, forgetting how much good there was mingled with their error and making it plausible— good that Catholics overlook very often. Change as little of that as you can ; and supplement it with the riches that Catholicism offers. You cannot abruptly change the whole structure of your mind, nor is there any reason to wish to do so. Go on saying your prayers night and morning as of old, in the same way as far as possible. Don't attempt strait-waistcoat methods of meditation ; but take up your Bible or à Kempis or St. Augustine's Confessions, and read quietly and think and pray as you feel moved. Begin perhaps with a Veni Creator and end with a Pater—and that will be formality enough. Or, better still, if you know Latin enough, recite slowly and intelligently some part of the daily office of the Church—the best of all prayers. And in fine, do try to be yourself, and don't try to be Père B. or somebody else. Christ's net holds all manner of fishes, even you and me ; we are not all sprats or herrings, but each a separate kind. Let us try to know ourselves, and then we shall know God ;

but if we disguise ourselves in other people's clothes
we shall never know ourselves or live, but shall be like
mummies swathed from head to foot and spiced, if
you will, but dead.

I don't often write like this, and perhaps you will
be scandalised at my warmth; but surely you will
some day say I was right.

Do you know Mrs. Craven's *Meditations*? I should
think her spirit and that of her school would be far
more congenial and helpful to you.

To the Same

RICHMOND, YORKS,
September 28, 1902.

I know you expect nothing of me in the way of correspondence, and may therefore cease to apologise for
my negligence. I feel that your lot has been cast in
troublous times and in a troublous *milieu*, and that
this tension in the Church of the old and new is the
worst thing possible for those who have the conflict
forced on their attention continually. I don't think,
however, you could have lived long in the choking
atmosphere of the old, with your essentially Protestant
hunger for inwardness of spiritual life; yet your no
less essentially Catholic desire of a sacramental and
external Church would have made Protestantism
impossible for you. If only you could have faith in
the fact that the so-called liberal movement in the
Church, in spite of all its vagueness and extravagances
and sub-divisions, and of its disfavour with the authorities, is really the *growing* and *living* extremity of the
Church and, when formed, will constitute the Catholicism of the future, you would, I think, leave details
alone, and be content to see in it evidence of the fact
that the Church grows and moves according to the
universal laws of all growth and movement, which are

never without travail and conflict—thesis, antithesis, and synthesis, over and over again, each new synthesis being but provisional, and requiring itself to be challenged as soon as its limitations come to light by experience.

To the Same

STORRINGTON, SUSSEX,
October 28, 1907.

Here I am at last, *arrivé*, i.e. excommunicated. An article in *La Grande Revue* (October 10) will tell you what I think about it. Beyond a new name of infamy it makes no change in my internal or external position or plans, and I hope you and my other friends will take it with the same stolid matter-of-course-ness. The date of my article was May 1904—which shows how little of a surprise it is to me. These are the death-agonies of the old, the birth-throes of the new, and we must expect a good deal of kicking and screaming. But God is God and Christ is Christ, " the same yesterday, to-day, and for ever." Let us try to be the same yesterday, to-day, and for ever, like the quiet stars and the eternal hills. Rome is but an ant-hill after all, and we should be ashamed of letting such insects trouble our central peace.

" Shut out the tumult of the world " (and of the Church), " and call unto thee Jesus thy Beloved." That is the best advice I can give you.

To N.

CLAPHAM,
February 6, 1908.

I want to acknowledge your " explosion " before going abroad for a few weeks. I hope to get to Storrington in the summer and see you. Meantime you are in pieces—like so many others. I feel sure the time has come to face the ugliest spectres boldly—as they are faced by the little brochure I have read to-day, *Lendemains de l'Encyclique.* My only comfort is that now the fat is in the fire there is nothing worse possible. If we survive this we are immortal. If——— As you know, I, rightly or wrongly, hold there is a limit to ecclesiastical as to civil authority —a time when resistance is duty and submission treason. If I believe the captain is unawares steering for the rocks I will not obey him. I am not infallible ; he may be right ; but I must go by my own moral certainties. Pius X is in the same case as a mad father, who orders his children to burn down the house.

Your vision is that of hundreds of priests ; to-morrow it will be that of thousands. That of Pius X is as incoherent and ugly as a nightmare. Ours is beautiful, and, apparently, coherent. Is it realisable ? Will it be realised ? Well, visions that are given independently to so many are usually prophetic of a proximate *parusia ;* they are the shadow of the coming event. That is my faith and hope. You will do better to vomit up " orthodoxy " altogether than to try and keep it down. You will never digest it. Your own similitude is quite just. Fancy yourself a Jew, A.D. 30, and ask yourself what was the *true* orthodoxy of that day—Christ's or Caiaphas's. Then, as now, one would hardly have dared to think of how much would have to go ; none but the strongest faith would have believed that such loss would have been such gain. Can one call oneself a Catholic honestly ? No, if Catholicism is a theory ; yes, if it stands for that historical community through whose fortunes and fluctuations and errors and experiences the truth is slowly threshed out. In that view the present crisis is a normal step in that process, an assurance of vitality. Pandemonium may endure for a night, but peace cometh in the morning.

The Catholicism of the Councils of Trent and Vatican was "a fond thing vainly invented." It was an hypothesis that had to be tried by experience and has served its turn in the discovery of truth. The community has outgrown it as the schoolboy outgrows his breeches. No patching will save it. Be silent and patient. "Suffer fools gladly"; for only fools are intolerant of fools. A—— is not the *orbis terrarum* and may judge very insecurely. If you are challenged you cannot lie. But short of that you are not bound to speak unless you are sure that it would tell for the general good.

To L. R.

MOORHURST, HOLMWOOD,
May 18, 1907.

I am very sorry to hear you have had such poor health of late, and hope the warm weather will bring you a respite.

You see where I have got to. Next week I go to my chronic address—Storrington, Sussex. No doubt I shall have to be in London fairly soon for one reason or another; in which case we must meet.

And now as to spiritual direction in any formal sense; even were I allowed the ordinary powers of a priest—which I am not—it is a position that I have never taken nor desire to take. I am always willing to give as well as to take suggestions; and to talk matters over as between friend and friend. But I can never feel that I have a right to speak with authority, or to be followed and obeyed. And then, for yourself, it is, of course, wise and right to exchange ideas with those whom you find helpful; but it is very bad to throw your responsibility on other shoulders more than you can avoid. The whole object of such outward help is to enable you to dispense with it sooner or later, and to make God your one great spiritual director. It is often better to make mistakes in trying to walk by oneself, than to be held up on each side. We are not learning or advancing when we are held ; but only when we are stumbling along and buying our own experience. Beware of directors and confessors. Keep to the old books and the old friends and the old thoughts by which God has led and consoled you in the past. Break with your past as little as possible.

To Mrs. U.

IVY HOUSE, CLAPHAM,
February 18, 1908.

I am never in or near N. I would ask you to come to London if I honestly thought I could be of the slightest service to you. But I should only say to you what I said in *The Much-abused Letter*, whose argument is quite unaffected by recent events. If Catholicism is the " theology " of Pius X and his Encyclical, or even of St. Thomas Aquinas, then neither you nor I are or can be Catholics. There we must agree with his Holiness. But if Catholicism means a belief in that living, continuous body of Christians called Catholic—a belief that it is the organ by which an ever truer idea of Christianity is slowly but infallibly worked out through many errors and blunders and fluctuations and contradictions, by all sorts of costly experiences good and evil ; that God leads it much as He led the stupid and recalcitrant people of Israel from Egypt towards a Land of Promise—then I think I am as good a Catholic as Pius X ; and, what matters very little if at all, a better theologian. To believe in Christ is to follow Him, not to define Him ; to put Him in the place of conscience which He simply incarnates.

To believe in His Church is again to follow Him, not alone, but in company with others of His household. Does your *inmost* conscience oblige you to anything else ? Are you not trying to guide yourself by the conscience of others instead of your own ? If it is your misfortune not to agree with the Encyclical, do you really feel it is your *fault* in any way that you know better ? Anything you need or ought to confess ? For myself, I know that the Church has blundered before, that she will blunder again. She is like a baby learning to walk. She will learn infallibly, not merely in spite of, but by means of, her blunders. It is the universal law of progress, and the Church is no exception.

To the Same

IVY HOUSE, CLAPHAM,
February 20, 1908.

As to your conjecture, your idea is not new. Either Strauss or Bauer has conjectured that Christ recovered from His trance and went away to some Essene monastery and died there in peace. There are a thousand ways of explaining the empty grave— all equally gratuitous and fanciful. If the only proof of the resurrection were the empty grave it would lack proof altogether. The proof is in the appearance of Christ to His Apostles and to St. Paul, who says nothing about empty graves (1 Cor. xv.). If Napoleon's coffin were found empty to-morrow no one would suppose his body had risen ; though if his body were still there we should know it had not risen. So with Christ's body : the empty tomb did not prove it had risen ; though had the tomb not been empty the body could not have risen.

But even if your difficulty were quite valid why should any honest difficulty keep you from the Sacraments ? Is it not that you still mix up faith with theology ? If you killed somebody by accident would you consider you had sinned ? Are not merely intellectual matters as completely out of your control ? Does your *own deepest conscience* say you do wrong to see as you see and think as you think ? Are you not looking in the mirror of some theologian's conscience and accepting what he would say of you as the verdict of your own conscience ? Madness lies that way. Nothing but *wilful* sin or *wilful* error should keep you from the medicine of your soul. You do wrong also to mention in confession what your *own* conscience does not accuse you about ; and you give your confessor an occasion of falsifying your conscience and making you scrupulous and uncomfortable. Never accuse yourself to your confessor of what you cannot first accuse yourself to God, alone on your knees. I think you would be ashamed to confess your intellectual difficulties to God—it would be so unreal.

To Mrs. Metcalfe

(Date uncertain.)

To stop between the several acts of your life, and refer them to God, is like stopping at every step of the road to remind yourself where you are going. It is impossible and quite useless. God has given you instincts and common-sense to tell you what you should do in each detail ; and so you should not ask each time for a special revelation on the subject.

St. Paul asked the question, " What wouldst Thou have me to do ? " *once*, at his conversion, and received a revealed answer. Our spiritual life is not a chain of sudden conversions. " But the saints have done so," you will say. As a married woman, probably you have once been " in love " ; and you know how, in that state, the thought of the beloved obtrudes itself and haunts us morning, noon, and night; how all our actions are done in that imagined presence; how all our idle thoughts turn thither, in spite of us; how the room brightens or darkens with that presence or absence. But in all this one is passive and not active; one can't escape from it if one would. Were one not in love with the person, the effort to imitate the effect of love would drive one mad. The saints *were* in love with God, and we are *not*. If you ask me for a recipe for falling in love with God or man, I don't know one. It can't be done by effort of any kind. Let us then accommodate ourselves to the *fact* that, though we should like to be, we are not " in love " with God; we love Him as dutiful servants and sons, but are not carried away by our love. This latter He does not ask from us, for it is not in our power; we may ask it of Him, for it is His to give to whom He wills. To *act* being in love, when one is not, is unreal and untruthful, and no good can come of it; while much harm may.

To the Same [1]

RICHMOND, YORKS,
June 29, 1901.

I heard of your illness—first of the worse fears, then of their groundlessness, from other sources. These depressing anxieties are so inseparable from your present state of health that words can do little or nothing to dispel them; they are as much an affliction from God's hands as the illness itself of which they are the necessary sequel. I am not sure that the prayer which asks God to stay the ruthless grinding—as it seems to us—of His will is nearly as good as the prayer which makes us lie still and say nothing, trusting that

[1] She was dying of cancer.

the seemingly ruthless law is governed by a higher love and wisdom than we can ever comprehend. To ask anything definite might, in some, argue a simpler and a stronger faith ; but for you I think there is a higher and more intelligent faith in a certain kind of fatalism, which takes each hour by itself, with its own burden, and studiously refuses to speculate or to look further. Even as a doctor I should say this was almost indispensable for the recovery of your health, just as fretfulness and worry, especially about spiritual matters, are almost fatal to the same end. May I recommend you the spirit that breathes in the poems for Tuesday, Wednesday, Friday, and Saturday of Holy Week in the *Christian Year*? Lines in those poems, as well as others familiar to you, will best serve to keep your soul tranquil and untroubled, while your more formal exercises will serve, at least, as a mute expression of your wish to do and bear all that God wants of you. That these latter should be hopelessly dry and wearisome is of no spiritual significance whatever.

Put interior rest before everything. God does not like fidgets. I will bring your case to the altar.

IV

CHANGE OF FAITH

Note

The first of these letters to L. R. was written nearly ten years before the later ones. Father Tyrrell had seen the correspondent in question at the time of his first letter, and had encouraged her to quiet reflection and delay, before taking any further step. He left London for Richmond in 1900, and saw no more of her for some years. Meanwhile she had fallen under the influence of a very different type of director, and had been hurried into the Roman Catholic Church without much consideration for her particular character and needs. The transplantation was not wholly successful, and gave rise to the later correspondence. She was a staunch friend to Father Tyrrell throughout his troubles.

To L. R.

WIMBLEDON COLLEGE, WIMBLEDON,
July 9, 1898.

On thinking over our conversation I feel sure that it would be premature were you to embark on anything like controversial reading at present. God is undoubtedly calling you to a life of closer union with Himself, and I personally know well that, had you been earlier familiarised with the Catholic religion, it would have satisfied superabundantly all those needs which you now feel unsatisfied. Still the human mind cannot easily and suddenly cast off its habitual ways of thought and begin to look at things from a totally new standpoint ; nor could any solid good be expected from such an effort. It would be very hard for us to throw ourselves heart and soul into sympathy with Chinese ways and customs ; and I think the Catholic conception of Christianity is almost as far removed from other forms—not excepting High Anglicanism, which resembles it only superficially, and has far less of its spirit than has evangelical Protestantism. All one wants in order to be in good faith and to satisfy God is a sincere and practical desire to know what is true and to be free from all unjust thoughts about the religion of others. If it be a sincere and practical desire you will take a little trouble to find out the truth; you will be slow to think evil of any religion, willing to believe the best. God does not give the full light of religion to all in this life ; but to all He gives abundance for salvation, though many shut their eyes and will not see. You need not fear being classed with these latter, seeing your whole trouble at present is lest you should in any way be wanting to the grace of God. If at any time you felt a clear command of conscience bidding you submit to the Catholic Church, it would be then time enough to put yourself under instruction and to consider in detail the many difficulties by which the mind is hindered from following the heart; but the heart must first be drawn. Meantime I think you will satisfy all justice if you strive to clear your mind of those common and almost vulgar travesties of Catholicism which have been current in this country for three centuries and exist in minds otherwise fair, charitable, and cultivated. Before considering the Church's claim to be Christ, it is well to see that at least she is not Anti-Christ, that she is not a monstrosity or an absurdity. I saw no trace of such narrow prejudices in you, but I fancy it is simply because you never thought about Rome, never discussed the subject with any Protestant seriously, so as to draw out the usual flood of calumnies by which we are assailed. Now, however, it may well be that you will get the benefit of all these commonplaces as soon as it is understood that you have really considered Rome as a remote possibility. But were you never to come a step nearer it is a part of Christian charity not to condemn the great mass of one's fellow-Christians, the millions of all generations who have been guided by Rome, without a hearing. For this end I think you should read Newman's *Present Position of Catholics in England ;* also his *Anglican Difficulties* (2 vols.) That I think will be quite enough for the present as far as the *mind* goes, unless perhaps you might read his *Apologia* again. But for the *spirit* I should recommend to you *The Creator and the Creature*, by Father Faber ; *All for Jesus*, by the same ; also *The Devout Life*, by St. Francis of Sales ; *The Sacred Heart*, by Father Dalgairns ; *The Life and Letters of St. Theresa*, and *The Life and Letters of St. Francis Xavier*, both by Father Coleridge. Catholicism is seen at high-water mark in Mrs. Craven's celebrated *Récit d'une Sœur*. Those who show some toleration for Catholicism will warn you against Jesuits as the most aggravated concentration of papistry. If you are curious to understand this you may read *The Jesuits : their History and Foundation*, by B. N. All these books are to be got through Burns & Oates ; but unless you get them through some intermediary you will probably find a paragraph in the papers announcing your conversion to Romanism.

Whatever happens it will be well to have read these things and to have lived a little with those strange people called saints. Above all, it is only by silence

and tranquillity of heart that one can hope to hear
the still small voice of Truth. A " visit to the Blessed
Sacrament," as we call it—that is, to go to the church
when all is quiet and to remain a little in wordless
prayer before the " Living Bread " from heaven—will
be a source of great spiritual strength. For a prayer,
I can recommend nothing better than à Kempis's
Imitation of Christ, Book III, c. 2.

I told Messrs. Longmans to send you a copy of my
meditations, of which some may help you, and the others
you can leave. May Our Lord perfect and further
your desire to know His truth and to do His will in
everything.

To the Same

16 OLD TOWN, CLAPHAM, S.W.,

February 1, 1907.

I am leaving London for a little while ; but when
I return shall be most pleased to call upon you
some day. I had heard through Mrs. T. that Father
N. had received you into the Church. I do sincerely
trust that you have there found all that you wanted
and that you do not blame me too much for having re-
tarded your steps in that direction. I often find that
my fears in such matters are unfounded, and that I
am more critical for others than they are for themselves.
To me, it is more important that people should be at
rest, and outside the currents of controversial excitement, than that they should rest here or there. For
that reason I dread, not a change for the better, but
the process of changing. However, I trust and pray
that, the process being over, the transplanting may be
for your greater and richer growth in the spirit.

17

To the Same

16 OLD TOWN, CLAPHAM, S.W.,
March 17, 1907.

I confess I was very angry with Father N. for all his tactlessness and stupidity ; but the truer and kinder interpretation is to be found by the recognition that in many respects he is an undeveloped specimen of humanity, and that what would be inexcusable in a grown man is excusable to the naïve self-confidence and self-delightedness of a vigorous boy in his teens. He is, I know, absolutely sincere and devoted, and in no sense a charlatan ; but the immaturity of his judgment makes him a dangerous guide for those who take him seriously as a grown-up person. Of course this is confidential.

I shall not regret your being in the Church if you can take it for what it really is—a means to serve you, not an end to be served. It caters for every kind and level of spiritual need, and you must find out and use just what suits and helps you ; you will find all that the Church of England offered you, and a good deal more ; and of that " more " some will nourish you and some will give you indigestion—so you must use your good sense and not let yourself be hustled and worried by doctors who know nothing about your constitution, and make their own stomachs a rule for other people's. I should say : Communion as often as you like ; and confession very rarely and, if possible, never. And, above all, avoid discussing religious questions with traditional Catholics, whether priests or layfolk. For your mind has been built up on a different system altogether, and it will be like a conversation between a dog and a fish. All their machinery is justified solely as a means of getting where you have got already ; namely, alone with God. Only, if they are narrow in wanting you to use crutches when you can walk without, you must not be Protestantly narrow in condemning crutches all round. Protestantism caters only for the elect and the " converted " ; Catholicism for all humanity—saints, scribes, pharisees, publicans, and sinners ; and for all moods and stages of each individual spiritual life ; for its infancy, youth, and old age ; for its healthy and sick periods. You may not want crutches to-day ; but you may sprain your ankle to-morrow. Or if you don't want crutches you may want spectacles, etc.

Well, I hope we shall soon meet and talk all this out.

To the Same

STORRINGTON, SUSSEX,
May 26, 1907.

I am here for a few weeks at all events, and so need not avail myself of your most kind invitation. I am so sorry to learn from Mrs. T. and yourself that you are still so far from well ; and yet more to gather from your second letter how troubled and puzzled you are by all these new ideas and prayers and practices. That is just what I feared for you ten years ago—the danger of transplanting a flower that is doing well where it is. I can hardly resist the impression that your inward life is being starved and worried to death. Most converts have been gradually prepared for the step through ritualism, and have grown accustomed to Roman ideas and Roman ways. You have bounced in, uninstructed and unpractised.

It is not a mere ceremony of reception that can make you a Romanist, but a certain set of principles and convictions and habits and inclinations which, for the most part, are utterly strange to you, owing to your education and entourage and disposition.

Father N. took no pains to understand you or instruct you. He played upon you by an appeal to your religious fears and your scrupulous desire to follow every call of grace. He wanted to land a fish, and, having landed it, he left it. You are just as much an Anglican to-day and just as little a Romanist as you were ten years ago. There is no question of your going back to what you have never left. The only question is whether, being what you are, you should remain an *apparent* Romanist or go back quietly to that form of religion through which God has hitherto spoken to you and sanctified you, and which, I am sure, He never wanted *you* to leave. You will complain of the limitations of the English Church—I know them ; but has Rome no limitations ? And why, then, do I myself remain a Roman ? For a whole bushel of reasons, not one of which would appeal to you. It is the best religion for me and for most, but not for all and not for *you*, just because transplanting is dangerous in late life, even though it be to a better soil. For the present I think you should try to see if it is possible just to find what you want in the Roman Communion and *to leave the rest*—on the lines I already suggested, and making as little change in your old Anglican ways as possible. If you find that unworkable or soul-starving—*then*, quietly and gradually, relapse into full Anglican communion, going to their services, first occasionally ; then frequently ; finally altogether.

To the Same

STORRINGTON, SUSSEX,
April 14, 1909.

I am sorry you have not yet been able to see Canon N.[1] If he agrees with me I shall have no doubt that

---

[1] An Anglican clergyman.

my advice was sound. No mere ceremony can make you a Roman Catholic unless your ideas and inner habits of feeling have been transformed; and in that case there can be no question of your leaving that Church, since you never were in it. You are just where you were when I first met you in 1898, only a little more puzzled and uncomfortable, like a fish suddenly taken out of the water and laid on the shore. All I said to you then I would say to you now. Much that perplexes you in the Roman Church is really bad and cannot be defended ; all that helps you, *you* can find in the Church of England. To be always distinguishing between what is and what is not genuinely Catholic would worry the life out of you and destroy your spiritual peace. Some of us professional theologians can manage to balance ourselves on a tight-rope ; but that is not your profession. The English Church is full of limitations ; but she does not ask you to approve of them. There you are allowed to pick and choose. In Rome you are not allowed. If you cannot take everything, you are told that you have no business there. Do remember that Churches are only helps to get to God. If you find that one walking-stick is too long or too short, you must choose another. We can't do without a stick altogether, but the less we rely on them the better. You will run more smoothly in your old grooves ; so get back to them as soon and as quietly as you can. Don't argue with N. N., etc.; simply say that you never were in the Church ; never had been instructed ; that it was all a mutual misunderstanding. Refuse to read ; refuse to argue ; refuse to be interviewed by Father N. or any priest.

To Sister B.

CATHOLIC CHURCH,
RICHMOND, YORKS,
December 15, 1900.

I write solely on the evidence of your own letter. A few minutes after I had read it I stumbled by chance on these words of Amiel's : *Toute voix double et partagée combattue dans la conscience n'est pas encore la voix de Dieu.* As far as mere controversy goes, the question can never be settled decisively one way or the other, except by those who can believe that their own knowledge is co-extensive with all that is to be known.   Given, however, other motives of belief, one cannot, of course, accept a position which appears to be false or immoral, and such appearance must be removed before one can obey more subtle and spiritual attractions.   From what you say I do not think you are likely to be a victim of the " logic " fallacy, which brings over to us a certain number of crude, impatient thinkers to whom the temper of faith is really unknown and who reinforce the section of narrow-minded extremists that delight in all that is mechanical and external in Catholicism, making an end of the means. Now, on your own showing, your tendency is mystical and contemplative ;   and so I am sure that I need say no more about this " rationalistic snare."   What I feel is that union with God is the great end, and just so far as the step in question might help or hinder that end, must we judge of it.   At present you have realised a great degree of union with God.   To doubt that would be high treason against your faculties. You could never have greater certainty of your duty to become a Roman Catholic than you have of that. Two reasons might incline you to the latter step : (1) that thereby you could attain closer union ; (2)

that by refraining you would forfeit your present
union. But it is only the second reason that should
move you. Many come over to us for their spiritual
betterment ; because in so many ways we can offer
a definite and established system of spiritual helps
which Anglicanism cannot offer to the same degree,
owing to its unhappy divisions. But they do not
regard it as a matter of life or death; of union with God
or of severance from Him. Hence they come over to
Rome not realising what is, after all, the essential
peculiarity (or scandal, if you will) of the Roman
claims. Now if the question has not presented itself
in this way to your conscience, and been *clearly*
answered, you are not only not bound to stir, but you
are bound not to stir. A spiritual earthquake is always
a shock to the inner life. If God sends it, if He makes
it *perfectly plain* to you that communion with Rome is
a duty, binding you under sin, then away with every
spiritual luxury in order to secure the one thing needful
and substantial.

But it is not yet like that with you. There is only the
voix double et partagée ; not the single, unambiguous
dictate of conscience. Most certainly if God wants
it of you, He will make it very clear to you. But
(speaking from my own Roman standpoint) He does
not want it of all ; and though, in the abstract, it is
at Jerusalem that men ought to worship, in the concrete it may be at Gerizim that God waits for them.
This, I think, is the sense underlying your paradox
that Rome may be the truth for others, but not for you.
We all know that we are blinded to many objectively
true aspects of duty ; but while the blindness remains
we must follow our conscience, howsoever erring. We
may be almost sure that others see better, and yet it is
our own light and not theirs that we must follow.
I would venture to go a little further and say that

supposing you were perfectly dissatisfied with Anglican claims to Catholicism, and yet could only see your way to a Gallican view (i.e. a pre-Vatican view) of the Roman Church, in such a case you could not in conscience join our Communion ; for to do so one must make a public profession that one accepts fully and cordially the Vatican claims. You would have then to regard yourself as in a state of subjectively justifiable schism.

I feel sure that any kind of anxiety about the question must be bad for your spiritual progress, which requires peace and tranquillity ; and so I say, *wait* till your present position strikes you clearly and undoubtedly as *sinful for you*. That it is unsatisfactory or less satisfactory is not a motive to attend to. There are limitations everywhere, even at the Béguinage or with the Trappistines. May I ask you to pray for me ?

To the Same

July 24, 1904.

I am sorry that the sedative influence of my former letter has begun to fail—on re-reading it I feel no desire to unsay what is there said. Before I go further let me say frankly that I have no business to speak as a *representative* Roman Catholic, and that my way of approaching the question would be vehemently disapproved by most of our clergy—as indeed my writings are to a great extent. It is possible that I am altogether wrong ; it is certain that, being human, I am not altogether right ; and so I aim only at helping you to form a judgment for yourself, not at judging for you.

When a man thinks of leaving a house because,e.g., the chimneys all smoke, in choosing another he will be inclined to attend solely to the chimneys and to forget the drains, which, in his old house, were quite satisfactory. When he has moved, at first he is conscious only of relief and pleasant contrast, but when the novelty of that contrast wears off other contrasts less pleasant are forced upon his attention, and perhaps he ends by thinking that smoky chimneys are a less evil than bad drainage. At present you can only think of the confusion and complexities of Anglicanism and of the comparative simplicity and clearness of the Roman Church, with its central monarchic government and consequent uniformity of confession and observance—all of which is good in its way, yet might be purchased by you at too great a cost. What makes it very hard for me to advise you is that, though I am convinced that to be in communion with Rome is one of the normal conditions of historical Christianity, and under certain circumstances a grave obligation, yet I do not believe one atom in the ordinary controversial quibbles about the Petrine texts, etc. ; and I feel that the reasons which weigh with you are just those which ought not to weigh with you. I believe the Roman Communion to be the authentic heir of the group of disciples who followed Christ. I hold every schism to have been a sin on the part of those who were driven out, and of those who drove them out ; that the English Church is a schism for which Rome was nine-tenths and England one-tenth responsible, and that the offending parties are bound by all means to heal the breach.

But if occasionally I have seen souls transplanted from English to Roman soil flourish where before they had languished, yet in most cases there seems little, if any, observable difference in their spiritual life, while in not a few a sort of sterilisation seems to result.

And this is the only thing worth considering ; for I assume you are not in search of a perfect theology or theory of Christianity, but of life and spiritual

vigour and perfection. Are you sure that what steri-
lises your spiritual life at present is not just an attach-
ment to certain ways and means of religion which are
quite separate from the one thing needful ? Do you
not know that generations of Christians, saints, and
martyrs lived and died without directly invoking the
saints ? and that the greater mystics even tended
to the disuse of such methods as they got nearer to
God ; nay, that the Sacred Humanity itself ceased
at last to be a help to them ? If it is one of the graces
of our Church to offer a richer variety of ways and
means than yours, it may also be a danger and a snare
if we come to rely on them as necessary, or to encumber
ourselves with an overabundance of them.

However, I do not know you well enough to say.
But if you told me that your peace of soul was radically
and. permanently shaken in the English Church and
in Christianity, and that you were convinced that
you could find God and peace only in Islam and in
communion with the Caliph, I would only say as now :
Look to your intentions, to your motives. " *Mutatio
locuum multos fefellit.*" " The desire of a change of
place," says à Kempis, " has deceived many a one."
It matters less *where* we are than *what* we are. " Wherever you go," says he, " you carry yourself along
with you," and, I might add, you carry God along with
you. You can be very Roman and very uncatholic ;
very Catholic and very unchristian. To be a Christian
by hook or by crook, that is the great end. Aim at
that alone and the others will come in just so far as
for you they are necessary means. But if you aim at
being Roman in the sectarian sense, you may easily
forget to be Christian.

If, however, your peace is really broken past mending,
then I think you should consult Father Maturin, who
knows you personally.

NOTE

Sister B. entered the Catholic Church years afterwards, having, as she wrote to a friend, satisfied herself that the conditions Father Tyrrell laid down were fulfilled.

To a Religious, troubled in his vocation

April 4, 1902.

None knows better than the undersigned the temptation to take the wings of a dove and fly away to the desert and be at rest. Nay, have I not made a certain compromise with it ? The Yorkshire shepherdesses are, however, too beefy to form a suitable complement of the tableau, and so I have taken Jack to my bosom as a *pis aller*. My cold reason tells me that this longing for simpler conditions, when life has grown complicated beyond endurance, enfolds an illusion similar to that which makes us often wish to be children again. But a man *cannot* when he is forty crawl back into his mother's womb ; its limitations would stifle him as soon as the first novelty of the situation had worn off. " Tessa " would reek of garlic and grease ; and would not have the wit to hold her tongue and simply look pretty and affectionate. And then, the Tessa *passée* ! No, if your convictions, or unconvictions, were not in the way, I should like to see you in a quiet little Anglican parsonage in the South of England with an intelligent, companionable wife, and two children guaranteed to remain aged six and eight for the rest of their lives ; and under a cultivated latitudinarian bishop who would allow you to call yourself a Catholic *in spe*, as a position quite within the limits of the capacious Anglican formularies.

To Mrs. S.

On reading your letter more than a month ago, I put it aside in hopes that I might have some clearer answer to give you ; but I see no reason now for longer delay. In every generation there are those who in some respects belong to the next but one, as well as others who belong to the last but one. Were you of the latter, instead of the former category, you might easily find all you need in the Roman communion. As it is you are of a large class of homeless souls, for whom the future may provide an asylum when it is too late. Had you been born and bred a Roman Catholic it might have been possible to show you a way of reading your religion which would have satisfied you as to your duty of adhesion ; but, as it is, it would, I think, involve too complete a rearrangement (and even restocking) of your religious ideas to be consistent with that sense of firm conviction which alone would justify your submission to the Church's claims. And though the reserves under which alone you ought to make such a submission are in themselves right, and would be approved by the great saints of the past, who knew that the Church was a means and not an end, yet, as things are at present, ninety-nine priests out of a hundred, and the whole Roman Curia to boot, would hold you no true Catholic were you to join us in the only spirit that I could justify.

The wish to be carried in another's arms, to be led blindfold, to be delivered from one's inevitable responsibilities, is more natural than supernatural ; and it is one on which a priesthood of any kind is naturally tempted to trade. And so far the aids offered by the Church are easily and constantly abused. Here the instincts which reveal themselves in your letter seem to me entirely right. It is only perhaps in your underestimate of the solidarity of all human souls in their relation to God, in your religious "individualism," that I think you are not quite true to the Christian spirit.

Practically I think you can consider yourself as belonging in spirit to the Church ; as excluded from its outward communion by circumstances for which none of us are directly responsible ; as a Catholic in hope and desire. This you have been from childhood. I do not believe it possible that you should suffer any *real* spiritual loss through no fault of your own ; though you may forfeit certain easements and comforts enjoyed by those who take their religion passively from other hands.

After all, " one thing is needful," and one only ; and the rest can take care of itself. If outward communion with the Roman Church is necessary for your life of prayer God will make it very much plainer to you than any discussion of doctrinal differences could ever do.

Note.—This lady, also, became a Roman Catholic in after-years.

V

LITERARY

To Professor Edmund G. Gardner

March 28, 1902.

MY DEAR GARDNER,

I am so dissatisfied with what I have said about *Desiderio* for the *Monthly Register*—writing, as I did, at short notice and pressed with many bothers about a book of my own which the Cardinal has just sat upon with all the weight of his elephantine personality—that I write to say how much more cordially I am in sympathy with its inspiring motives than was possible to say in a suspected ecclesiastical review. One feels more and more—*di quanto mal fu madre quella dote*—that mill-stone that Constantine is supposed to have tied round the Church's neck ; and how superficial is the diagnosis that attributes the decay of religion to " Free-Masons " and liberals and atheists, without inquiring into the cause of this cause, and finding it in the Churchmen who have slain their Church. At the present moment every movement of Rome is determined with reference to the temporal power, and the interests of real religion are almost scoffed at, except so far as piety makes a convenient cloak for policy. Witness the disgraceful *volte-face* as to the Catholic democratic movement. Leo XIII has steadily betrayed every hope that he raised, smiling at liberty to approach and meeting her with a blow in the teeth,

time after time. Whence are we to look for the Veltro ?
I may be wrong, but I feel a thunderstorm gathering
in the atmosphere, and predict the downfall of political Catholicism. Let us hope that a Christian Catholicism may rise from its honoured ashes.

Your book fanned much smouldering indignation
into flame. Little wonder, as I have said, that men
turned back to Nature in search of something true and
real, and struck against a religion that was either
shamelessly dead in worldliness and formalism, or
else—as in the hands of fanatical reformers—sourly
puritanical and hostile to that full Christianity which
appeals to sense and spirit alike in due proportions.
Of course your book will be called " shocking " by
many well meaning Catholics, who will fail to seize
its true drift. I have lent it to two or three good
judges who are unanimous as to its merits. As a
novel it seems to me to move up to its culmination
very easily and naturally ; and the tragedy is a most
happy conception. What have other critics said,
I wonder ? I am too much out of the run to know.

To the Hon. Emily Lawless

RICHMOND, YORKS,
August 25, 1904.

I am sure I should have written sooner but for fear
of disappointing your hope of getting back better
nursery rhymes than your own. My muse is a very
erratic and dry old cow and only favours me by fits
and starts, principally at seasons of tranquillity and
idleness. As there is no sign of a yield, I will defer
no longer to thank you very sincerely for *Maria Edgworth*, about whom I was shamefully ignorant till
you instructed me. I had known her through Lock-
hart's *Life of Scott*; and when I came here (1900) I

found her *Tales of Fashionable Life*, which puzzled me
very much by their mingling of life and death, nature
and convention, attraction and repulsion. But your
book explains it all. It was precisely the Sandford
and Merton spirit that gorgonised me—what she had
derived from her impossible father and his more impossible friend, Mr. Day. Surely the religion and morality
of the eighteenth century was just as false and hollow-
hearted as its irreligion and immorality ; and we owe
an infinite debt of gratitude to the revolution that
drew us back to Nature and taught us to, at least,
profess a horror of cant. As far as good-will is concerned, I suppose both Day and Edgworth were really
good men, and that part of their goodness was their
profound deference to the conventional code of thought,
speech and conduct of their *milieu*, which simply hid
souls from one another, like a uniform mask hiding
men's faces and rendering them indistinguishable.
So masked, souls could not know one another, nor
know even themselves ; and the result was a horrible
untruthfulness of life and heart. Men *could* not say
what they meant or were, but only what they *ought*
to mean and be. Only the blacklegs and scapegraces
could afford to be true and natural. I think, for
all our faults, we are infinitely more real and truthful
to-day. Thus only, or in some such way, could I
conceive that there is any salvation for the Sandford-
Day-Edgworth type, if Christ is to be the criterion
and judge ; they were pharisees, not of their own free
choice, but in virtue of the pressure of a pharisaic
Time-Spirit. Miss Edgworth's was a stronger individuality, which to a great extent resisted that pressure
successfully. Do you not notice its influence even in
Scott's heroes and heroines, with their dead marble
perfection and monotony ? Whence the anomaly, that
they simply furnish what Patmore calls " the Point of

Rest," or the line of mediocrity by divergence from which his other characters gain life and interest. I found your book so full of life that I did not read it very critically. Perhaps the end seemed a little hurried ; but that may be only because you prepared me to think so.

As to the "Nothing-Matters" philosophy, I fear it breaks down on closer observation. We really mean Nothing compared with just that Something which, at the time, we feel, does matter profoundly. It should rather be : "Nothing *else* matters." When I am ill I feel nothing matters—*except* health ; when well, nothing *except* work, etc. When we say "*all* is vanity*" (as Mr. Stiggins said in reference to taps) we make a reserve in regard to some particular vanity like pineapple rum, warm, with a slice of lemon in it. In fact Stoicism is the most ghastly of our many philosophical grimaces ; the most painful to sustain. When God slaps us we should scream. At all events, to say "I don't care a button" is impertinent. I am not *quite* sure about Mr. Peter Price's attitude ; it may be a little too independent and almost defiant. Things went from bad to worse with the job, till he dropped his stoicism and began cursing and swearing. He should have begun when the oxen and asses were stolen. But he said "Nothing matters" and simply did without them ; and so the powers had to pinch harder and harder to make him scream. We must take things as they are to *us*, there and then, with our present strength and light ; and not as they might be to God or to angels, or to ourselves in wholly altered conditions. Of course there is a true sense in which "Nothing Matters" might be affixed as a legend on the Crucifix ; but there again the great "except" is quite obvious. I fall back more and more on à Kempis as (with all its serious limitations of Stoicism

18

and Buddhism) the wisest reading of life and the best comforter in trouble. I *think* you have seen my Preface to it ; but in case not I send you an offprint.

I dare not ask if you are better in health ; I can only hope that you are not worse, that you are gradually getting reconciled to these new limitations.

To the Same

RICHMOND, YORKS,
March 17, 1905.

It is a good day to write to you on ; though I am not wearing the shamrock this year, being somewhat out of temper with my native land—the Peer Gynt among peoples. I am shocked to see that January 25 is the date of your letter ; but your script is so like one of my voluminous correspondents that by accident I bundled your letter away with his and only found it this morning. I am taking for granted that you are still in Park Street listening from your sofa to the brisk flow of life outside, and feeling perhaps a little bit out of it all—a feeling that I know very well, though for very different reasons. I wish one's desire for life and action would vary directly, and not inversely as so often happens, with one's opportunities and health. No rheumatism is more irritating than the sense of what one might be doing during the waste days and weeks when one's head is muddled or one's hands are tied. My chief gravamen against convents is the misery of women who do not know what really ails them is the pent-up energy of head, heart, and hand, and the attempt to build up a full life out of trifles and straws and scruples. How much better for such to be thrown into the arena of this " wicked " world to struggle with sin and sorrow and trouble, even were they to fall seven times a day. All are not like that ; there are prayerful, quiet, docile natures whom the convent shelters and suits ; but the spoilt lives are too many. Schopenhauer makes pain more bearable than ennui ; hell more bearable than heaven ; and of course he is right, as he means it. But ennui is just that sense of suppressed vitality which is unknown to the dead or the dead-alive. A toad is never *ennuyé*. However the world of books is open to us, even if the book of the world is stiff-backed ; and travelling there is cheap and easy. I have just put down Oscar Wilde's *De Profundis*, which I read twice on end in one day. The beauty of style fairly swept me off my legs. Though that is by no means all ; for as a human document it is intensely interesting and illuminating. Though it is the work of a man who has lived for artistic expression and is a *poseur*, and to whom his own life with all its lights and shades must necessarily be a theme of artistic contemplation and treatment, yet, in spite of some of the reviewers, I think there is sincerity here ; that disgrace and sorrow sunk him below the glittering surface of life to the solid, under-lying reality. It may well be that had society forgiven and received him again he would have risen like a cork to the surface, and bobbed about as before for the rest of his days ; but as a fact he seems to have had the grace of dying " real." The great difficulty for the artistic, and especially the dramatic, temperament is that of " coming to itself " (as the Gospel says). It is so enamoured of rôles and parts and poses that the real personality is lost and forgotten altogether. I made an excursion to Bookland with Sir Alfred Lyall on the tracks of Lord Dufferin—a most pleasing personality, an idealised Irishman in many respects, whom I have known only through his vivid and witty *Letters from High Latitudes*. Though the lines lay for him in very pleasant places, and success was as his shadow, yet in no sense does he irritate.

Perhaps it was some sort of natural humility and detachment from his success ; but I think it is partly the wonderful bravery of the man, which makes one confident that he would have borne trouble well and cheerfully ; whereas, I feel, C. would have run away ; or, if caught, would have lost his temper.

I am greatly pleased that you sympathise with my Preface to à Kempis. With all his faults I love him still, and he lives in my waistcoat pocket year after year. The Fioretti delight me, as little children at play delight me ; but they cannot help me in the world of which St. Francis knew nothing.

I have just made your namesake, who is here, read *Grania*. It is one of my test-books for the stability of friendship. He has borne the test well and is satisfactorily enthusiastic. I do hope your pains stop gnawing at intervals, and that it is not always dead Lent with you with never a Laetare-Sunday stuck in.

To Laurence Housman

November 28, 1904.

MY DEAR SAINT,

First of all in reply to yours of December 9. I am quite in agreement with what you say in the beginning ; though less satisfied with your concluding remark, which, however, throws some light upon what goes between. Yes, I think so ; though under the reserves you refer to. But would it not be better to wait before deciding one way or the other ? Still, there is much in what you say at the foot of p. 2, which, taken in connection with your parenthesis on p. 27, rather bears out my contention.

And now for *Easter Dawn ;* the idea is excellent and even " orthodox," save that you attach more value to the reality symbolised by the bodily resurrection than to the symbol—which is always a note of heresy. The letter quickeneth, the spirit profiteth nothing. Don't you sometimes trust your sense to an inadequate vehicle ? How many will miss the point of " where His feet had been " ! and will wonder : Why not where His head, or His form ? Of course, this is an argument for writing prose and giving up poetry altogether. As a professional " proser " my whole energy goes in eliminating ambiguities, which are, of course, the *materia ex qua* of the poet.

" With eyes dim—think the world void, not finding Him," seems to want a tonic. As to Mark Rutherford, we are not so divergent as you think. What I admire is the awful, depressing truthfulness of the man ; his limpid sincerity of style ; his Wordsworthian eye for the significance of the seemingly paltry and mediocre ; his ruthless self-confession. That itself is a species of greatness compatible with much smallness and squalor. Nay, I sometimes think with Pascal it is man's only greatness to feel his meanness, and not merely his misery. Byron poses as an aggrieved archangel and is really bursting with a sense of his spiritual importance. Still, I don't feel *sure* I should like M. R. personally any more than I should like Hardy, whose views of life are equally depressing and un-inspiring, yet true with that kind of one-sided truth-fulness which is all we can manage, and which makes it necessary to hear all sides of life in turn, and to take no one aspect, however truthfully drawn, as adequate. It is the singular merit of M. R. to confess that his views lead to nothing, either practical or speculative· " George Lucy " (*Pages from a Journal*, p. 200) has simply failed to find any clear meaning in life, and says so frankly and honestly. I dare say this is what fetches F. B. if she could explain herself. So pleased that Shad is back on the sleepers. It is the comfort-ablest part, which shall not be taken from him.

To the Same

DEAR LAMB,

It is good of you to seek the lost shepherd in his beery wanderings. He means well, but can't live up to the part. He will be in London for a few days to-morrow, and could drop in on Thursday, about 3.30 or 4, to tea and such-like. If that won't do he might shift it on to Friday, or back to Wednesday, if you drop a card to " The Lost Shepherd, 16 Old Town, Clapham, S.W."

I have meditated on Langtsi old and young and Mrs.[1] Perhaps the motif should not have been executed on a china plate. The public translates slowly, and all gospels should be in the vernacular. But we'll talk of that. Woe to the Tikipins who see more than their masters, and seduce the Mee-mees from their masters' sons ; and blessed are they who work on the flat and have no perspective. So much I feel ; but your three strings to your moral bow must be untwisted for me.

To V.

Before it grows dim in memory I will write down my impressions of the *Garden of Allah.* Androvsky's confession, as a fine piece of psychological analysis, is perhaps the only thing that interested me profoundly in the book ; and then, the subsequent struggle ending in his return. But I think the book is profoundly mischievous, appealing strongly, as it does, to popular sentimentality and romanticism in favour of a false and fanatical asceticism. Every valid vow must be *de bono meliori ;* it must not exclude any better alter-

[1] *The Chinese Lantern.* Laurence Housman.

native. In the young monk's revolt against the
narrowness and unreality of Trappist life, in favour
of the fulness of the possibilities of a natural life in
the school of humanity ; in his feeling that with all
its risks and temptations this latter is a divine, as
the former is a human, institution, there is an instinctive truth and justice which the author ought
to have acknowledged, for, indeed, what he treats
as a fallacy and temptation (p. 501) is perfectly true ;
that the asceticism of the glass-eating dervishes and of
the Trappists are one *in principle*, and are equally
strange to the spirit of Christ. It is a superstitious
conception of a vow that regards it as irrevocable,
absolutely, simply *qua* vow. Had A. vowed to eat
glass all his days, would Hichens have thought it
necessary to bring him back from a lapse into a saner
dietary to a régime of empty bottles ? The finale
is simply a triumph of fanaticism on both sides. Had
Boris and Domini been a pair of healthy-minded
Protestants they might have saved their souls and
found more profitable forms of sacrifice in other
directions. Here again we meet another inveterate
fallacy of piety, both Protestant and Catholic : the
notion that the love of God is on the same plane with
creature love, and that it can enter into competition
with it, as having a definite and exclusive object.
It has an object *immanent* in, and confused with that
of every created love ; and simply imparts a quality
to this latter, but is not another love alongside of it,
as Neo-platonists have taught us. The monastic idea
of loving God in Himself, and out of creatures, leads
to mere image-worship, though the images are mental.
This is an instance of the implicit Deism (versus
Immanental Theism) that runs through all religious
thought ; which makes us look on faith as on the plane
of knowledge and therefore capable of conflict ; or

which places spiritual jurisdiction on the same plane
and in competition with temporal jurisdiction. The
book is one that will please Roman Catholics very
much ; but those who look further will only feel what
a very terrible thing religion may be when it is mingled
with fanaticism. Count Anteoni is rather an old
donkey, and perhaps Islam was a better faith than
he deserved. I could not but contrast the ease with
which Hardy makes Egdon Heath into a personality
with Hichens's elaborate and incessant endeavours to
galvanise the desert into life. The desert-people,
on the other hand, seem more real and convincing.

To Miss Dora Williams

RICHMOND, YORKS,
November 19, 1904.

I have got down to W. in my correspondence, and,
as D. W. comes before W. W., I must reply to you before
" your brother." How methodical ! you will say.
Yes, I have started the system on the spot and will
stick to it for at least a day. " Your brother," to
emphasise my respect for your admonition about the
use of Christian names—about which I have carefully
examined my conscience : at first, with an impression
that I followed no rule at all in the matter; later,
a law loomed through the chaos of phenomena—a
law that makes me instinctively speak to people in
their own language. He who is Willie for you, is
Willie for me *to you*. For me *to myself* I find he and
all acquaintances are simply nameless—they are what
they are, according to their essential quiddity ; naked
and nameless. Familiarity is to me as hair-oil or
treacle ; but a conscious primness often makes me
studiously free and easy. All of which is much ado
about nothing and does not matter in the least. Much
more serious are your night thoughts and astral

revelations. As, however, they are given not as what
you think, but as what you think our friend L. would
think, to him I address myself.

"My dear L.—if you will pardon the seeming
familiarity—what the devil do you mean ? Have
I not as your spiritual director been warning you
these several years against the perils of a versatility
so rapid and manifold that it has never allowed any
one of these flitting ghosts of personality to fix itself
and grow strong and substantial and exercise rule
over the sheol of shades and bring them into subjection
to itself. The least specialised play-actor who can
jump into any clothes and get up any part goes home
and puts on fustian and is himself again, and holds
his stage-life no more than his dream-life ; but you,
my friend, go to bed in tights and never twice in the
like costume. If you sleep it is with one eye open and
fixed on a mirror, and with great admiration of the
slumberer's pose. Have I not likened you even to
the Prodigal who pawned his overcoat and then came
to his coat, thence to his waistcoat, to his shirt, to his
undervest, and at last ' he came to himself ' ? And
have I not prayed that your last end might be like his ?
And does it become you now to rush forth from your
glass tenement with a handful of stones and set to work
to pelt my windows ? If I am a father, where is my
honour ? I suppose I must be grateful that you seek
my eternal origin in so roomy, so brilliant a world
as Sirius, and am willing to believe you did not reflect
on its incandescence or wish to draw a moral therefrom.
It is on the ' irresponsible ' manner of its twinkling,
its frequent changes of colour, that you lay stress as
pointing it out as the stage of our former acquaintance.
I understand you to say that the majority of its
denizens was made up of those *me-s* into which my
terrestrial self might be resolved by some sort of

atomic psycho-chemic analysis ; the remainder being,
no doubt, a considerable multitude of your own *you-s*
and the *they-s* of the remainder of our friends. Heaven
forbid I should misunderstand you—but such, I fancy,
is the nature of your feeble *Tu quoque* argument.
And then you transfer to me the troubles and gropings
of your own lost, miserable soul, vainly seeking its own
identity, long forfeited and laid asleep upstairs in the
cradle of oblivion, its innocent thumb in its innocent
mouth. My dear L. (or disciple—for this is a most
intimate moment of our spiritual relationship), do
you not know the difference between mobocracy
and democracy ; between the crowd and the people ;
between unorganised and organised multiplicity—
which latter is the highest kind of unity, compared
with which the unity of simplicity is an empty symbol ?
Given a steady governing end, purpose, interest, the
bigger the multitude the better ; take this away, the
bigger the worse. A spirit as will is characterised
by the end ; by a common end that multitude of
spirits which every man is, potentially, infused into
one. None can tell from without whether this unity
exists or no. The poorly equipped often seem simpler
and more knit together in their lives ; but surely it is
the simplicity of poverty and nothing more. It is
easy to keep a room tidy whose furniture is a three-
legged stool and no more. No, my dear friend,
there is no suck-a-thumb Hermes upstairs ; but
there are ten thousand devils downstairs who, left
to themselves, might no doubt play the devil in a quite
unpredictable variety of ways, but are at present
very serviceable coal-carriers, stokers, bottle-washers
to their prince, be his name Beelzebub, or what you
will—that is for you to find out. No doubt he is frail
and mortal for all his immateriality ; he nods at
times with Homer ; or slumbers outright for days at

a time—and then there are ructions below stairs.
But Lord help them when he is on his legs again!

" Try again, L., and perhaps you'll shy straighter
next time.   As it is, my windows are unbroken.
I can see out, you cannot see in.   Get your own mended,
and you will enjoy a like advantage.

"Ever your fond Pa."

Such in tone and substance would be my reply.
Yet maybe that a somewhat guilty conscience has led
me to accuse by excusing myself.

Now I must write to E. W., F. W., G. W., etc., etc.,
and so your brother may hear from me in a few days.

To the Same

RICHMOND, YORKS,
December 31, 1904.

At last I am in a condition to report on the
Phœnix [1] and *Die Bestimmung*.   It is hard to combine
them in one review, so I will take them in order.
" The *Phœnix* beguiled me and I did eat " ; that is
to say, I read on greedily to the end,. to the great damage
of my other duties.   And that, with a childlike un-
questioning faith which is highly complimentary to
the author's equally childlike and convincing mendacity.   The illusion is of course due to the smooth
continuity between the mythical and real ; and to
the wonderful reality and truthfulness of this latter.
But the personality of the Phœnix, with its curious
blend of vanity and amiability, is very fascinating,
and so familiar that I must have met the same soul
either in life or in fiction or in prenatal life.   The
situations are most unique—the cats, the cow and the
burglar in the basement parlour, and the solemn

[1] *The Phœnix and the Carpet*, E. Nesbit.

Te Deum in the Insurance Office, being perhaps the most unexpected. A world where such things are possible would be worth living for. It is the growing sense of determinism, of the unlikelihood of " something turning up," that destroys our *joie de vivre*, our Micawberish buoyancy. If the All is perfectly rational then I must pray with Laurence Housman :

> Give darkness that it may be dark
> And heal my eyes of light,

and to be delivered from the ennui of the so-called Beatific Vision.

Die Bestimmung des Gelehrten is certainly very inspiring, very eloquent, very profound. I dare say that in his fourth lecture he is carried away by his zeal and inclined to make the Gelehrter a saint, apostle, priest, sage, ruler, and everything ; and thus to overpass what belongs to him strictly *as such*, and not merely by a sort of congruity or fitness. Thus I do not think that a good life and example is required of the *Gelehrter* in any *special* sense. Aristotle's Ethics are not more or less fruitful by reason of his personal conduct. All I would say is that an immoral man destroys a certain moral taste which is as needful for moral judgment as the palate is for tea-judging. But the work of the G., as such, stops with the sound moral judgment.[1] In our sceptical, dilettante attitude in regard to learning and philosophy, the earnestness and unshaken faith of Fichte seems to belong to the days of anthropocentric vanity, when the divine dignity and destiny of man were unquestioned axioms ; and when we hear that he was horribly " ragged " by his pupils we cannot but suspect he must have been lacking in that saving humour which prevents a man taking anything, least of all himself, too seriously ; and this,

[1] *Life*, vol. ii. p. 10.

not out of levity, but as the fruit of an outlook into those immensities in which our greatest philosophers seem considerably less than chirping grasshoppers.

This is surely what we feel and love in our Shakespeare ; what we miss in Dante. One point in the second lecture dislikes me, if I understand it right; He implies that the unattainable ideal is *absolutely,* not relatively, the same perfection for all men. But he rightly admits that individuals are radically different in disposition. Hence *I* should say the goal of society is the perfection of each according to his individuality ; not a uniformity of result, but the unity of a harmony or organism. Laws, as such, suppose roughly that men are alike—which they are not. The true development of society means the gradual abandonment of the rough expedient of laws in the measure that each becomes a law to himself ; no two according to the same pattern. This, I think, is *de facto* the course of social progress—away from militarism which droves men like sheep and aims at perfect uniformity. But I dare say this is what F. means, unless he was dominated; by scholastic survivals.

With best New Year wishes to you and to him you call Will.

To the Same

January 12, 1905.

You are a most letter-provoking correspondent ; your tune always ends on *Si* or *Re*, so that I am forced to supply the *Do* or go mad.

Those lines [1] imply the Cat-theory of the universe which must be reckoned with, *sc.* the mixture of good and evil, kindness and cruelty, in the world (prescinding from the human soul) is far better explained by an

---

[1] Reference to a work by Mr. Laurence Housman.

all-governing Cat than by Paley's "good man in the skies"; for puss allows the mouse little runs and counterfeit liberties and escapes; and smiles at his gambols and dandles him lovingly in velvet paws, but all with a view to a final grab and crunch. It is easier to suppose that an evil agency would do good for evil ends than that a good agency would do evil for good ends—so that, if we leave inward human goodness out of account, as the old apologists so often did, the argument from design makes for the Cat-theory. Now it were better in that case that the mouse should not know the truth, but should live in merciful ignorance.

(2) I do not mean the space and time immensities, but the spiritual immensities; the immensity of the knowable compared with the known. When I think of the difference between the savage and the cultured outlook; between that of earlier and later times; when I think what the privation of a single sense like sight would have meant for human experience and understanding; or what the addition of another sense would mean; and how *infinitely* unlikely it is that we exhaust the possible kinds of sense-experience, I cannot resist the deep conviction that our physical insignificance in the universe of space and time is the analogue of our mental and moral insignificance. And this is not *agnosticism*, because the difference between zero and the most infinitesimal *something* is again infinite. Compared with microbes we are very great and very wise, but compared with what stretches out beyond we are practically as minute as they. It is a truth we ought not to dwell on; for self-respect is a *sine qua non* of moral effort, and the conclusion that "nothing matters" is a very false one, though it *seems* to follow from the truth. The microbe matters much; *capilli capitis vestri omnes numerati*

sunt. Fichte's earnestness is altogether good, so it be just touched with the sense of those heights and depths, which we must forget if we would walk straight without reeling.

I am delighted that you differ and criticise ; else I should feel responsible and write you articles and essays instead of silly letters. As to your PS., the reason is—but I really must stop.

To the Same

RICHMOND, YORKS,
January 30, 1905.

My will, which Schopenhauer informs me is only another aspect of my body, has been somewhat indisposed in consequence of recent over-exertions of one kind or another, and responds but faintly to reason and duty, as the tail of a chrysalis to the poke of an inquisitive finger. The reason why (I seem to be always defending myself at the bar of your most unauthorised tribunal) I did not enquire in my last, and do not enquire in my present, how you are, is simply that such a question refers to the present moment of enquiry and has no sense except through a telephone. Your answer arrives a week or so later to tell me how you were, not when I asked, not when I receive your reply, but at a moment that has ceased to be interesting. You may be quite ill when I am reading your assurance that you are quite well. However, to satisfy you, I hereby enquire how you will be at the moment this reaches and shall have been previous to my receipt of your answer.

(2) I still hold to the Cat-theory *in the form stated,* sc. as the best hypothesis to explain all experience *exclusive* of that of human goodness ; i.e. if we cut off the head of the whole body of experience, that (and not Paley's Good Man) is what the acephalous corpse

suggests. Indeed, we have there the foundation of that evil principle which has been personified as the devil. Not that the determinism of Nature is really outside and apart from God, but that it is so relatively to our necessary way of taking things, which puts a sort of opposition between the head and body of our experience. You really agree with me when you say that love " can't reveal himself to reason, only to the heart of man." Quite so ; reason shows me a cat and a snake ; Psyche's sisters were partly right. I don't deny the heart-view ; but you mustn't deny the head-view—though I should prefer to contrast the views as complete and partial. Yesterday I read with delight *Zuletzt muss er siegen ; denn ihm sind wir schon durch die Geburt anheimgefallen, und er spielt nur eine Weile mit seiner Beute, bevor er sie verschlingt.* There is my dear old puss again, the ruthless " wheel of things," from whose claws and teeth we are all seeking deliverance if we are wise, whether with the wisdom of Buddha and à Kempis or with that of Christ. The latter is, I think, the greater faith, both as nobler and as further removed from superficial plausibility. I wish you would read Eucken's *Wahrheitsgehalt der Religion.* He is righter than anyone I know. I was very sorry to hear that " Will " had been so seedy when you wrote last. Aren't you both coming up here soon ?

To the Same

RICHMOND, YORKS,
March 6, 1905.

As a translation the *Trip to the Moon* reads very smooth and pleasant, and is, I should think, a difficult feat from the nature of the matter.

But as for Lucian's part of the performance, I cannot

but wonder whether we should think much of it if we did not know its antiquity and classical authority. Is it a patch on Jules Verne's *Journey to the Centre of the Earth*, etc. ? I feel sure you could have done something much better and more pointed with a like theme. I am weary of the classical tyranny. On re-reading the *Tale of a Tub* lately I asked my inmost conscience, and it pronounced it, not merely coarse (that is nothing) but laborious and awkward ; so utterly wanting in Sterne's finesse and Rabelaisian frolicsomeness and buffoonery. There is clever nonsense and stupid nonsense ; and of the latter there is a good deal in the *Tale ;* far less in *Gulliver.* Clever nonsense is wisdom walking on its head for diversion. Stupid nonsense is folly on its feet, or wisdom reeling drunk. *Roma locuta est ; causa finita.*

Thanks for the garlic. We agree in one sense—in the wearing of the green ; but we differ in another ; for the shamrock is not so odoriferous, and is altogether more modest. The Sassenach may yet tremble before our united forces.

So glad you didn't like my letter to Mrs. Stracy. You dread the grim side of truth and hug your Fichte, and call it faith. Give me the faith of the mouse who dies squeaking out : " O lovely Pussy ! O Pussy, my love ! What a lovely Pussy you are, you are ; what a lovely Pussy you are ! "

To the Same

March 15, 1905.

Please justify the following logical sequence ; " A. B. fails to admire the humour of Lucian's *Trip to the Moon, ergo* A. B. is opposed to compulsory Greek at the University of Cambridge." Or again : " *ergo* he fails to admire Lucian altogether and Aristophanes as well." Or this sequence : " A. B. protests against

19

the tyranny of the classics, *ergo* he protests against the classics, *ergo* he would abolish Greek at the Universities." What about the equation " Classics = Latin and Greek " ? Is not the *Tale of a Tub* a classic ? Is the Greek Test or the Latin Vulgate a classic ? If one's humour is the flower of one's philosophy, one's reason is the root. What a cleavage, then, is this from top to toe of the fair tree of friendship !

Let Mrs. Stracy have the *Wahrheitsgehalt* so long as I get it back again. If Eucken or anyone else were to me such an idol as Fichte is to you I would help to stone him with my own hands. Absolute detachment is the first requisite of an untroubled eye for truth. For lack of this, and not for any imagined mental infirmity, it is easier for a camel to enter the Kingdom of Heaven than for a woman to pass through the eye of truth's needle. They must always " sit under " somebody, and on the rock of this fact all Churches are built.

In reply to your question as to what I am writing now, I reply, Absolutely nothing. I am much interested in Volkelt's theory of *Erkentnisstheorestischvoraussetzunglosigkeit,* and for the time being nothing seems to me of any consequence whatever. If there is an act of blind faith involved in the simplest *Urteil,* where are we or where aren't we ? But you have no soul for these profoundly actual and living questions of the hour. Talking of profundities, have you read *De Profundis* ? I would rather have written that book than the Epistle to the Romans or *Alice's Adventures.* Perhaps if I sink as low I may rise as high ; or perhaps one needs to be in gaol to stand outside life and see it in its true perspective ; cf. the Tinker of Bedford, Silvio Pellico, Ignatius Loyola, etc. One needs social and spiritual as well as bodily isolation.

It was not an Irishman, but a father of the Christian

Church, who retailed the traditional belief about the
asp. I read it first in Rodriguez' *Christian Perfection*.
It may very well be true, especially when we know that
the scorpion combs its back hair with its tail-prong—
ex uno disce omnes.

NOTE

By special request this article, which appeared in
The Weekly Register of May 27, 1899, has taken a place
amongst the correspondence. It was one of an invited series on "Books that have influenced Me,"
to which various writers contributed. I may add
that it was the only book of its class selected—other
writers making their choice more gravely and con-
ventionally.

BOOKS THAT HAVE INFLUENCED ME

Alice's Adventures in Wonderland.
Through the Looking Glass.

It may, I think, be maintained in general that the
books we first read have most to do with the shaping
of our minds; that what is sown earlier sinks deeper,
and spreads its fibres further through our life; that
those influences which have been acting on us longer,
through the quiet accumulation of their fruits year
by year, have contributed more to our personality than
those to which we were afterwards subjected. What
enters the stream of life at its sources—be it sweet
or bitter—usually determines its character more
fundamentally than what later tributaries may bring
to it.

Among these books of childhood there is one—or
rather two, which may be regarded as one—whose
preponderating influence I feel bound to acknowledge,

not only as having made at the time a singularly definite and sensible impression still fresh in memory ; not only as one whose subsequent influence I can trace with tolerable clearness, as a silver thread in a silken skein ; but also as one the potency of whose spell has waxed rather than waned under the searching ordeal of reperusal and of oft-renewed familiarity— a book which I have never outgrown or left behind ; which has ever some freshness to offer, untasted before.

So it is with our study of Nature, and of those great art-works which make Nature their theme—the object ever exceeds our desire, enlarges it, and still exceeds it. It is because Shakespeare and George Eliot interest us, not in what is peculiar and accidental to human nature in this or that individual, but in human nature itself as we recognise it in ourselves and in all men, that they mean more for us in the measure that we know more of our common humanity. There is a certain kind of noble " popularity " which attaches to these time-defying works, appealing, as they do, not to the coat-regarding multitudes, but to every inward reflective mind that finds in mankind a central object of observant interest and kindly affection. Such is the " popularity," strangely wide-spread and per- sistent, of *Alice's Adventures*—a book whose life-long influence upon my own and many another mind it would be untruthful and ungrateful to disown.

Truly, as there are numbers whose admiration for Shakespeare is a conscious or unconscious affectation, an effect of blind imitativeness or of obsequious hypocrisy, so some considerable amount of the en- thusiasmi for *Alice* is strained and insincere, like that of the court-officers for the Emperor of China's invisible clothes. The fear of being proved dull or obtuse will force many to see, or seem to see, what they cannot see, nay, what is not there to be seen.

Minds, narrowly utilitarian, unsuspicious of the deep use of things useless, and of the sense of nonsense, are to be found at times labouring out some solemn exposition of what they could only pardon as a cunning allegory ; searching for some solid substratum of congenial dulness underlying all this beaded froth of fancy ; hunting after and chuckling over some dismal political, philosophical, or mathematical allusion, undreamt of by the writer ; distinguishing the mystical, the allegorical, the anagogical, from the disreputable literal sense. That there should be just no meaning whatever, no more design than in the figures we find in the glowing embers, no more Dutch-gardening than in the tangle and undergrowth of Nature's forests, is a conception quite alien to such gravely constituted minds, whose providential function in human society is analogous to that of the straw-packing in a case of champagne-bottles. Whatever their capabilities might have been originally, for them *Alice* has come into the world too late ; the evil she might have forestalled has established itself finally ; the cartilages of perennial youthfulness have ossified irretrievably, and by nothing short of a miracle can those who have once allowed themselves to grow old return again to the open-minded innocence and receptivity that preceded the closing of the cranial suture.

It is not, however, precisely as a masterpiece of artistic and graceful nonsense that this book has won a just pre-eminence ; though that were no small praise. For in these days, when a narrow and tyrannical science broods like a nightmare over human life, and steadily explains away all apparent variety by some iron law of monotonous uniformity, and wraps her wettest blankets round our warmest fancies, and finds the goal of her ambition in the reduction of our fair cosmos to a congeries of homogeneous atoms or primordial pills which some blind force has worked up into a sort of tapioca pudding—in these days, I say, nonsense expresses the revolt of healthy reason against this oppressive cultus of uniformity, and bids fair to rise to the level of a fine art. Nay, if it be true that we understand all things in pairs, each in the light of its opposite ; if, as the schoolmen say, *eadem est scientia de contrariis ;* if black and white, evil and good, belong to the same science, the same art, the same taste ; if the grotesque be an object of æsthetics co-ordinately with the beautiful ; if none can be so delicately and incisively rude as the expert in good manners : surely it is not wonderful that an artistic sense of delight in the incoherent, the unexpected, for its own sake, should be most keenly developed in an age which a sense of all-pervading uniformity is driving to desperation.

Now, though *Alice* gives expression and relief to this pent-up rebelliousness, it is not in this that her greatest merit lies. In Lear's works and others of the class we find a sufficient tonic against the malaria of a scientific climate, a peak of refuge from the rising deluge of dulness which threatens to overwhelm us when knowledge shall have stripped life of its redeeming illusions, and shall have turned all its colour and music into vibrations of a silent and colourless medium. In a primitive society, with a conception of the world as unscientific and bizarre as that of an infant, Lear's pictures and rhymes would fall flat, simply as untruthful —as bad history and imperfect portraiture. Their lawlessness would wake no joy in a world where lawlessness was commonplace. In an Abyssinian hagiography I have lately seen devout illustrations every bit as wild, and, for aught my ignorance of the language can tell, the letterpress may have been quite in keeping. For like reason, it is to the wisdom-stifled "grown-ups," rather than to the children, that such nonsense is as welcome as a cool hand on a fevered brow.

But in addition to all this, it is especially as expressing and fixing in type the unspoilt child-mind of every age and country—universally and eternally the same—that this book is so beneficial and influential. No child could have performed the task for want of the powers of self-dissection and comparison, and literary utterance ; no adult of the rare few who could, like " Lewis Carroll," root up their buried and forgotten child-self from the depths of their subliminal consciousness, had deemed the work worth doing for its own sake. Hitherto, children's books had been written with a view to improvement—open or insidious ; with a view, that is, to the very process by which the child-mind, as God made it, is changed into something different, for better or for worse. Even the *Water Babies*, in which Cousin Cramchild is so deservedly denounced, is itself designedly an improving book, differing from *Sandford and Merton* only in style and doctrine. It does not portray the child-mind to itself in its heathen nakedness just for the joy of contemplation, but with a mean *arrière pensée* of combining instruction with amusement.

Children, if healthy, read *Alice* with profound interest, but with unbroken gravity ; for to the child there is little ridiculous in what to us is so incoherent and unexpected. The spell for them lies in finding a grown-up mind so much in tune with their own, and bold enough to give the respectability of print to such dreamings as they are taught by their prosy elders to be ashamed of and to keep locked up in the secret of their busy little brains. Their surprise is like that of a puppy beholding its reflex in a glass. Here is the world as they know it, and not as it is said to be ;

here is no tiresome sequence or dull consistency, but events and remarks wander on or break off capriciously as in dreams, when the sense-gates are slammed in the face of orderly reality with its tiresome contradiction of fancy. Experience soon creates habits of expectation, and changes the disorderly kitten, to whom head-foremost or tail-foremost is a matter of indifference, into the sedate cat, victimised by the fallacy of uniformity into believing that what has been, so far, must therefore be of necessity and eternally. The human kitten is still worse off, for not only does its own growing experience tend to limit fallaciously its idea of what is possible ; but by education the accumulated experience of the race is brought to bear upon it to the same end. Not only does the child, once burnt, leap to the absurd inconsequence that fire necessarily burns, but society formulates this into a dogma and gives it the full weight of its authority. Previously, cold fire was quite unthinkable (as it is) ; thenceforth it becomes intrinsically ridiculous. And so with a vast body of beliefs which we wisely hold to throughout life solely because we have always heard them asserted, or because they have not been contradicted within the narrow limits of our own experience, but which we have no right to regard as eternal necessities. It were madness, indeed, not to accept the guidance of society or of our own unvaried experience, or to attempt to sift all such beliefs to the bottom before acting upon them ; but it is by confounding what is usual with what is necessary that our mind, under social influence, loses its freedom of imagination, and comes to limit the possible by the actual. If we never took off our clothes we should soon begin to mistake them for part of ourselves ; and, similarly, we come to mistake opinions we continually repeat, for opinions we have intelligently formed ;

and what is usually said, for what we really think ;
and what we infer, for what we actually see ; and there
are times when our only chance of getting at the
truth is to throw off the heaped-up experiences under
which our child-mind lies buried, and to look at things
with the fresh retina of our first consciousness ere
fallacies of uniformity had crippled our freedom of
perception.

It is in encouraging us in our defiance of that false
necessity, which the adult mind imports into the order
of things really contingent, and in helping us to get
back to the child's unspoilt view of the world ; to
see things once more as we really do see them, and
not as we want to see them, and therefore seem to
see them ; to look straight and not asquint into the face
of truth, that these books will act as a lubricant to our
life-rusted mind, and will enable us to turn intellectual
back-somersaults at an age when we should be otherwise corpulent and unbendable. When the root-
causes of all things shall at last be laid bare, I shall
not be surprised if it prove that *Alice* has had more
to do with many a conversion than the theologians,
controversialists, philosophers, and other grave and
reputable persons who were too hastily credited with
the result.

> " ' In my youth,' said the sage, as he shook his grey locks,
> ' I kept all my limbs very supple
> By the use of this ointment (one shilling a box) :
> Pray allow me to sell you a couple ! ' "

VI

STRAY REMARKS AND SENTENCES FROM CONVERSATION AND LETTERS

Patching.—I do feel more and more that religion ought not to need so much defending and patching up. A point comes when we cease darning our stockings and throw them away. I suppose if we could get no others we should go on darning.

To a friend who aspired to a Cardinal's hat.—I wish I had your sensibility to hats—*oculos habeo et non video.* My artistic sense woke late in life and I shall never recover lost ground.

About Popes.—Could you translate *Tu es Petrus* " You're a brick"?

Isolation.—Is it a fair test of life? " What am I to myself when everything is gone?" I should say " Nothing," a mere punctured balloon.

Money.—I am sorry to hear of your financial destitution ; I always thought you would be able to bail me out in an emergency. To be hampered by lack of so absurd a thing as money is of all our mortal humiliations the grievousest—one of those things that *should* not be true.

Planchette.—Talking of mysticism, a beastly planchette of a friend of mine has tapped my subconsciousness and is finding out all my secrets. I feel like a pot with the lid off.

Scandal argument.—It is not the hundreds who would *now* be scandalised who prepare the way for the millions of the future ; on the contrary they hinder that preparation which is the work of those other hundreds who would now be edified by plain speaking and are scandalised by silence. Let the scandal be given, since scandal there must be, to the dying cause and not to the living. I would not " kill and eat the babies if the adults were famine-stricken." I would kill the adults and make them into meat-extract for the babies, as representing the future.

Love of God.—I feel that such love of God as you and I talk about is the luxury of a few happy and imaginative temperaments, and that, in the lump, man was not created or designed for the love of God in that mystical sense, but for the love of man. But that is a passing phase of realism, and I hope soon to resume the blinkers of idealism when the wind shifts from the East.

Tigers.—Tell Rollo (a small boy) that tigers would " like God " if they could get at Him, but there are poor pickings on a spirit.

Weariness.—*Defecit caro mea et cor meum*, the last ten days or so ; enormous inertia and world-weariness ; partly, I fancy, from having finished all jobs in hand, and seeing nothing more to say or do. Still mild Wordsworth has soothed me with his one-eyed outlook on the peaceful side of life ; and I have sat on a cold tombstone, listening to his incomparable prosy old parson's gossip, till I am stiff with lumbago and propriety.

Poetry.—The many things we could not see till Wordsworth gave us eyes. The function of the poet : " Whereas I was blind, now I see."

Right proportion.--Aquinas not greater, but less for being made infallible ; Mary belittled by titles as by tinsel—well-meant, ill-judged. The world is greater, not less, for Wordsworth's simplification of it,

Modernism.—A philosophy of Catholic experience or practice, distinguishing what is life-giving and permanent in beliefs and usages—what saints have lived on. It tries to reconcile this with modern knowledge. It seeks a fuller and deeper, not a thinner and shallower explanation.

Parousia.—It is the approach of a " new order " that wakes religion and unites sects. Cataracts are normal and necessary to the stream of progress. We feel things cannot possibly go on as now.

Polytheism.—A better expression of the divine than anthropomorphic deism. No room for *all* good qualities in one man. Jahveh cannot be at once Apollo and the Man of Sorrows, Minerva and St. Francis.

Apostolic weakness.—We help less by our ideas than by the way we got to them—desire, folly, sin are conditions of health, wisdom, goodness. We can all contribute to progress by our miseries, if in no other way.

Councils.—Councils do not debate on dogmas for whose decision the Church waits as in a scholastic dispute ; they debate as to what actually *is* the morally unanimous belief.

Polygamy.—There was no " hardness of heart " in the Old Testament " friends of God." When did it grow *wrong* ? Surely not religiously. *Ergo* only by social authority. Yet bigamy is the basis of our argument against divorce. Physical divorce is less evil than rational and spiritual. Are two cats, tied together by the tails, an image of Christ and His Church ?

Acts of submission.—B.'s letter (of submission) ought to, but does not, edify me. At that rate where should we be ? Did Christ sit down and bite His nails and wait for miracles ? I suppose we are all apt to canonise our weaknesses. I canonise my temper.

Free will and Providence.—A curiously weak letter

of J. H. Newman to Father Whitty has come out in
The Standard—the same fanatical conviction of a
special mission and work that appears so often, and yet
a recognition of the thwarting circumstances as the
" Blessed Will of God." What a muddle! If the work
impulse is from God, the obstacle is from God only
in the sense that the devil is from God. Is the devil's
will the " Blessed Will of God " ? The truth is that
God never pokes His finger into the clockwork one
way or the other, and faith of the best sort begins
with an appreciation of that ruthless fact.

Last Words.—I am glad God is to judge me, and not
any of His servants. (A month before his death.)

PRINTED IN GREAT BRITAIN
BY HAZELL, WATSON AND VINEY, LD.,
LONDON AND AYLESBURY.

Printed in the United States
101520LV00001B/192/A